Ultimate ONNX for Deep Learning Optimization

Design, Optimize, and Deploy Deep Learning Models Using ONNX for Scalable Production and Edge AI Systems

Meet Patel

www.orangeava.com

First Published: December 2025

Published By: Orange Education Pvt Ltd, AVA®

Address: 9, Daryaganj, Delhi, 110002, India

275 New North Road Islington Suite 1314 London,
N1 7AA, United Kingdom

ISBN (PBK): 978-93-49887-20-6
ISBN (E-BOOK): 978-93-49887-34-3

Scan the QR code to explore our entire catalogue

www.orangeava.com

Dedicated To

To My Parents, Shri. Dilipbhai Patel and Smt. Leenaben Patel,

The Roots of My Tree and the Architects of My Character.

To My Wife, Dhairyaa Parikh,

for Being the Most Beautiful Chapter in My Story.

To the Infinite Universe around Me,

for Its Boundless Wonder and Wisdom.

About the Author

Meet Patel is a machine learning engineer with over seven years of expertise dedicated to a singular challenge, that is, making Artificial Intelligence (AI) faster, smaller, and more efficient. His passion lies in unlocking the potential of AI on resource-constrained devices, pushing models from the lab into the real world.

His transition into AI from a mechanical engineering background underscores a journey fueled by curiosity and self-motivation. He was driven by a passion to master the intricacies of machine learning. Meet has extensive hands-on experience in taking models from initial research and training through advanced optimization techniques such as quantization, pruning, and knowledge distillation, all the way to compiler level enhancements and final deployment.

His hands-on experience includes deploying a wide array of models, spanning computer vision and Large Language Models (LLMs), onto various edge platforms. He has architected core optimization tools, developed custom high performance operators, and designed distributed training strategies to scale AI efficiently.

This book is a culmination of his practical experience. It connects the scattered pieces of the ONNX and edge deployment ecosystem into a single, coherent guide. His aim is to empower his fellow developers to overcome the hurdles of deployment, and build systems that are not just intelligent, but also practical and performant where it matters most.

Through this book, he hopes to share the conviction that with the right tools and understanding, any developer can master the crucial final step of the ML journey, and bring their models to life at the edge.

About the Technical Reviewer

Heflin Stephen Raj S is an AI engineer and innovator specializing in advanced natural language processing, transformer architectures, ONNX, and edge intelligence. With a strong foundation in data science and emerging technologies, he has consistently transformed cutting-edge research into scalable, high-impact solutions that drive business value, and enhance user experiences worldwide.

At *Zoho*, Heflin serves as a *Member Technical Staff* (NLP), where he builds AI-powered capabilities that elevate automation across a product ecosystem used by over 20 million people, each month. His work spans text classification, semantic search, and optimized model deployment across both cloud and on-premise environments. Previously, he contributed to *CodeOps*, engineering APIs that reduced infrastructure costs, and to *Webnexs*, where he developed enterprise-grade chatbots, forecasting systems, and CRMs that streamlined operations for diverse organizations.

Heflin is also a notable contributor to the global open-source community. He identified and resolved a critical bug in Microsoft's ONNX Runtime that affected training workflows on Windows; his fix was merged into the official branch, strengthening a widely adopted AI framework. His personal projects reflect similar innovation such as *Nalam*, a bilingual health chatbot, was selected for *Twilio*'s Impact Access program, while his *Covid-19 dashboard* was featured in Streamlit's weekly and monthly showcases for its intuitive design and real-time insights.

A dedicated educator and community leader, Heflin has delivered talks at Google Developer Groups Chennai events, including DevFest, covering transformers, BERT, Sentence-BERT, and emerging trends in large language models.

Driven by curiosity and impact, Heflin continues to advance ONNX, edge intelligence, and real-world AI deployment, while mentoring the next generation of innovators.

Acknowledgments

First and foremost, I owe an immeasurable debt of gratitude to my parents. Their unwavering support and sacrifices laid the foundation of my journey, and enabled me to reach for the heights I enjoy today in my career.

To my lovely wife, no words are sufficient. This book would simply not exist without her constant encouragement, boundless patience, and steadfast affection. She was my anchor throughout this demanding process, and her support gave me the strength and space to see it through to completion.

My professional journey has been profoundly shaped by the incredible opportunities and challenges I encountered in the industry. I am deeply grateful to the companies, colleagues and mentors who placed their trust in me, providing the complex problem statements and real-world exposure that became the crucible for my understanding of the ONNX ecosystem. The lessons learned there are the bedrock of this book.

A special thank you goes to the entire team at Orange Education Pvt. Ltd., my editors, reviewers, and production staff. Their guidance, expertise, and proactive approach were invaluable. They not only shepherded this project with great skill but also helped me refine my ideas, and complete this work within a demanding timeframe.

Finally, I would like to express a quiet thanks to the universe, for the serendipitous opportunities, the lessons learned from challenges, and the simple fortune that allowed me to undertake and complete this journey. It is a privilege to present this work of mine to the readers.

Preface

The field of machine learning experienced a pivotal "aha" moment with the introduction of AlexNet, triggering a period of rapid and relentless innovation. Since then, a diverse array of models has emerged from research labs, capable of solving complex, real-world problems. This progress is accelerated by two key drivers: The development of more efficient models and the library support that enables their deployment, whether in the cloud or at the edge.

This book, *Ultimate* ONNX *for Deep Learning Optimization* focuses squarely on the latter, specifically deploying models to edge devices, and leverages the ONNX ecosystem to do so. ONNX's versatility makes it possible to deploy models to virtually any system, understanding it is crucial for any Machine Learning (ML) Engineer looking to master the practical side of the ML lifecycle.

Within these pages, we will explore the tools of the ONNX ecosystem, and the practical techniques used in real-world model deployment. Filled with code examples and accompanying Jupyter Notebooks, this book takes a hands-on approach. While a basic understanding of machine learning will help you grasp the concepts more deeply, our journey is designed to be accessible and immediately applicable.

A Glimpse Inside

The book is structured into 13 chapters to guide you from the core or foundation to the advanced concepts:

Chapter 1 introduces the domain of edge computing and the ONNX. We explore its pros and cons, compare it with other deployment tools, and establish why ONNX is a superior choice for getting started with edge AI.

Chapter 2 helps in setting up the system for ONNX. We will explore the components of an ONNX model, visualize it using Netron, and get hands-on by running a model with ONNX Runtime.

Chapter 3 covers the conversion process, teaching how to export the trained models from PyTorch, TensorFlow, and Scikit-learn into ONNX format, and understanding the mechanics under the hood.

Chapter 4 dives into graph optimization, a key technique for removing redundancy to make models faster. We will use ONNX Simplifier and ONNX Runtime to apply optimizations, and measure their impact on performance.

Chapter 5 tackles model quantization, a necessity for resource-constrained edge devices. We will learn the math behind converting high-precision models to lower precision, apply it to a BERT model, and evaluate the trade-off between speed and accuracy.

Chapter 6 discusses model pruning, which identifies and removes redundant weights to create lighter and faster models. We will use PyTorch's pruning APIs, and evaluate the effects on model performance.

Chapter 7 explores knowledge distillation, a technique for training smaller, efficient "student" models to mimic larger "teacher" models. We shall apply this to create a distilled variant of a ResNet model.

Chapter 8 is a practical walkthrough of deploying models to edge devices. Focusing on the Raspberry Pi, we will learn the nuances of deployment, including how to build ONNX Runtime for a target device, and use its C++ APIs for an end-to-end example.

Chapters 9, 10, and 11 are comprehensive case studies. We will deploy three different model types to an edge device: an object detection model (YOLOv12), a speech transcription model (OpenAI's Whisper), and a small language model (SmolLM2). Each chapter covers the full cycle from export and optimization to quantization and deployment, addressing practical challenges along the way.

Chapter 12 delves into advanced ONNX concepts. We will learn to construct models from scratch using ONNX Script, and implement custom operators by using ONNX native APIs, ONNX Script, and PyTorch export.

Chapter 13 concludes by discussing the best practices and safety considerations for edge deployment. We then look ahead to the future of ONNX and edge AI, exploring upcoming trends, features, and tools.

Thus, we hope that this book empowers you to break down the barriers between training a model, and deploying it in the real world. The power of edge AI is immense, and with ONNX as your toolkit, you are well-equipped to harness it!

Get a Free eBook

We hope you are enjoying your recently purchased book! Your feedback is incredibly valuable to us, and to all other readers looking for great books.

If you found this book helpful or enjoyable, we would truly appreciate it, if you could take a moment to leave a short review with a 5 star rating on Amazon. It helps us grow, and lets other readers discover our books.

As a thank you, we would love to send you a free digital copy of this book, and a **30%** discount code on your next cart value on our official websites:

www.orangeava.com

www.orangeava.in (For Indian Subcontinent)

☑ **Here's how:**

Leave a review for the book on Amazon.

Take a screenshot of your review, and send an email to **info@orangeava.com** (it can be just the confirmation screen).

Once, we receive your screenshot, we will send you the digital file, within 24 hours.

Thank you so much for your support – it means a lot to us!

Downloading the code bundles and colored images

Please follow the links or scan the QR codes to download the ***Code Bundles and Images*** of the book:

https://github.com/ava-orange-education/Ultimate-ONNX-for-Deep-Learning-Optimization

The code bundles and images of the book are also hosted on ***https://rebrand.ly/7ad1e8***

In case there's an update to the code, it will be updated on the existing GitHub repository.

Errata

We take immense pride in our work at **Orange Education Pvt Ltd,** and follow best practices to ensure the accuracy of our content to provide an indulging reading experience to our subscribers. Our readers are our mirrors, and we use their inputs to reflect and improve upon human errors, if any, that may have occurred during the publishing processes involved. To let us maintain the quality and help us reach out to any readers who might be having difficulties due to any unforeseen errors, please write to us at :

errata@orangeava.com

Your support, suggestions, and feedback are highly appreciated.

DID YOU KNOW

Did you know that Orange Education Pvt Ltd offers eBook versions of every book published, with PDF and ePub files available? You can upgrade to the eBook version at **www.orangeava.com** and as a print book customer, you are entitled to a discount on the eBook copy. Get in touch with us at: **info@orangeava.com** for more details.

At **www.orangeava.com**, you can also read a collection of free technical articles, sign up for a range of free newsletters, and receive exclusive discounts and offers on Print Books and eBooks.

PIRACY

If you come across any illegal copies of our works in any form on the internet, we would be grateful if you would provide us with the location address or website name. Please contact us at **info@orangeava.com** with a link to the material.

ARE YOU INTERESTED IN AUTHORING WITH US?

If there is a topic that you have expertise in, and you are interested in either writing or contributing to a book, please write to us at **business@orangeava.com**. We are on a journey to help developers and tech professionals to gain insights on the present technological advancements and innovations happening across the globe and build a community that believes Knowledge is best acquired by sharing and learning with others. Please reach out to us to learn what our audience demands and how you can be part of this educational reform. We also welcome ideas from tech experts and help them build learning and development content for their domains.

REVIEWS

Please leave a review. Once you have read and used this book, why not leave a review on the site that you purchased it from? Potential readers can then see and use your unbiased opinion to make purchase decisions. We at Orange Education would love to know what you think about our products, and our authors can learn from your feedback. Thank you!

For more information about Orange Education, please visit **www.orangeava.com**.

Table of Contents

Chapter 1
Introduction to ONNX and Edge Computing

Introduction

In this chapter, we will be understanding the fundamentals of the ONNX framework and edge computing paradigm. We will learn more about the ONNX framework, its ecosystem and the relevance of the ecosystem in edge computing.

The chapter will also explain edge computing and key differences compared to cloud computing. The benefits and challenges associated with edge computing are also discussed in detail along with real-world examples of edge computing.

The later part of the chapter discusses the overall deep learning inference optimization pipeline, and different ONNX tools that can be useful in the entire inference pipeline. At last, we will compare the ONNX ecosystem with other available tools and libraries, along with their benefits and limitations.

Structure

In this chapter, we will cover the following topics:

- Overview of ONNX (Open Neural Network Exchange)
- Key Concepts and Importance of Edge Computing
- Benefits of Edge Computing
- Challenges in Deploying AI Models on Edge Devices
- Real World Examples of Edge AI Applications
- Overview of Deep Learning Inference Pipeline
- Applicability of ONNX Ecosystem in Edge Computing
- Competing Frameworks for Model Deployment

Overview of ONNX (Open Neural Network Exchange)

ONNX (Open Neural Network Exchange)[1] is an open-source deep learning framework initially developed by Facebook. Subsequently, the collaborative efforts of Microsoft and Facebook led to its release into the public domain in September 2017[2]. Later on, other companies like AMD, Arm, Baidu, Huawei, HuggingFace, IBM, Intel, Mediatek, Nvidia, and Qualcomm have extended their support for a common framework to accelerate development in the field of deep learning.

The main aim of ONNX was to facilitate interoperability within the framework, where researchers, practitioners and engineers can develop deep learning models in a single framework such as Pytorch, Caffe, Tensorflow, and Keras, translate it to another framework for further integration, or directly deploy it using ONNX's ecosystem on a given target device.

ONNX offers a common interface and abstraction of a deep learning model. This makes collaboration easy among different teams with different skill sets. It means that an engineer well-versed with Tensorflow models can also play with Pytorch models without much effort.

ONNX provides support for range of programming languages such as C++, Python, C#, Java and others. This makes deploying trained models very efficient and smooth. The model can be trained on any training framework such as Pytorch, Tensorflow, or Keras using Python language. Then the trained model can be converted into an ONNX model, which is based on the Protobuf format to serialize it. This ONNX model can be used in different deployment scenarios using respective programming language APIs.

The ecosystem developed around ONNX has been the key factor for its successful adoption. The open source tools like ONNX Simplifier and ONNX Optimizer optimize the ONNX graph, which removes redundant nodes and fuses mathematically equivalent nodes. Such optimizations make the ONNX model efficient when executed on target devices. On the other hand, Netron provides a nice graphical interface to visualize the ONNX graph structure. The ONNX Runtime[3], which is developed by Microsoft, can quantize and run the model on a variety of target devices such as Nvidia GPUs, AMD GPUs, Intel CPUs, AMD CPUs, RaspberryPi, Android Phones and other FPGAs.

---

[1] ONNX Homepage (https://onnx.ai/) and Github (https://github.com/onnx/onnx)

[2] https://azure.microsoft.com/en-us/blog/microsoft-and-facebook-create-open-ecosystem-for-ai-model-interoperability/

[3] https://onnxruntime.ai/

Besides ONNX, there have been other training frameworks that provide their own version of runtime libraries. For instance, Tensorflow provides TFLite/LiteRT[4] and Pytorch provides Pytorch ExecuTorch[5]. The primary limitation of such runtimes is that the model which needs to be deployed has to be of Pytorch or Tensorflow format. For instance, a model trained in PyTorch must be converted to the TensorFlow graph format to be deployed with TFLite, and vice versa.

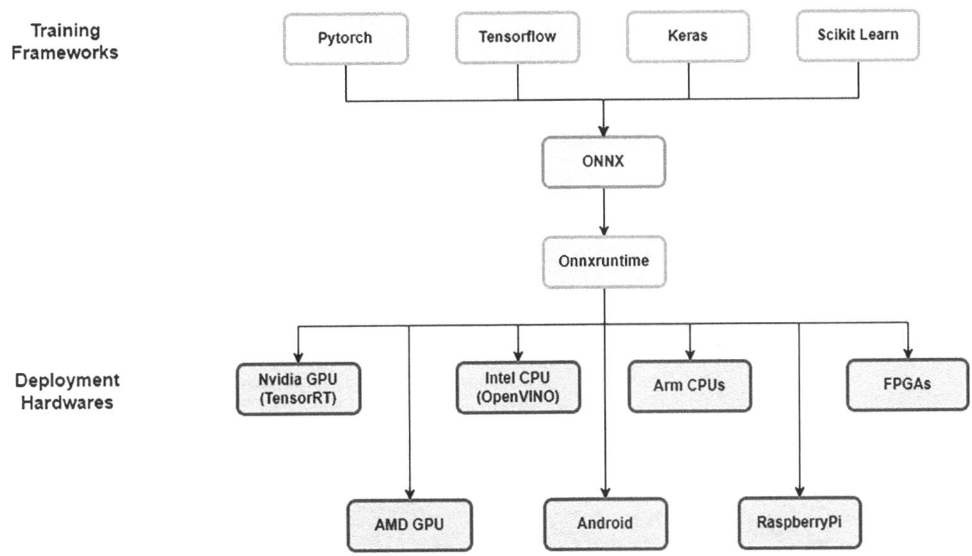

Figure 1.1: *Overview of the ONNX ecosystem where different framework models can be converted to the ONNX framework and the same can be deployed on different hardwares using ONNX Runtime*

From the machine learning development point of view, the entire ONNX ecosystem will give ease of choosing the training framework. If we were to deploy a Pytorch trained model on Android devices, we do not need to worry about translating it to TFLite. If the model is trained on Tensorflow and we want to deploy it on a web-based interface, then we can deploy it using the ONNX ecosystem. Such a strong ecosystem will reduce the barrier to entry for any developer and expedite development.

Understanding Edge Computing

Now that we know about ONNX, let us try learning about edge computing.

Traditionally, there have been two different types of computing models for processing data: Cloud Computing and Edge Computing. These categories are based on where the data is actually processed.

[4] https://ai.google.dev/edge/litert
[5] https://pytorch.org/projects/executorch/

The data used for processing is usually generated by sensors. These sensors can be cameras, voice recorders, LiDAR sensors, satellite imaginary sensors, heat sensors, and electronic devices that measure the various parameters of the environment around them. These sensors are devices with low power and low resources requirements. Their purpose is to just collect correct data consistently and reliably. The generated data can have magnitudes of a few MBs in a day to several GBs in a given second. An example of such sensors is the LHC (Large Hadron Collider) at CERN (Conseil Européen pour la Recherche Nucléaire), where sophisticated sensors are used to identify the trajectory of the particles and measure their energy. All this happens in a fraction of seconds, and the data generated by each process is on the scale of several GBs. This data would undergo further processing before it can be used to generate proper insights.

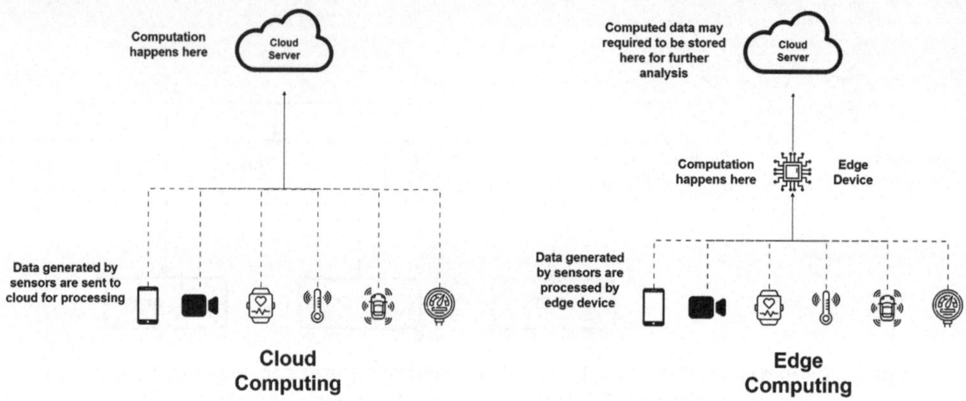

***Figure 1.2**: Visualization of Cloud Computing and Edge Computing*

As shown in the image, the different sensory devices send the data to the cloud server for processing in Cloud Computing. In case of Edge Computing, the data is processed locally or nearby to the sensor using an edge device.

In Cloud Computing, the generated data is sent to a centralized server with higher computation capabilities to process large chunks of it. Based on processing, various conclusions, visualizations and analytical operations can be performed on the data. Based on different types of use cases, either the results are returned to the source, or are stored on the cloud device. An example of such cloud computing is Amazon Echo Dot, or any speech recognition assistant like Siri or OK Google that captures the user's voice and the voice data is sent to a centralized server for further processing after which the results are sent back to the device.

In case of edge computing, the computation is performed at or near the source of data to reduce the overall latency of the execution. This is achieved through equipment such as Internet of Things (IoT) devices, smart cameras, electronic sensors, voice recorders, LiDAR sensors, and so on. Usually in Edge Computing, such sensory devices are coupled with an entire system that has limited computation capabilities. Sensory devices capture data, while supporting hardware processes it locally. These devices bring the computation capabilities to the edge of a network or device, paving way for efficient and faster data processing, reduced latency, real time computation and increased bandwidth.

Benefits of Edge Computing

Having grasped the basics of edge computing, let us direct our attention to its benefits:

- Reduced Latency and Real Time Processing: Since the data is processed nearby to the source of data, the data transfer time is minimized, which eventually improves overall latency and enables real time execution.
- Improved Bandwidth Efficiency: As the data is processed locally, edge computing reduces the amount of data sent to the central server over the network. This reduces bandwidth requirements and the overall load on the network, making the system efficient.
- Better Privacy and Security: In edge computing, data is generated, stored and processed locally. Hence, the misuse of sensitive data is prevented, which safeguards privacy.
- Cost Savings: By reducing the amount of data sent to the cloud, edge computing can minimize operational costs of data transfer, cloud storage and computational resources in central servers.

Challenges in Edge Computing

Edge computing brings its own challenges due to its characteristics. We will now discuss them in detail:

- **Limited Computation Power**: Edge devices usually have less processing power and storage compared to centralized cloud based infrastructure. This can limit the complexity of tasks that are handled by edge devices, especially in resource intensive applications like big data and deep learning.
- **Reliability:** Edge devices are prone to fail due to factors like extreme weather conditions, power outages, connectivity issues, and hardware malfunctions. This can disrupt operations, especially in remote or safety-critical applications, where uptime is essential.
- **Scalability:** Since edge devices are spread across large geographical locations, scaling such deployments requires manual effort, thereby increasing overall operational costs. On the other hand, cloud infrastructure providers enable

the customer to seamlessly and dynamically scale the resources as and when needed.

- **Safety:** As the data is processed locally, one can maintain data security. However, since edge devices are often located in less secure environments, they are vulnerable to physical tempering, large scale cyber-attack and unauthorized access. Historical and recent examples demonstrate the potential of targeted sabotage. A famous early case is the Stuxnet worm, which in the late 2000s caused Iran's nuclear centrifuges to physically fail. In a more recent, physical example, a 2024 operation led to the synchronous detonation of pagers and communication devices used by Hamas operatives.
- **Maintenance and Updates:** Edge devices often require regular software updates and fixes, which can be challenging to implement across a large number of geographically distributed devices. The remote location of these devices makes it difficult to perform maintenance or apply fixes, rendering them vulnerable.

Edge Computing Examples

With a clear understanding of edge computing and its benefits and challenges, it will be helpful to understand some of its real-world applications. This will give us a brief overview of edge computing applications that are commonly used in our surroundings.

- **Autonomous Vehicles:** Self driving cars are equipped with many modern sensors like Lidar, cameras, and radars. These sensors generate vast amounts of data that need to be processed in real time to make split-second decisions for navigation and safety, as autonomous driving is a safety-critical application.
- **Smart Cities:** In smart cities, traffic lights, surveillance cameras, sensors for air quality, and other IoT devices collect data in real-time. Edge computing allows for locally processing this data to manage traffic flows, monitor pollution, and detect accidents without sending all the data to the cloud, which can be too slow or bandwidth-intensive.
- **Manufacturing:** In the manufacturing industry, edge computing helps in monitoring the health of mechanical machinery and its performance in real time. It identifies any abnormality in the operation such as vibration, sound, or temperature, and detects potential failures for preventive maintenance, which can improve the performance of the equipment.
- **Healthcare:** In the healthcare industry, edge devices can be used as wearable trackers to monitor vital signals such as heart rate, blood sugar level, and so on. These devices record and process data in real time and send an alert signal in case of any abnormal readings.

- **Locally Executed Chatbots on Mobile Phones:** Recent advancements of LLMs have enabled the usage of lightweight and accurate models which can run locally on mobile phones. They enable users to interact with the LLMs via a chat interface.
- **AI-Based Photo Editing on Mobile Phones:** Nowadays, there are many applications such as Google Photos, Snapchat, Instagram, and others, where you can visually enhance photos and allow the user to extract text from images.
- **Drone Operations:** Drone manufacturers like DJI provide functionality in their drones to lock and track the given human object. This allows the user to make stunning videos while trekking or travelling. All such tracking and processing happens within the limited compute capacity of a tiny, lightweight drone.
- **Call Transcription and Speech Translation:** With the rise of speech recognition models, it is possible to transcribe and summarize calls on mobile phones without the need to send the recordings to the cloud server. The same is helpful in translating speech from one language into another language which makes the communication very efficient across geography.
- **Driver Monitoring Systems:** Human-driven cars are equipped with cameras inside the cockpit, which continuously analyze the driver in real time. If there are any signs of distraction like using your phone, looking sideways, or drowsiness, then such systems alert the driver and decelerate the car to prevent accidents.
- **Face Recognition-Based Attendance System:** Many companies and academic institutions use a Face Recognition-based attendance system to capture a person's face and mark their attendance. Such systems perform the required computation inside the edge devices itself to detect impersonation.

Deep Learning Inference Optimization Pipeline

Deep learning models are usually trained on GPUs hosted on cloud or in-premise. Once models have been trained, they undergo the following steps before they are ready for deployment on edge devices:

- **Pruning**
    - Pruning is a technique which identifies redundant weights from the trained model. It takes an algorithmic approach to trim down the overall architecture of the model.
    - This makes the model lightweight with minimal impact on accuracy. If the edge device has sufficient resources, then you may skip this step.

- **Distillation**
  - Usually, pruned models are a trimmed down variant of the original model, which might have lost a good amount of accuracy due to reduced number of parameters. There have been other instances where one needs to develop small scale variants from models that are already proven and trained.
  - In such cases, distillation techniques can train smaller models from larger reference models, which can make smaller models more accurate than supervised training-based models.
- **Graph Optimizations**
  - Once the trained model is obtained it might contain many redundant nodes and parameters that can be either removed from the graph or fused together with other nodes and parameters.
  - The trained graph would undergo several optimizations such as Constant Folding, NoOp Removal, Dead Code Elimination, and Kernel Fusion, which can make it more efficient during execution.
- **Quantization**
  - A model is usually trained on FP32 or FP16 precision as higher precision provides higher stability in the gradients during the process. Fundamentally, the core computation in any deep learning model is the MAC operation (Multiply and Accumulate), which is usually found in Matmul or Convolution operation.
  - Usage of lower precision like INT8 for MAC operations is more efficient compared to higher precision ones like FP16 and FP32 as it consumes less computation cycles. Hence, it has been the industry standard that an FP16 or FP32 trained model should be converted into an INT8 precision model for deployment to reduce the size of the model and improve its execution.
  - Lower precision is obtained by tracking the activation range of all the nodes of the trained FP32 or FP16 model. The activation range from FP32 or FP16 range is then shrunk into the INT8 range by grouping several activations into different buckets of the latter range. This methodology is called Post Training Quantization (PTQ), which might result in loss of precision and quantization, while impacting accuracy.
  - To overcome this issue, there have been techniques such as Quantization Aware Training (QAT), that fine tune the model to minimize the loss of accuracy from using lower precision during inference and deployment.

Figure 1.3 presents these different stages at a high level in sequential order. In subsequent chapters, we will examine each stage in detail, exploring how they function and contribute to making the model more suitable and efficient for edge deployment.

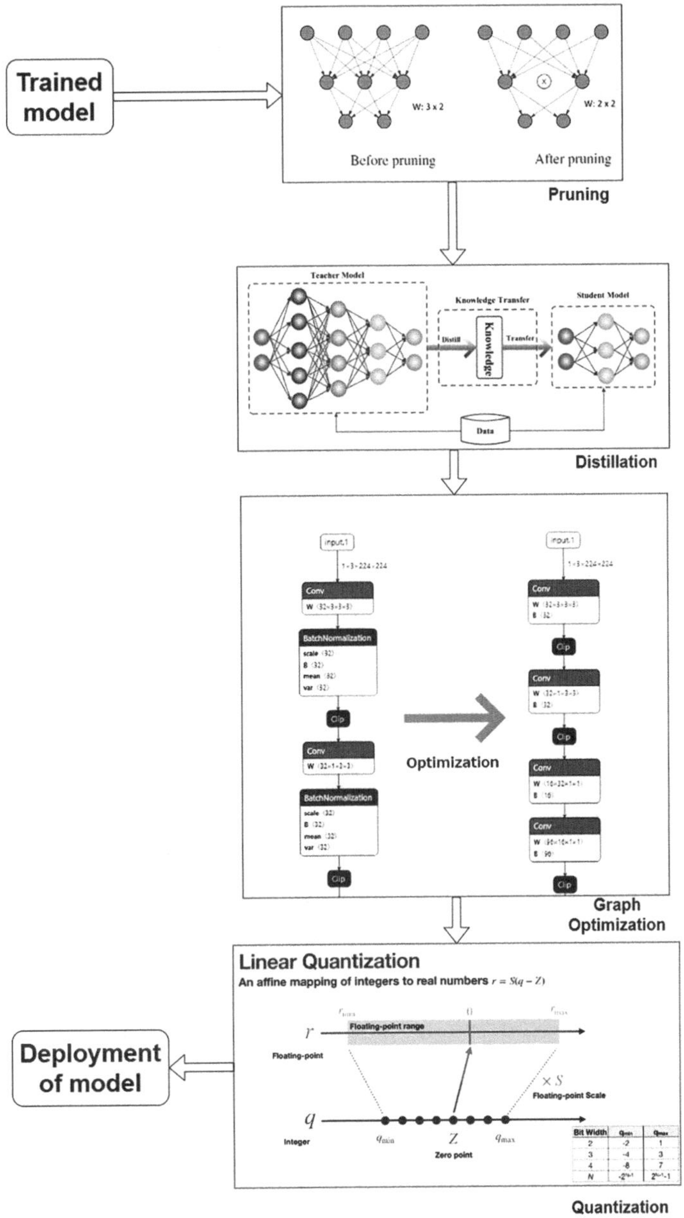

Figure 1.3: *Overview of Deep Learning inference optimization flow* (Source: Pruning[6], *Distillation*[7], *Graph Optimization*[8], *Quantization*[9])

---

[6] https://pohsoonchang.medium.com/neural-network-pruning-update-cda56343e5a2
[7] https://neptune.ai/blog/knowledge-distillation
[8] https://becominghuman.ai/a-deep-dive-into-onnx-onnx-runtime-part-2-785b523e0cca
[9] https://www.coditation.com/blog/how-to-optimize-large-deep-learning-models-using-quantization

Leveraging the ONNX Ecosystem for Edge Computing

The framework's success is driven by an ecosystem that provides a complete, interoperable toolchain for edge deployment. ONNX has been adopted successfully because of the rich and open source ecosystem around the framework that consist of the following features:

- **Framework conversion tools**
  - The Pytorch library has built in APIs[10] that allows the user to export a given Pytorch-trained model into an ONNX equivalent one.
  - For the Tensorflow library, an open source tool tf2onnx[11] exists to help users convert a Tensorflow or Keras-trained model into an ONNX model.
  - For models trained on classic machine learning algorithms using scikit-learn module, the sklearn-onnx[12] tool helps the user export the model into an ONNX model to deploy it on various devices.
- **Pre-Trained Models**: ONNX repo maintainers have to continuously keep track of widely used pre-trained models on their modelzoo[13], which can be directly used for the deployment. Such models include ResNets, YOLO, GPT2, and BERT.
- **Model Visualization Tools**: To visualize ONNX models, industry standard tools like Netron[14] allow users to visualize the entire graph of an ONNX model and its architecture.
- **Optimization Tools**
  - Training frameworks provide support to prune weights and make the model lightweight by removing redundant weights.
  - The models exported from training frameworks such as Pytorch and Tensorflow can have many redundant operators, which are important from a training point of view, but are redundant from a deployment perspective. Examples of such operators are Dropout and Batchnorm after each Convolution operator. Such operators either can be removed from the graph or can be fused together to form a unified operator, which is the mathematical equivalent of the former. Tools such as ONNX Optimizer[15],

[10] https://pytorch.org/tutorials//beginner/onnx/export_simple_model_to_onnx_tutorial.html
[11] https://github.com/onnx/tensorflow-onnx
[12] https://github.com/onnx/sklearn-onnx
[13] https://github.com/onnx/models
[14] https://github.com/lutzroeder/netron
[15] https://github.com/daquexian/onnx-simplifier

ONNX Simplifier[16], and ONNX Runtime can automatically identify the scope of optimization and apply it. Applying such graph optimizations quickens the execution of the model.

- Once the optimized model is obtained, ONNX Runtime can further improve the execution by quantizing the model from Float32 precision into Int8 precision. By lowering the precision, the size of the model is reduced and computation would become faster. Both are favorable characteristics which are important for edge computing.

- **Inference Tools**: Optimized and quantized models can be deployed using ONNX Runtime, which supports different edge device configurations. These include Android Phones, AMD CPUs, Arm CPUs, FPGA devices, Intel CPUs, Jetson Nano, Nvidia GPUs, and RaspberryPi. As the overall binary size of the ONNX Runtime library is very less, it is suitable to deploy on edge devices with space constraints.

Competing Libraries for Edge Computing

Over the past years, there have been many edge computing libraries which serve different purposes to different use cases.

- **TFLite:** The TFLite library has been developed and maintained by the Tensorflow team to enable the execution of models on Android and Arm-based devices. Models from any training framework have to be converted to TFLite format first to use it.
- **OpenVINO:** Intel developed the OpenVINO[17] library to accelerate the execution of models on its hardware. It is a collection of tools that take models from major training frameworks and convert it into OpenVINO-specific format to execute on Intel CPUs, GPUs, and NPUs.
- **TensorRT:** Nvidia has a range of AI accelerators starting from edge computing devices like Jetson Nano to workstation scale GPUs like A100 and H100. These devices are based on the CUDA technology. To provide a unified experience to users, Nvidia developed the TensorRT[18] library to optimize the execution of models on Nvidia hardware.
- **TVM:** Apache TVM[19] is an open-source Machine Learning Compiler stack, which provides diverse support to training frameworks and deployment hardwares. It enables users to optimize and run the model on Intel, Nvidia, AMD, and Arm-based devices.

---

[16] https://github.com/onnx/optimizer
[17] https://www.intel.com/content/www/us/en/developer/tools/openvino-toolkit/overview.html
[18] https://developer.nvidia.com/tensorrt
[19] https://tvm.apache.org/

- **Pytorch ExecuTorch:** To compete with Tensorflow's TFLite framework and overcome the shortcomings of the same, Pytorch has developed Pytorch ExecuTorch to easily deploy models on Android and iOS devices.
- **ArmNN:** ArmNN[20] is developed by Arm to facilitate the efficient conversion, optimization, and execution of models across Arm Cortex-A CPUs and Arm Mali GPUs.

Sr. No.	Edge computing library	Training Frameworks							
		TensorFlow	TFLite	Pytorch	Keras	Jax	Scikit Learn	ONNX	Paddle-Paddle
1	LiteRT (TFLite)	✓	✓	✓	✓	✓	✗	✗	✗
2	OpenVINO	✓	✓	✓	✓	✗	✗	✓	✓
3	TensorRT	✓	✗	✓	✓	✗	✗	✓	✗
4	Apache TVM	✓	✓	✓	✓	✗	✗	✓	✓
5	Pytorch ExecuTorch	✗	✗	✓	✗	✗	✗	✗	✗
6	ArmNN	✓	✓	✗	✗	✗	✗	✓	✗
7	ONNX Runtime	✓	✓	✓	✓	✗	✓	✓	✓

Table 1.1: *Table showing the supported training frameworks by different edge computing libraries*

Table 1.1 and *Table* 1.2 summarize the training frameworks and hardwares supported by these edge computing libraries. As we can see, each of these libraries is developed keeping a particular goal in mind. Hence, each has its own benefits and limitations. The end user should choose the library that satisfies all edge computing requirements.

Sr. No.	Edge computing library	Hardwares								
		Arm CPU (e.g. RaspberryPi)	Mobiles		Intel			AMD GPU	Nvidia	
			Android	iOS	CPU	GPU	NPU		Jetson Nano	GPU
1	LiteRT (TFLite)	✓	✓	✗	✗	✗	✗	✗	✗	✗
2	OpenVINO	✗	✗	✗	✓	✓	✓	✗	✗	✗
3	TensorRT	✗	✗	✗	✗	✗	✗	✗	✓	✓
4	Apache TVM	✓	✗	✗	✗	✓	✗	✓	✓	✓

[20] https://github.com/ARM-software/armnn

5	Pytorch ExecuTorch	✓	✓	✓	✗	✗	✗	✗	✗	✗
6	ArmNN	✓	✓	✗	✗	✗	✗	✗	✗	✗
7	ONNX Runtime	✓	✓	✗	✓	✓	✓	✓	✗	✗

Table 1.2: *Table showing the supported hardwares by different edge computing libraries*

Conclusion

In this chapter, we delved deeper into the edge computing paradigm, exploring its benefits and challenges and also examined various real-world use cases of edge computing.

Additionally, we explored the ONNX framework and its ecosystem. Later in the chapter, we discussed the deep learning inference pipeline and compared different competing frameworks suitable for edge computing. This analysis not only highlights ONNX's role in the edge ecosystem but also provides the context needed to justify its adoption for portable and efficient model deployment.

In the next chapter, we will learn about various components of an ONNX model, while visualizing it and using ONNX Runtime to run a sample model for hands-on practice.

CHAPTER 2

Getting Started with ONNX

Introduction

In the previous chapter, we learned about edge computing and got a detailed idea about the ONNX ecosystem. Now, we will dive deeper into the ONNX framework and its core components. The chapter then transitions to a practical tutorial where we will visualize a sample model using Netron to understand the graphical representation of the model. We will then use ONNX Runtime to run the model and try to get outputs from it. This chapter is designed to provide readers a hands-on experience as they work with ONNX. To allow readers to experiment further, we have also linked a Jupyter Notebook with this chapter. By the end of this chapter, you will have a practical foundation for inspecting and executing models with the ONNX runtime.

Structure

This chapter will address the following topics:

- Setting Up the Environment for ONNX
- Visualizing the ONNX Model with Netron
- Overview of the ONNX Model Architecture
- Executing the ONNX Model via ONNX Runtime

Setting up the Environment for ONNX

To set up a Python virtual environment for ONNX, we need to install ONNX, ONNX Runtime, and ONNX Simplifier packages. This environment will serve as a common interface for all the chapters in the book.

Make sure to perform the following steps to set up a Python virtual environment:

1. Install Python 3.10
   a. **For Windows:**

      Download and install python 3.10 from the link https://www.python.org/downloads/windows

   b. **For Linux:**

```
sudo apt update
sudo apt install -y software-properties-common
sudo add-apt-repository ppa:deadsnakes/ppa
sudo apt update
sudo apt install -y python3.10
sudo apt install python3.10-venv
curl -sSL https://bootstrap.pypa.io/get-pip.py -o get-pip.py
&& python get-pip.py
```

   c. Verify the installation by executing the below command in the command prompt.

```
python3 -version
```

2. Set up the virtual environment that will be used throughout this book.

```
python -m venv ./onnx_env
```

3. Activate the environment as per the requirements of the Operating System
   a. **For Windows**

```
./onnx_env/Scripts/activate
```

   b. **For Linux**

```
source ./onnx_env/bin/activate
```

4. Install Jupyter Notebook, ONNX, ONNX Runtime and ONNX Simplifier packages

```
pip install jupyter==1.1.1 notebook==7.4.4 onnx==1.18.0 onnxrun-
time==1.22.0 onnx-simplifier==0.4.36
```

5. Once the dependencies are set up, clone the git repo[1] for this book.
6. After cloning, move into the root directory of the cloned repo and start the Jupyter Notebook server by executing "**`jupyter notebook`**" from the command line. Once the server starts, a URL starting with "**`http://localhost:8888`**" will be displayed on the console. Click the URL or copy and paste it in a browser to start the Jupyter Notebook interface.

[1] https://github.com/ava-orange-education/Ultimate-ONNX-for-Optimizing-Deep-Learning-Models

7. We will be following the Jupyter Notebook from this chapter for the following sections.

Visualizing the ONNX Model with Netron

Before exploring the different components of the ONNX model, let us visualize the model and understand its graphical representation:

Firstly, let us download a sample model. We will use ResNet18 from the ONNX Model Zoo[2].

Once the model is downloaded, visit the Netron tool on the URL: **`https://netron.app/`**.

Open the downloaded model in the Netron tool. The model is illustrated in *Figure 2.1*. Alternatively, readers can follow the Jupyter Notebook for this chapter as mentioned earlier.

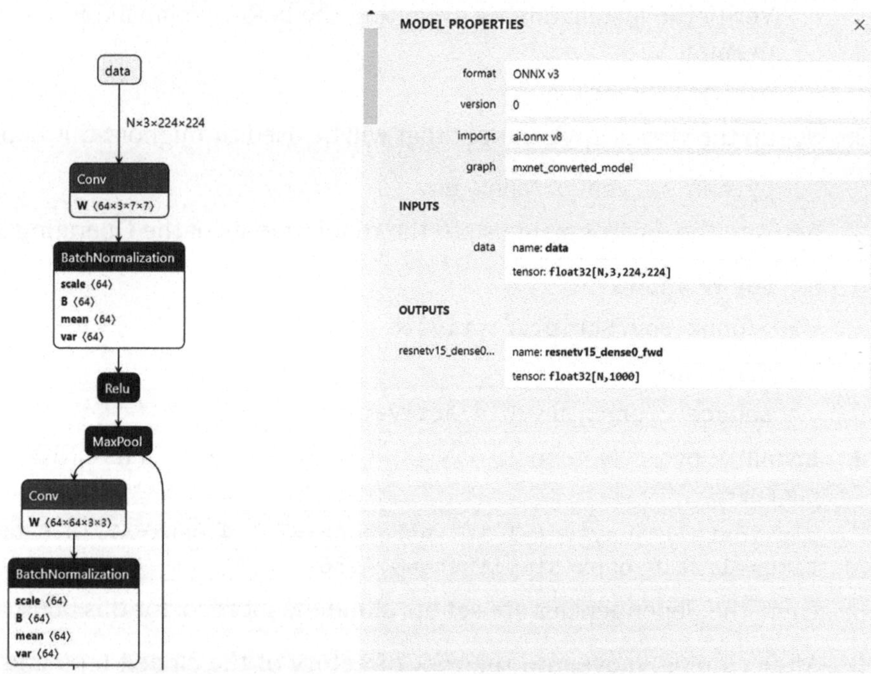

Figure 2.1: *ResNet18 model visualized in Netron tool*

On the right pane, Netron will provide an overview of the inputs and outputs of the model such as its shape, data type, and name. On the left side, we will see a graphical view of the ResNet18 model. The model starts with an input named "**`data`**" with the shape **`[N, 3, 224, 224]`**. The input is followed by a Convolution node.

[2] https://github.com/onnx/models/tree/main/validated/vision/classification/resnet

Clicking the Convolution node shows us the node properties, its inputs and outputs. Each node can have different attributes, inputs, and outputs. As shown in *Figure* 2.2, the selected Convolution node has attributes such as **`dilation`**, **`group`**, **`kernel_shape`**, **`pads`**, and **`strides`**. It has an input named X from the graph input "**`data`**". The other input named W comes from the "**`resnetv15_conv0_weight`**" named initializer. The initializer contains an ONNX graph that stores constant tensors such as weights and biases.

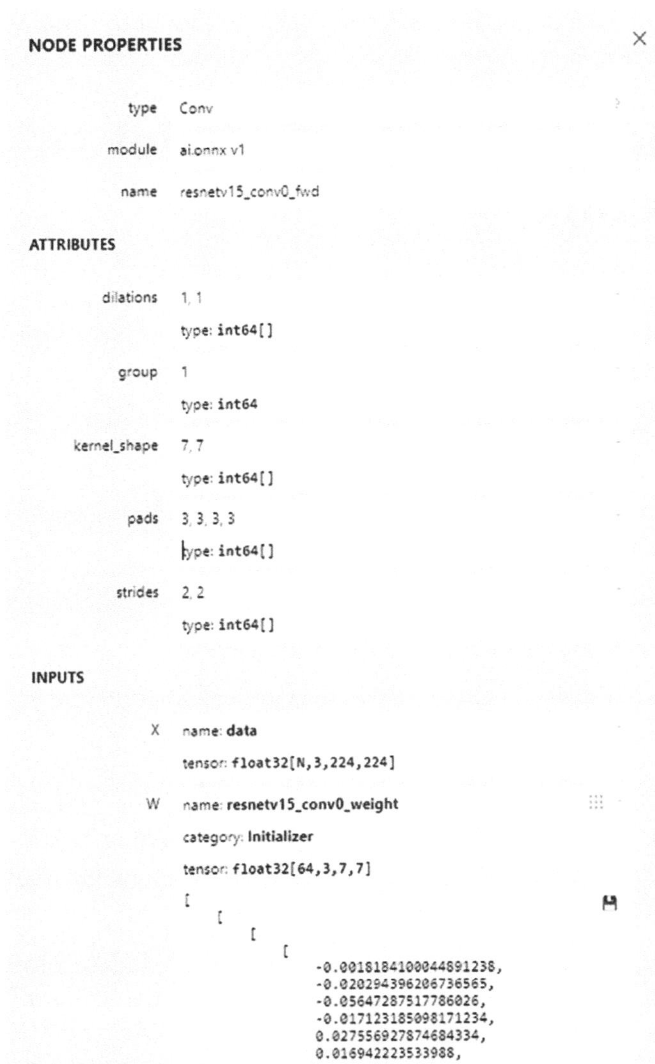

Figure 2.2: *Convolution node and its properties visualized in Netron tool*

The output of the Convolution node is passed into the BatchNormalization node. This is evident from the output tensor of the Convolution node, "**`resnetv15_conv0_fwd`**", which is the input for the BatchNormalization node.

By looking at the entire model in terms of its nodes and edges, we can think of it as directed acyclic graph data structure. Each node's output can be fed to some other node's input.

The entire graph can be checked by scrolling. At the end of the graph, we will see "**`resnetv15_dense0_fwd`**" as graph output with **`float32`** data type and **`[N, 1000]`** shape. Since this model is trained on **`[224, 224]`** resolution on ImageNet dataset, when we feed the image with this dimension to "**`data`**" input, the "**`resnetv15_dense0_fwd`**" output will be generated. Readers can play with the model to explore different nodes and their properties.

Overview of the ONNX Model Architecture

Now that we have visually inspected it, it will be easier for us to understand the core components of an ONNX model. Firstly, we will load the previously downloaded ResNet18 model in ONNX. *Figure* 2.3 shows us the code used to load the model in ONNX. The Jupyter Notebook for this chapter can be used to walk through the provided code.

Load the model in ONNX

```
import onnx
model = onnx.load("resnet18-v1-7.onnx")
```

```
# Onnx models are stored as ModelProto object.
print("Onnx model stored as: ", type(model))
```

```
Onnx model stored as:  <class 'onnx.onnx_ml_pb2.ModelProto'>
```

Figure 2.3: *Code showing loading of ONNX model*

The ONNX framework leverages Protobuf[3] to represent and serialize machine learning models. This helps in easy sharing and deployment across different platforms and tools. Protobuf (Protocol Buffers) is a language-agnostic, platform-neutral data serialization format developed by Google.

On a high level, the ONNX model is made up of a ModelProto[4] structure. The ModelProto object contains several GraphProto objects. Each GraphProto object can contain multiple NodeProto. NodeProto can contain different AttributeProto and TensorProto. This structural hierarchy is demonstrated in *Figure* 2.4 as follows:

[3] https://protobuf.dev/
[4] https://onnx.ai/onnx/api/classes.html

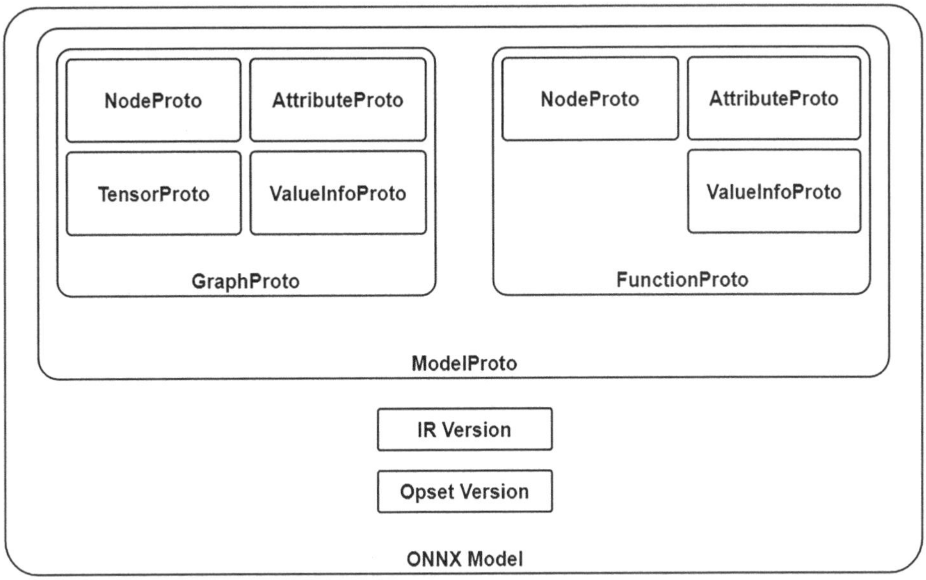

Figure 2.4: ONNX *model structure*

The following sections explore each of these Protobuf structures in more detail:

- **`ModelProto`:** It contains model description, **`GraphProto`** and **`FunctionProto`**. When we load the ONNX model, we will get **`ModelProto`** representation. It can contain one or more **`GraphProtos`** and one or more **`FunctionProtos`**.
- **`GraphProto`:** **`GraphProto`** structure defines the overall computational graph of the model. It includes **`NodeProtos`**, **`TensorProtos`**, **`AttributeProtos`**, and **`ValueInfoProtos`**.
- **`NodeProto`:** **`NodeProto`** defines individual nodes in graphs. Each node can have various input tensors, output tensors and attributes. Different types of nodes can be defined by the "**`op_type`**" property of the node. Different types of nodes can have different types of attributes. *Figure* 2.5 shows a sample Convolution node from the ResNet18 model.

```
# Each GraphProto object contains NodeProto objects.
print(f"Total nodes in graph: {len(graph.node)}\n")

first_conv_node = graph.node[0]
print(f"First convolution node: \n\n{first_conv_node}")
```

```
Total nodes in graph: 69

First convolution node:

input: "data"
input: "resnetv15_conv0_weight"
output: "resnetv15_conv0_fwd"
name: "resnetv15_conv0_fwd"
op_type: "Conv"
attribute {
  name: "dilations"
  ints: 1
  ints: 1
  type: INTS
}
attribute {
  name: "group"
  i: 1
  type: INT
}
attribute {
  name: "kernel_shape"
  ints: 7
  ints: 7
  type: INTS
}
attribute {
  name: "pads"
  ints: 3
  ints: 3
  ints: 3
  ints: 3
  type: INTS
}
attribute {
  name: "strides"
  ints: 2
  ints: 2
  type: INTS
}
```

Figure 2.5: *Sample NodeProto structure*

- **`AttributeProto`:** Attributes associated with each node are stored as **`AttributeProto`**. **`AttributeProto`** can contain a scalar value and an array of numbers, where each attribute has a name and associated value. *Figure* 2.6 shows the attribute values stored in the Convolution node mentioned above.

```
# Node's attribute which is stored as AttributeProto can be accessed as below.

print("Attribute type: ", type(first_conv_node.attribute[0]))

print(f"Node: {first_conv_node.name}\n")
for attr in first_conv_node.attribute:
    print(f"Attribute name: {attr.name}, value: {onnx.helper.get_attribute_value(attr)}")

Attribute type:  <class 'onnx.onnx_ml_pb2.AttributeProto'>
Node: resnetv15_conv0_fwd

Attribute name: dilations, value: [1, 1]
Attribute name: group, value: 1
Attribute name: kernel_shape, value: [7, 7]
Attribute name: pads, value: [3, 3, 3, 3]
Attribute name: strides, value: [2, 2]
```

Figure 2.6: *Values stored in* **`AttributeProto`**

- **`TensorProto`:** Trained weights of Machine Learning models are stored as **`TensorProto`**. The **`TensorProto`** are stored in the "**`initializer`**" property of the **`ModelProto`**. The **`TensorProto`** are referenced as input in the **`NodeProto`**. In *Figure* 2.5, the input "**`resnet15_conv0_fwd`**" is trained weights of the Convolution layer, stored as "**`initializer`**". The value of the same can be accessed as shown in *Figure* 2.7.

```
[10]: # Actual tensor value from initializer can be obtained as below.

      first_init = graph.initializer[0]
      first_init_value = onnx.numpy_helper.to_array(first_init)
      print("First initializer")
      print("name: ", first_init.name)
      print("shape: ", first_init_value.shape)
      print("dtype: ", first_init_value.dtype)
      print("value: ", first_init_value)

      First initializer
      name:  resnetv15_conv0_weight
      shape:  (64, 3, 7, 7)
      dtype:  float32
      value:  [[[[-1.81841000e-03 -2.02943962e-02 -5.64728752e-02 ...  2.75569279e-02
           1.69422235e-02 -2.61198264e-02]
         [-1.91061497e-02 -1.50184799e-02 -1.39287570e-02 ...  4.68977951e-02
           1.36066740e-02 -2.65738834e-02]
         [-2.26846598e-02 -8.33997782e-03  1.50225367e-02 ...  4.97992784e-02
           2.60790698e-02 -1.42802447e-02]
         ...
         [ 7.68385781e-03  3.75749506e-02  4.59949709e-02 ...  6.16705380e-02
           5.27052656e-02 -5.58289466e-03]
         [ 1.11488421e-02  3.37563045e-02  4.41418886e-02 ...  5.52862063e-02
           8.68887547e-03 -4.06390540e-02]
         [-3.80610190e-02  4.65004565e-03  5.96935414e-02 ...  7.75443390e-02
           9.65741347e-04 -7.41245821e-02]]
```

Figure 2.7: *Convolution node's weights stored as initializer*

- **ValueInfoProto:** The graph structure of the model is defined using nodes and edges. Nodes have inputs coming from graph input, some other node's output or initializer. Node's output is either connected with some other node's input or it is a graph output. All these edges are tensors which can optionally have the shape and datatype information. The information for each tensor is stored as **ValueInfoProto**. The shape and datatype information is important from an optimization standpoint. If any operator is doing redundant work, then it can be identified via the shape and datatype information. For example, a Cast node converts a given tensor's data type into boolean. If the given input itself is Boolean, then the cast node is redundant. To identify this, we need data type information of the input tensor. If the shape and datatype information is not present for the given tensor, then they can be populated by running the shape inference. *Figure* 2.8 shows a code snippet to get the value info associated with the preceding Convolution node's output:

```
# Each node's input and output tensors have shape and data type
# information. This info is stored as ValueInfoProto structure of GraphProto.

all_value_infos = model.graph.value_info
print("Total number of value info : ", len(all_value_infos))

# There are no value info available in graph because intermediate nodes
# doesn't have any shape information. This information can be obtained by
# performing shape inference.
model = onnx.shape_inference.infer_shapes(model)

all_value_infos = model.graph.value_info
print("Total number of value info : ", len(all_value_infos))

first_tensor_val_info = all_value_infos[0]
print("Value Info type: ", type(first_tensor_val_info))
print("\nFirst tensor's value info: ", first_tensor_val_info)
```

```
Total number of value info :  0
Total number of value info :  68
Value Info type:  <class 'onnx.onnx_ml_pb2.ValueInfoProto'>

First tensor's value info:  name: "resnetv15_conv0_fwd"
type {
  tensor_type {
    elem_type: 1
    shape {
      dim {
        dim_param: "N"
      }
      dim {
        dim_value: 64
      }
      dim {
        dim_value: 112
      }
      dim {
        dim_value: 112
      }
    }
  }
}
```

Figure 2.8: ONNX *Shape Inference and* ***ValueInfoProto*** *visualization*

- **Graph Input and Output:** ONNX **`ModelProto`** also contains information about graph inputs and outputs. These are stored as **`ValueInfoProto`** but are included explicitly in the "**`input`**" and "**`output`**" property of **`ModelProto`**. Unlike other intermediate tensors, these inputs and outputs should mandatorily contain the shape and datatype information. *Figure* 2.9 shows the input and output information of the ResNet18 model. Note that it shows 103 numbers of inputs, but in reality, only one input shall be present in the model. The older versions (with **`IR version < 4`**) of the ONNX model have conventions to show initializers as graph inputs. Therefore, the rest 102 of them are initializers.

```
# Model Input and Output
print("Total inputs of graph: ", len(graph.input))
print("Total outputs of graph: ", len(graph.output))

print("\n\nOutput of graph: ", graph.output[0])
```

```
Total inputs of graph:  103
Total outputs of graph:  1


Output of graph:  name: "resnetv15_dense0_fwd"
type {
  tensor_type {
    elem_type: 1
    shape {
      dim {
        dim_param: "N"
      }
      dim {
        dim_value: 1000
      }
    }
  }
}
```

Figure 2.9: ONNX *Graph input and output inspection*

- **`FunctionProto:`** It defines a function. While it is not a complete model itself, it can be used to define custom operators within a model. For example, consider a case where a user needs to develop functionality for the new activation function PReLU, assuming that ONNX does not support it. The user can then define the PReLU operator via **`FunctionProto`** to support such models.

- **IR Version:** ONNX is a generic graph representation with specific schema. Over time, it has undergone many iterations, where each is defined by an IR (Intermediate Representation) version.
- **Model Opset:** ONNX continually updates and improves the list of supported operators, as defined by the opset version. As the opset version increases, there may be incremental changes to the schema of specific operators, such as in the Convolution operator. Every new opset version introduces new operators.

Executing the ONNX Model via ONNX Runtime

Until now, we have inspected the ONNX model visually while learning about its core components. Now, we can try running it through ONNX Runtime.

To do this, we will try to run the ResNet18 model downloaded previously. We need to prepare input data to feed it to the model first. Since the ResNet18 model is trained on ImageNet dataset with 1000 classes and `224 x 224` resolution, we will load the image using `opencv2` (version 4.11.0.86) package and preprocess it according to *ImageNet preprocessing*[5]. *Figure* 2.10 shows the image preprocessing code for the ResNet18 model.

[5] https://github.com/onnx/models/blob/main/validated/vision/classification/imagenet_preprocess.py

```
# Load and preprocess the image as per
# https://github.com/onnx/models/tree/main/validated/vision/classification/resnet

import cv2
import numpy as np

def preprocess_image(image_path):
    # Step 1: Read the image using OpenCV
    image = cv2.imread(image_path)

    # Step 2: Resize the image to 224x224 (ResNet18 input size)
    image = cv2.resize(image, (224, 224))

    # Step 3: Convert the image from BGR to RGB
    image = cv2.cvtColor(image, cv2.COLOR_BGR2RGB)

    # Step 4: Normalize the image using the mean and std of ImageNet
    # Normalize pixel values to the range [0, 1]
    image = image / 255.0

    # ImageNet Mean and Std
    mean = np.array([0.485, 0.456, 0.406])
    std = np.array([0.229, 0.224, 0.225])

    # Normalize based on ImageNet statistics
    image = (image - mean) / std

    # Step 5: Convert the image to a numpy array with shape (224, 224, 3)
    # Step 6: Add an extra batch dimension (1, 224, 224, 3)
    image = np.expand_dims(image, axis=0)

    # Step 7: Convert NHWC layout image into NCHW layout
    image = np.transpose(image, (0, 3, 1, 2))

    # Convert image to float32 for model compatibility
    image = image.astype(np.float32)

    return image

# Example usage:
image_path = 'Photo_of_a_kitten.jpg'
preprocessed_image = preprocess_image(image_path)

print("Input shape: ", preprocessed_image.shape)  # Should be (1, 3, 224, 224)
```

```
Input shape:  (1, 3, 224, 224)
```

Figure 2.10: *Image preprocessing for ResNet18 model*

Figure 2.11 shows a sample code snippet to load the ONNX graph in ONNX Runtime and run the model. To execute it, ONNX Runtime first needs to load the model and create a session. Once the session is created, we can pass required preprocessed input data in a numpy array form to the session and get the actual output. By default, ONNX Runtime executes the model on the CPU backend. However, it can be changed through the "**provider**" argument while creating the session. ONNX Runtime provides different backends, that are termed as Execution Providers[6] such as TensorRT for GPU execution, OpenVINO for CPU execution, TVM for Arm CPU execution, and so on.

```
# Run model in onnxruntime

import onnxruntime as ort

# By default, onnxruntime executes model on CPU. So if we dont
# provide CPU execution provider then it will run on CPU by default.
execution_provider_list = ['CPUExecutionProvider']

# uncomment below line to execute model on Nvidia GPU. Make sure
# to install onnxruntime-gpu using "pip install onnxruntime-gpu"
# execution_provider_list = ['CUDAExecutionProvider']

session = ort.InferenceSession("resnet18-v1-7.onnx",
                               providers=execution_provider_list)
input_data = {"data" : preprocessed_image}
model_output = session.run(None, input_data)

print("Total outputs: ", len(model_output))
print("Output shape: ", model_output[0].shape)
```

```
Total outputs:  1
Output shape:  (1, 1000)
```

Figure 2.11: *Sample code to run the model using ONNX Runtime*

The output of this ResNet model is logits with the shape **[1, 1000]**. To get the class probability, we need to apply Softmax activation on logits. Post that we can get the top-5 classes with highest probability in descending order as per *Figure* 2.12. To execute it, we have used the image of a cat and the ResNet18 model identified it as "Persian Cat" with 59.64 % probability.

[6] https://onnxruntime.ai/docs/execution-providers/

```
# Model will generate logits for 1000 classes of imagenet. We will need to apply softmax

def softmax(x):
    return np.exp(x) / np.sum(np.exp(x))

probabilities = softmax(model_output[0])
# [1, 1000]

top_5_indices = np.argsort(-probabilities[0])[:5]

for i, idx in enumerate(top_5_indices):
    class_name = class_mapping[f'{idx}']
    class_prob = probabilities[0, idx]*100
    print(f"Top-{i+1} predicted class: {class_name}, probability: {class_prob:.2f} %")

Top-1 predicted class: Persian_cat, probability: 59.64 %
Top-2 predicted class: window_screen, probability: 13.59 %
Top-3 predicted class: tabby, probability: 3.34 %
Top-4 predicted class: bow_tie, probability: 2.89 %
Top-5 predicted class: hamster, probability: 2.79 %
```

Figure 2.12: *Post processing of the model outputs*

Alternatively, the readers can follow and execute all the above steps via the provided Jupyter Notebook.

Conclusion

In this chapter, we set up an environment and visualized the ONNX model using Netron and the ONNX library. Understanding the key components of the ONNX model would help the readers grasp the concepts in later chapters. Later on, we executed the ResNet18 model using ONNX Runtime and interpreted the outputs as well.

Furthermore, we took ResNet18 as a reference model and directly used it as an off-the-shelf model. The next chapter will see us export the ONNX model from various training frameworks such as Pytorch, Tensorflow, and Scikit learn. Since the models are trained on the mentioned frameworks, learning about them will take us a step closer to the end-to-end use of these trained models.

CHAPTER 3
ONNX Integration with Deep Learning Frameworks

Introduction

The last chapter was all about ONNX and its ecosystem. In this chapter, we will learn how to obtain an ONNX model from trained Pytorch, TensorFlow, and Scikit-Learn models. These libraries offer strong support for training traditional machine learning models such as Decision Trees and Random Forests, as well as for modern deep learning models such as ResNets, YOLO, BERT, GPT, and more. Understanding how to export an ONNX model from these frameworks will be helpful when we look at the entire lifecycle of the model, which usually begins from training and ends at the deployment stage.

Structure

In this chapter, we will cover the following topics:

- General Ideas about Model Conversion
- Converting Pytorch Model into ONNX
- Converting a Simple Pytorch Model to ONNX
- Converting ResNet Pytorch Model to ONNX
- Converting TensorFlow 2.0 Model into ONNX
- Converting a Simple TensorFlow Model to ONNX
- Converting ResNet TensorFlow Model to ONNX
- Converting Scikit-Learn Model into ONNX

General Ideas about Model Conversion

When we convert a model from one framework to another, we will just translate it from one representation into another. The internal working of the model will remain the same. *Figure* 3.1 shows the overall model conversion workflow:

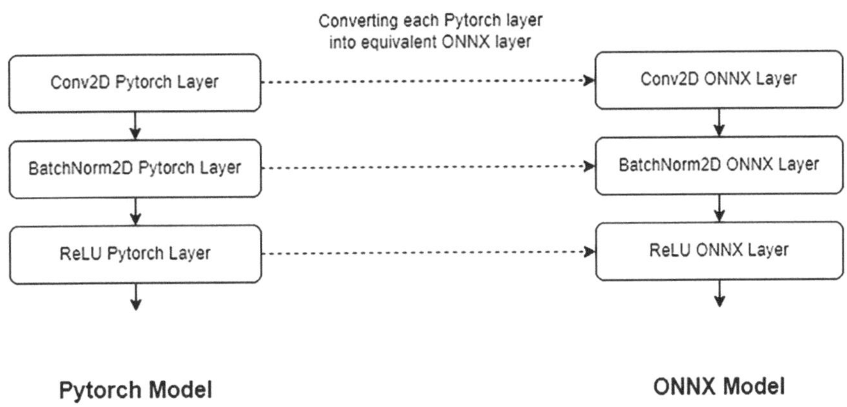

Figure 3.1: *Image representing overall model conversion flow*

For example, a ResNet18 model might consist of layers such as Convolution, Relu, MaxPool, and so on. The Pytorch representation of the ResNet18 model will contain a Pytorch-interpretable representation of all these layers. A Convolution layer is defined in Pytorch. When we convert it into an ONNX model, the same Pytorch-interpretable Convolution layer will convert into an equivalent ONNX interpretable layer. There will be a one-to-one mapping of each layer from Pytorch into its ONNX counterpart. The same holds true when the user is converting models from frameworks such as TensorFlow or Keras.

Converting Pytorch Model into ONNX

Now that we have a general idea of the conversion process, we will dive deeper into each of the frameworks. First, we will understand the conversion process for Pytorch models.

Let us set up dependencies for loading Pytorch models, and exporting the same to ONNX models. Readers can refer to *Pytorch website*[1] for installing the latest version of Pytorch or execute the commands shown in *Figure* 3.2. Readers can follow the Jupyter Notebook for this chapter from *the book's repo*[2]. We will be using the same environment which we have used in earlier chapters.

[1] https://pytorch.org/get-started/locally/
[2] https://github.com/ava-orange-education/Ultimate-ONNX-for-Optimizing-Deep-Learning-Models

```
# Note: Please make sure the notebook-2 python dependencies are
#       also installed in the environment.

# Install pytorch prerequisites
!pip install onnx==1.18.0 onnxruntime==1.22.0 netron==8.4.3
!pip install torch==2.6.0 torchvision==0.21.0 torchaudio==2.6.0 \
    --index-url https://download.pytorch.org/whl/cpu
!pip install matplotlib==3.10.0
```

Figure 3.2: Pytorch dependencies installation

Converting a Simple Pytorch Model to ONNX

Now that we have installed the PyTorch dependencies, let us create a simple 2-layer neural network in PyTorch first. Then we will try to convert it into the ONNX version.

```
import torch
import torch.nn as nn

# Define a 2-layer neural network
class TwoLayerNet(nn.Module):
    def __init__(self, input_size, hidden_size, output_size):
        super(TwoLayerNet, self).__init__()
        self.fc1 = nn.Linear(input_size, hidden_size)  # First fully connected layer
        self.relu = nn.ReLU()                          # ReLU activation
        self.fc2 = nn.Linear(hidden_size, output_size) # Second fully connected layer

    def forward(self, x):
        x = self.fc1(x)     # Pass input through first layer
        x = self.relu(x)    # Apply ReLU activation
        x = self.fc2(x)     # Pass through second layer
        return x

# Example usage
input_size = 10       # Size of input features
hidden_size = 20      # Size of hidden layer
output_size = 2       # Size of output (e.g., binary classification)
model = TwoLayerNet(input_size, hidden_size, output_size)

# Dummy input for tracing the model (batch_size=1 for demonstration)
dummy_input = torch.randn(1, input_size)

# Dummy execution of the model.
dummy_output = model(dummy_input)
print(f"Dummy input shape: {dummy_input.shape}")
print(f"Dummy output shape: {dummy_output.shape}")
```

Figure 3.3: Pytorch model for two-layer neural network

Figure 3.3 shows an example of a two-layer neural network implemented in PyTorch. The network consists of an input layer, a hidden layer with ReLU activation, and an output layer. This is a simple feedforward model suitable for tasks like regression or classification, depending on the final activation function.

The PyTorch model is defined as a subclass of **`nn.Module`**, where the **`__init__`** method initializes the two linear layers (**`fc1`** and **`fc2`**), and the **`forward`** method defines the computation flow: the input passes through the first layer, followed by a ReLU activation, and then through the second layer. No final activation like softmax is applied here, but it can be added if needed for a specific use case. The model takes an input of size **`[batch, 10]`**, transforms it through the hidden layer of size 20, and produces an output of size **`[batch, 2]`**.

```
# Export the model to ONNX
onnx_path = "two_layer_net_pt.onnx"
torch.onnx.export(
    model,                          # PyTorch model to export
    (dummy_input,),                 # Dummy input for tracing
    onnx_path,                      # Output ONNX file path
    input_names=["input"],          # Name for the input tensor
    output_names=["output"],        # Name for the output tensor
    dynamic_axes={
        "input": {0: "batch_size"},   # Allow dynamic batch size for input
        "output": {0: "batch_size"}   # Allow dynamic batch size for output
    }
)
```

Figure 3.4: ONNX *conversion of Pytorch model*

To convert this simple two-layer PyTorch neural network model into ONNX, we will follow code as shown in *Figure* 3.4. The **`torch.onnx.export`** function is used for this conversion. Readers can find more about this API from Pytorch documentation[3]. The key parameters here include the model object itself, a dummy input tensor used to trace the computation graph, the output ONNX file path, and optional metadata like input and output names for better readability. The **`dynamic_axes`** parameter allows specifying dynamic dimensions (like batch size), making the model more flexible for different input sizes during inference.

The export process involves running a dummy input through the **`forward`** method of the model to record the operations, which are then saved in the ONNX format. The operations which are traced during this export are one by one translated into its ONNX representation. In other words, the first and second linear layers are translated to Gemm ONNX nodes, whereas the ReLU layer is translated to the Relu ONNX node. The input "**`x`**", which is passed to the forward method, is named as "**`input`**" in the ONNX

[3] https://pytorch.org/docs/stable/onnx_torchscript.html#torch.onnx.export

model, and the final tensor that has been returned from the forward method is named as "**`output`**" in the ONNX model.

It is important to note that the dummy input used for tracing has a shape of **`[1, 10]`**, as shown in *Figure* 3.3. However, because the **`dynamic_axes`** parameter was used during export to designate the 0th dimension of both the "**`input`**" and "**`output`**" tensors as "**`batch_size`**", the exported model defines these shapes dynamically as **`["batch_size", 10]`** and **`["batch_size", 2]`**, respectively. Without the **`dynamic_axes`** parameter, the shapes would have been fixed at **`[1, 10]`** and **`[1, 2]`**. Therefore, when we visualize the exported model using Netron, its structure will appear as depicted in *Figure* 3.5.

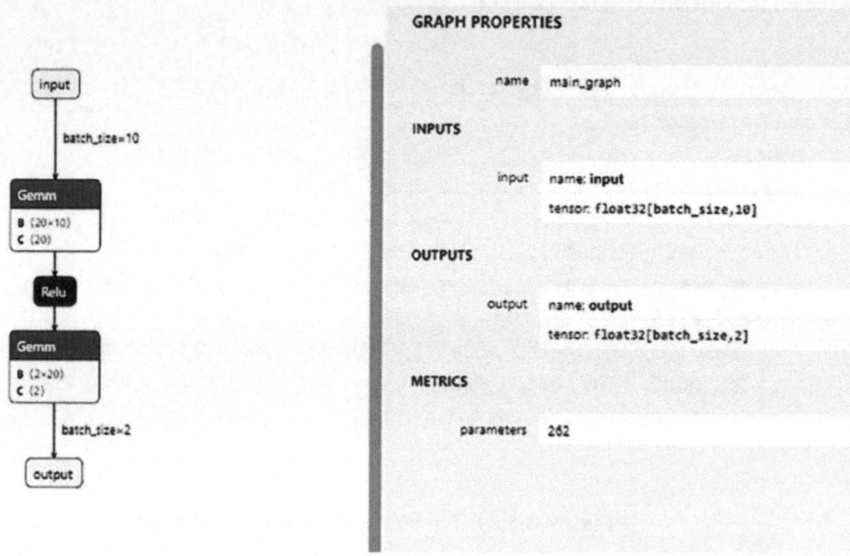

***Figure* 3.5:** ONNX *model visualized using Netron*

Converting ResNet Pytorch Model to ONNX

Now, we will load the pre-trained ResNet50 model from the **`torchvision.model`**. The **`torchvision`**[4] library provides a collection of pre-trained vision models along with their preprocessing image transforms. *Figure* 3.6 shows a sample code to load the ResNet50 model.

[4] https://pytorch.org/vision/stable/index.html

```
import torch
import torchvision.transforms as transforms
from torchvision import models
from PIL import Image
import requests
import matplotlib.pyplot as plt
import torch.nn as nn

# Load the pre-trained ResNet-50 model
model = models.resnet50(pretrained=True)

# Set the model to evaluation mode.
# This disables dropout and puts batch normalization layers in eval mode.
model.eval()
```

Figure 3.6: *ResNet50 Pytorch model loading*

Just like we have done in the previous chapter's inference example, we will read the image, preprocess it, and then feed the preprocessed image to the model. The outputs from the model will be logits. We will apply the Softmax activation function to convert raw logits into probabilities. Here, we will perform ImageNet preprocessing as the ResNet50 model is already trained with it. *Figure* 3.7 shows the required preprocessing transformations.

```
# Define image transform (preprocessing)
transform = transforms.Compose([
    # Resize the image to 256x256
    transforms.Resize(256),
    # Crop to 224x224 (ResNet input size)
    transforms.CenterCrop(224),
    # Convert the image to a tensor
    transforms.ToTensor(),
    # Normalize with the same stats as the training data
    transforms.Normalize(mean=[0.485, 0.456, 0.406],
                         std=[0.229, 0.224, 0.225]),
])
```

Figure 3.7: *ResNet50 ImageNet preprocessing transforms*

Figure 3.8 and *Figure* 3.9 show the overall code to load the image, preprocess it, and then generate the outputs from the model. It also shows the code to find the predicted class and its probability. In Pytorch, the model will be executed when we pass appropriate Pytorch tensors. The line "**`logits = model(image)`**" actually runs the model by taking the image tensor as input and generating the logits tensor as output.

```
# Function to load image from a URL
def load_image(image_path):
    if image_path.startswith('http'):
        response = requests.get(image_path, stream=True)
        img = Image.open(response.raw)
    else:
        img = Image.open(image_path)
    return img

# Inference function
def infer_image(image_path):
    # Load and preprocess the image
    image = load_image(image_path)
    image = transform(image).unsqueeze(0)  # Add batch dimension (1, 3, 224, 224)

    # Move image to the appropriate device (GPU or CPU)
    device = torch.device("cuda" if torch.cuda.is_available() else "cpu")
    model.to(device)
    image = image.to(device)

    # Perform inference
    with torch.no_grad():
        logits = model(image)
        probs = torch.nn.functional.softmax(logits)

    # Get the predicted class
    predicted_prob, predicted_class = probs.max(1)

    # Load the ImageNet class labels
    LABELS_URL = "https://storage.googleapis.com/download.tensorflow.org/data/imagenet_class_index.json"
    response = requests.get(LABELS_URL)
    class_idx = response.json()

    # Map predicted class index to label
    predicted_label = class_idx[str(predicted_class.item())][1]

    return predicted_prob[0], predicted_label
```

Figure 3.8: *ResNet50 inference function which loads the image, applies preprocessing, feeds the same and generates the class probabilities.*

```
# Example usage
image_path = 'cat.jpg'  # Change this to the path of your image
probability, class_label = infer_image(image_path)

print(f"Predicted label: {class_label}, Confidence score: {probability:.2f}")

# Optionally, display the image and the prediction
image = load_image(image_path)
plt.imshow(image)
plt.title(f"Prediction: {class_label} ({probability:.2f})")
plt.show()
```

Figure 3.9: *ResNet50 model execution code*

When we feed the image of the cat shown in *Figure* 3.10 to the model, we see that it is indeed predicted to be the "`Tiger Cat`" class, which is a breed of cat, with a probability of `0.41`. The exact breed might not be correct, but the model is at least able to narrow it down to a category.

Figure 3.10: *ResNet50 model output when the image of a cat is fed to the model*

So far, we have loaded the ResNet50 model and tried running the same using Pytorch library. Now let us try to convert this Pytorch model into the ONNX model. For this, we will use the previous API "**`torch.onnx.export`**" to convert the Pytorch model into an ONNX model. As discussed earlier, this API expects us to pass a Pytorch model instance, a sample input acceptable to the model, the output path of the ONNX model, and optional names for the model's inputs and outputs. *Figure 3.11* shows the usage of the same. Here, the model is imported from **`torchvision`**, and it is worth checking out its implementation to understand which parameters the **`forward`** method of the class accepts. To inspect the **`forward`** method in detail, readers can refer to source code of ResNet implementation[5]. As this model is trained on ImageNet dataset, it expects an input of shape **`[1, 3, 224, 224]`**. Once this code is executed, the generated ONNX model will be present at the output path provided to the API. Here, we have not used **`dynamic_axes`** argument while exporting; hence the generated model will be of fixed shape. Readers can experiment with this argument further, if needed.

5 https://github.com/pytorch/vision/blob/b818d320a14a2e6d9d9f28853e9e7beae703e52e/torchvision/models/resnet.py#L284

```
import os
os.makedirs("./exported_models/torch/", exist_ok=True)
output_path = "./exported_models/torch/resnet18_torch.onnx"

dummy_input = torch.randn(1, 3, 224, 224, dtype=torch.float32)

torch.onnx.export(
    model,
    (dummy_input,),
    output_path,
    input_names=["input"],
    output_names=["logits"],
)

print(f"ONNX model has been saved to {output_path}")
```

***Figure 3.11:** ResNet50 Pytorch to ONNX model conversion*

Now, let us try to visualize the converted ONNX model using Netron. *Figure 3.12* shows the ResNet50 ONNX model visualized in Netron. As we can see, the ResNet50 model has residual connections in the graph. Also, the model's input and output names are as per what we have added in the code while exporting.

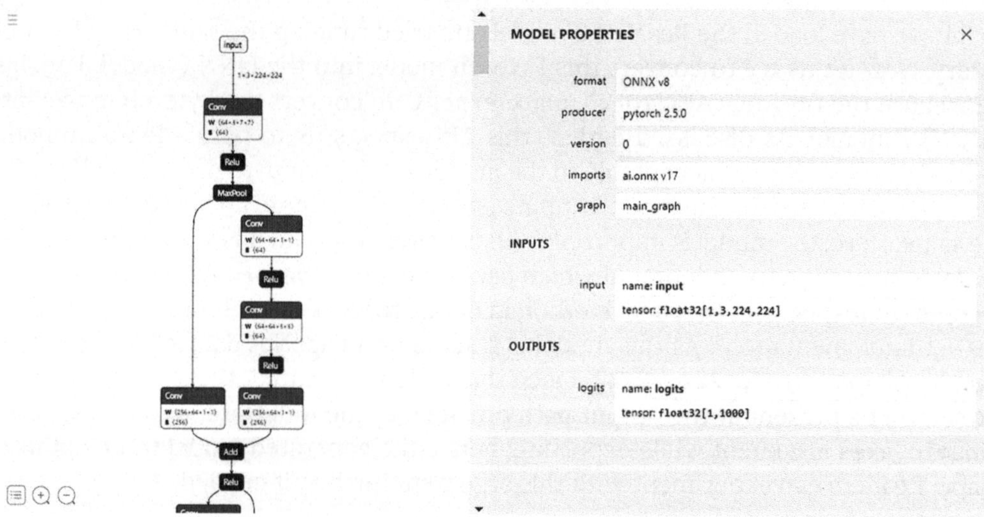

***Figure 3.12:** ResNet50 ONNX model visualized in Netron*

Converting TensorFlow 2.0 Model into ONNX

In the previous section, we learned about the Pytorch model and its conversion into ONNX. Now, we will understand the same for TensorFlow models. TensorFlow has been used in the industry for many years and its APIs have undergone significant changes over time. There are a few open-source models and codes that still use TensorFlow 1.0 APIs. Currently, the TensorFlow 2.X version is a widely used version. With the shift in the TensorFlow version, the model representation within TensorFlow has changed as well. Earlier in TensorFlow 1.X, the Protobuf-based frozen graph (**graphdef**) was used, which was later replaced by a saved model format. After the merger of Keras into TensorFlow during 2.X, Keras models are now supported in TensorFlow 2.X. For this chapter, we will only consider TensorFlow 2.X models and their APIs.

As we did in the previous sections, we first need to install the dependencies to load the model and a conversion utility called **tf2onnx**. Readers can look at TensorFlow website[6] for installing the TensorFlow python package, or execute the command shown in *Figure* 3.13. At the time of writing this chapter, the latest available version of the TensorFlow package was **2.19**.

```
# Install tensorflow dependencies
!pip install tensorflow==2.19.0 tf2onnx==1.16.1
```

Figure 3.13: *TensorFlow dependencies installation*

Converting a Simple TensorFlow Model to ONNX

Now that we have the TensorFlow dependencies in place, let us try to create the same 2-layer neural network in TensorFlow, which we created earlier with PyTorch. Then, we will convert the same into the ONNX version.

Figure 3.14 shows an example of a two-layer neural network implemented in TensorFlow. Similar to the earlier Pytorch model, this model also consists of an input layer, a hidden dense layer with ReLU activation, and an output layer.

In TensorFlow, the model is defined as a subclass of **tf.keras.Model**, where the layers are initialized in the **__init__** method. The **call** method defines the forward pass, where input data flows through these layers sequentially. In our example, the first dense layer transforms the input to a hidden representation, followed by a ReLU activation, while the second dense layer produces the final output. The model takes an input tensor of shape **[batch_size, 10]** and outputs predictions of shape **[batch_size, 2]**.

[6] https://www.tensorflow.org/install/pip#linux

```
import tensorflow as tf
import tf2onnx

class TwoLayerNet(tf.keras.Model):
    def __init__(self, input_dim, hidden_dim, output_dim):
        super(TwoLayerNet, self).__init__()
        self.dense1 = tf.keras.layers.Dense(hidden_dim, activation='relu')
        self.dense2 = tf.keras.layers.Dense(output_dim)

    def call(self, inputs):
        x = self.dense1(inputs)
        return self.dense2(x)

# Create and compile the model
input_dim = 10
hidden_dim = 20
output_dim = 2
model = TwoLayerNet(input_dim, hidden_dim, output_dim)
model.compile(optimizer='adam', loss='mse')

# Create dummy input data for tracing
dummy_input = tf.random.normal([1, input_dim])

# Dummy execution of the model.
dummy_output = model(dummy_input)
print(f"Dummy input shape: {dummy_input.shape}")
print(f"Dummy output shape: {dummy_output.shape}")
```

Figure 3.14: *TensorFlow model for two-layer neural network*

To export this model to ONNX format, we use the **tf2onnx**[7] library, which converts TensorFlow models to a standardized ONNX format. As shown in Figure 3.15, the conversion process involves calling **tf2onnx.convert.from_keras** with the model, input signature, and output path. The **input_signature** parameter is crucial as it defines the expected shape and data type of the inputs, which directly correspond to the specifications in the **call** method. When dealing with more complex models, the **@tf.function decorator** can be used on the **call** function to create explicit signatures, though in this case, the default conversion works well. Before conversion, we also need to explicitly set the **output_names** attribute of the **model** object as it will be used internally by the **tf2onnx** module during the export.

[7] https://github.com/onnx/tensorflow-onnx

```
# Export to ONNX
onnx_path = "two_layer_net_tf.onnx"
model.output_names = ["output"]

model_proto, _ = tf2onnx.convert.from_keras(
    model,
    input_signature=[tf.TensorSpec(shape=[None, input_dim], dtype=tf.float32, name='input')],
    output_path=onnx_path
)

print(f"Model exported to {onnx_path}")
```

Figure 3.15: *ONNX conversion of TensorFlow model*

Similar to **`torch.onnx.export`**, the **`tf2onnx.convert.from_keras`** function handles the conversion by tracing the model's computation graph using the provided example input. It maps each layer in the TensorFlow model to equivalent ONNX operators. In our example, the Dense layers of the TensorFlow model are converted to the Matmul layer of ONNX, whereas the Relu activation associated with the Dense layer is converted to the Relu ONNX node. The exported ONNX model is visualized in *Figure* 3.16.

The **`input_signature`** parameter must match the expected input shape defined in the model's **`call`** method. Here, **`None`** is typically used to represent the batch dimension, providing flexibility for variable batch sizes at runtime. This outcome is visually confirmed in *Figure* 3.16, where the tensor shapes reflect this dynamic axis. For models with multiple inputs, additional **`TensorSpec`** entries would be included in the input signature.

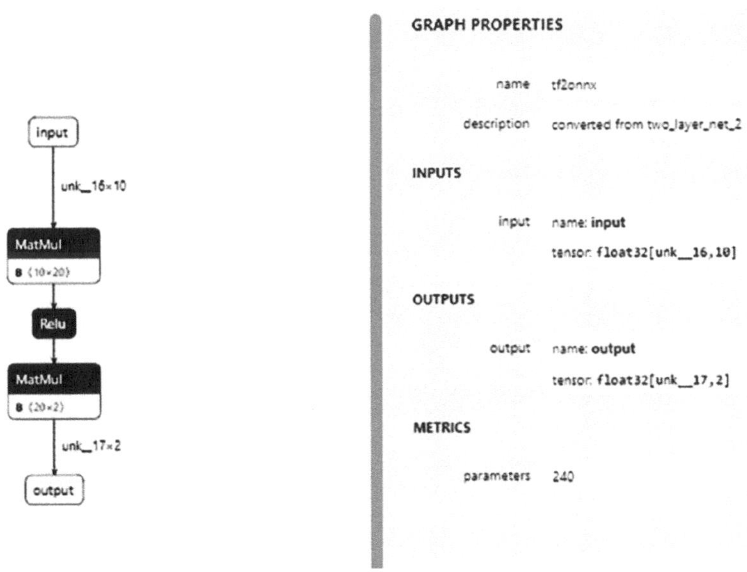

Figure 3.16: *ONNX model visualized through Netron*

Converting ResNet TensorFlow model to ONNX

Let us try to do the same with the ResNet50 model. We can load the same ResNet50 model, but this time we will load it using TensorFlow APIs. Just like Torchvision, the TensorFlow library also has built-in APIs to load pre-trained models. *Figure* 3.17 shows the code to load the ResNet50 ImageNet pre-trained model using TensorFlow APIs. In *Figure* 3.17, **`model.summary()`** generates a layer-by-layer summary of the ResNet50 model for better understanding.

```
import tensorflow as tf
import numpy as np
import requests
from PIL import Image
import matplotlib.pyplot as plt

# Load the pre-trained ResNet-18 model from TensorFlow Keras Applications
model = tf.keras.applications.ResNet50(weights='imagenet')

model.summary()
```

***Figure* 3.17:** *ResNet50 TensorFlow model loading*

Now that the model is loaded, we need to set up the image loading and preprocessing for this TensorFlow model, which are very similar to the PyTorch code we used earlier.

```
# Image Preprocessing function for ResNet input
def preprocess_image(image_path):
    # Load the image
    if image_path.startswith('http'):
        response = requests.get(image_path, stream=True)
        img = Image.open(response.raw)
    else:
        img = Image.open(image_path)

    # Resize the image to (224, 224) as ResNet models expect 224x224 input
    img = img.resize((224, 224))

    # Convert the image to numpy array and preprocess it for ResNet50
    img_array = np.array(img)

    # Preprocess the image using ResNet50's preprocessing function
    img_array = tf.keras.applications.resnet50.preprocess_input(img_array)

    # Expand dimensions to create a batch of size 1
    img_array = np.expand_dims(img_array, axis=0)

    return img_array

# Function for performing inference
def infer_image(image_path):
    # Preprocess the input image
    image = preprocess_image(image_path)

    # Perform inference using the pre-trained ResNet model
    predictions = model.predict(image)

    # Decode the predictions to class labels
    decoded_predictions = tf.keras.applications.resnet50.decode_predictions(predictions, top=3)[0]

    # Get the predicted label and confidence
    top_class_id, top_label, top_score = decoded_predictions[0]
    return top_label, top_class_id, top_score
```

Figure 3.18: ResNet50 *image preprocessing and inference functions*

Figure 3.18 and *Figure* 3.19 show the image loading, preprocessing, and model execution code. In TensorFlow, the model execution happens when we call "**`model.predict(image)`**" or "**`model(image)`**". Both the approaches invoke the **`call`** method of the model. The **`predict`** method is usually fed with the appropriate TensorFlow tensor, which the model expects and uses to generate the required output. In our case, it generates the "**`predictions`**" tensor, which represents the probability of each class instead of logits. The "**`predictions`**" tensor is passed to the "**`decode_predictions`**" API to obtain the predicted class probabilities and class labels.

```
# Example usage
image_path = 'cat.jpg'  # Replace with the path to your image
class_label, class_id, score = infer_image(image_path)

print(f"Predicted label: {class_label}, Confidence score: {score:.2f}")

# Optionally, display the image and prediction
image = Image.open(image_path)
plt.imshow(image)
plt.title(f"Prediction: {class_label} ({score:.2f})")
plt.show()
```

***Figure 3.19:** ResNet50 model execution code*

When we feed the same image of the cat to the TensorFlow model, the results will be as per *Figure* 3.20. The model can predict the image as the "**Tiger Cat**" class with a probability of **0.43**. There is a minor difference between the prediction of the TensorFlow model and the Pytorch model. This is due to the implementation of image interpolation and resizing used by these frameworks. The image preprocessing has slight differences between the frameworks, as these models are trained differently.

***Figure 3.20:** ResNet50 model output when the image of a cat is fed to the model*

To convert this ResNet50 TensorFlow model, we will use the "**tf2onnx.convert.from_keras**" API provided by **tf2onnx** utility to take the loaded TensorFlow model. Optionally, it takes the input specification, which the model is expected to. The ResNet model in our example requires input tensors of shape **[batch_size, 224, 224, 3]** with **float32** precision. Here, **batch_size** represents the dynamic dimension that accommodates varying numbers of input samples, while the fixed dimensions (**224 × 224 × 3**) correspond to standard RGB image inputs. Unlike in the previous example, where we explicitly defined **model.output_names**, here the **output_names** attribute is internally stored in the model's definition since the model is a pretrained one from the TensorFlow APIs. Here, we have not specified the **output_path** argument of **tf2onnx.convert.from_keras**. Instead, we will use the first-returned value from the API, which is an in-memory ONNX model. This in-memory ONNX model can be saved to the disk using "**onnx.save_model**". *Figure* 3.21 shows the entire code to convert the TensorFlow model into the ONNX model. Readers can check the **tf2onnx** documentation to understand how to convert the frozen graph and TFLite representation into an ONNX model.

```
import tf2onnx
import onnx

print(f"TF model output names: {model.output_names}")

# Convert the TensorFlow model to ONNX
# API documentation: https://github.com/onnx/tensorflow-onnx?tab=readme-ov-file#from_keras-tf-20-and-newer
onnx_model, _ = tf2onnx.convert.from_keras(
                    model,
                    input_signature=[tf.TensorSpec([None, 224, 224, 3], tf.float32, name="input")])

os.makedirs("./exported_models/tensorflow/", exist_ok=True)
output_path = "./exported_models/tensorflow/resnet50_tf.onnx"

# Save the ONNX model to a file
onnx.save_model(onnx_model, output_path)
```

Figure 3.21: *ResNet50 TensorFlow to ONNX conversion*

Once the ONNX model is obtained, we can load it using the Netron tool to visualize it. *Figure* 3.22 shows the same. The visualized ResNet50 model looks similar to what we have seen in the earlier PyTorch section.

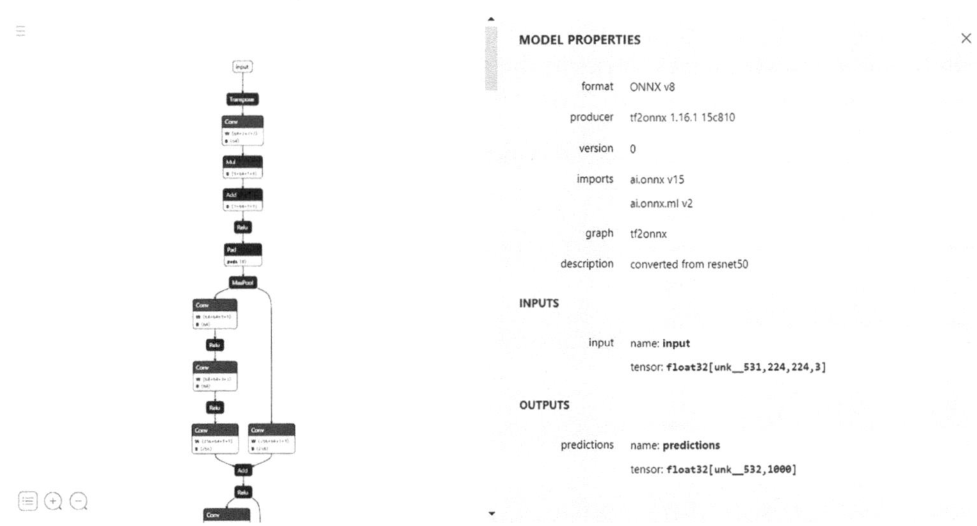

Figure 3.22: *ResNet50 TensorFlow to ONNX converted model*

Converting Scikit Learn Model into ONNX

So far, we have learned about the Pytorch and TensorFlow libraries, which provide many modern Deep Learning models. For classical Machine Learning models such as Decision Trees, Random Forests, and SVM, the Scikit-Learn library provides the necessary boilerplate code to train them on custom datasets. As there is no widely recognized standard benchmark for classical Machine Learning algorithms (unlike ImageNet in modern Deep Learning), we will train a classical Machine Learning model on a sample dataset and then convert it into ONNX.

First, we will install the required dependencies. As per *Figure* 3.23, we will install "**scikit-learn**" and "**skl2onnx**" packages.

```
# Installing scikit-learn dependencies
!pip install scikit-learn==1.7.0 skl2onnx==1.19.1
```

Figure 3.23: *Installing Scikit Learn dependencies*

For training, we will use the IRIS dataset[8] which is a small dataset of 3 different species of iris flowers–setosa, versicolor, and virginica. The dataset contains 4 features Sepal Length, Sepal Width, Petal Length, and Petal Width for each observation. The goal of the training is to classify the given observation of 4 features into one of the iris flower categories. For this, we will use a Decision Tree classifier from the Scikit-Learn library. The algorithm constructs a tree structure, where each node evaluates a specific condition based on the input features. As data traverses the tree, each condition determines which branch to follow and guides the sample toward a leaf node. The final prediction is made when the sample reaches a leaf node, which assigns the most probable class label based on the training data. These splitting conditions are learned during training by analyzing patterns in the data to maximize predictive accuracy. We will split the dataset into 80-20 splits of train and test sets.

Figure 3.24 shows the code to load the dataset, train the Decision Tree classifier, and visualize the trained Decision Tree.

[8] https://www.geeksforgeeks.org/iris-dataset/

```
import numpy as np
from sklearn.datasets import load_iris
from sklearn.model_selection import train_test_split
from sklearn.tree import DecisionTreeClassifier, plot_tree
from sklearn.metrics import accuracy_score
from sklearn.tree import export_text

# Load the Iris dataset
iris = load_iris()
X = iris.data  # Features (sepal length, sepal width, petal length, petal width)
y = iris.target  # Target (species)

# Split the dataset into training and testing sets (80% train, 20% test)
X_train, X_test, y_train, y_test = train_test_split(X, y,
                                                    test_size=0.2,
                                                    random_state=42)

# Create a Decision Tree Classifier model
clf = DecisionTreeClassifier(random_state=42)

# Train the model on the training data
clf.fit(X_train, y_train)

# Make predictions on the test set
y_pred = clf.predict(X_test)

# Evaluate the model
accuracy = accuracy_score(y_test, y_pred)
print(f"Accuracy of the Decision Tree Classifier: {accuracy:.2f}")

# Plot the Decision Tree
plt.figure(figsize=(20, 20))
plot_tree(clf, filled=True, feature_names=iris.feature_names,
          class_names=iris.target_names, rounded=True, proportion=False)
plt.title("Decision Tree trained on Iris dataset")
plt.show()
```

Figure 3.24: *Code to train Decision Tree classifier and visualize the same*

Figure 3.25 shows the trained Decision Tree classifier. The leaf nodes in the decision tree assign final classifications to each sample. The first child node of the root (in orange) directly classifies samples as setosa species. Moving deeper into the tree, the green leaf nodes correspond to versicolor classifications, while the purple nodes represent virginica species predictions. This color-coded structure visually demonstrates how samples traverse different paths in the tree to reach their final classifications.

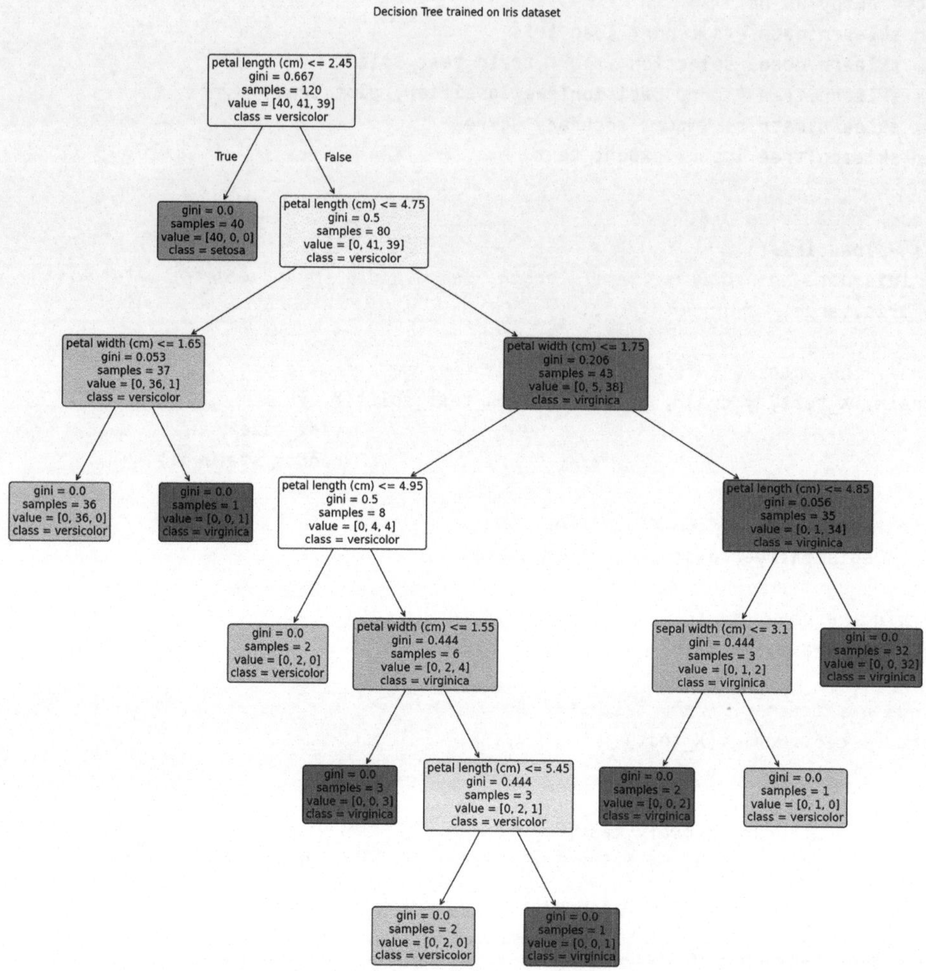

Figure 3.25: *Trained Decision Tree classifier visualized*

Once we have the Scikit-Learn trained model, we can convert that into an ONNX representation using the **`skl2onnx`** library. The **`skl2onnx`** library supports the majority of the Scikit Learn algorithms as mentioned in *its documentation*[9]. The **`skl2onnx`** library provides a high-level API named "**`to_onnx`**" to convert the supported Scikit Learn algorithms into ONNX representation. The "**`to_onnx`**" method expects a Scikit-Learn model object and a sample input, for which we will use the first sample from our dataset. The method returns an in-memory ONNX model object that can then be serialized and saved to the disk. *Figure* 3.26 shows the code to convert the trained Decision Tree classifier into the ONNX model.

[9] https://onnx.ai/sklearn-onnx/supported.html

```
# Convert into ONNX format.
from skl2onnx import to_onnx

os.makedirs("./exported_models/sklearn/", exist_ok=True)
output_path = "./exported_models/sklearn/decision_tree_sklearn.onnx"

onnx_model = to_onnx(clf, X[:1])
with open(output_path, "wb") as f:
    f.write(onnx_model.SerializeToString())
```

Figure 3.26: *Decision Tree classifier converted into* ONNX

The ONNX-converted model can be visualized using Netron, as shown in *Figure 3.27*. In the ONNX representation, the Decision Tree classifier appears as a **`TreeEnsembleClassifier`** node. The model requires input features with shape **`[batch_size, 4]`**, matching the original four-dimensional iris dataset features. For each input sample, the model outputs both class probabilities and predicted labels.

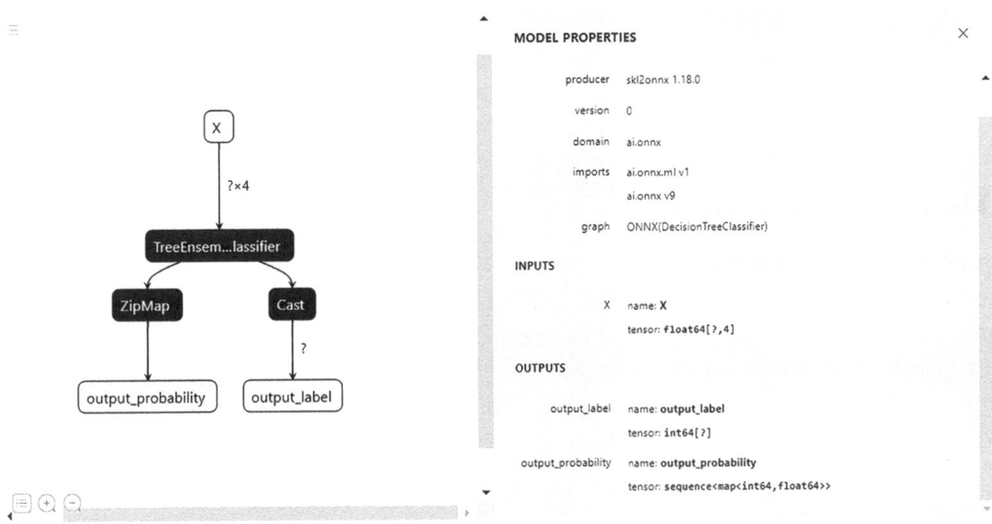

Figure 3.27: *Decision Tree classifier converted into* ONNX

Conclusion

In this chapter, we learned about ONNX model conversion from Pytorch, TensorFlow, and Scikit-Learn models. We understood the tools and APIs used for the same. Here, we took an example of a simple 2-layer neural network, ResNet50 model, and a Decision Tree classifier. The same concepts can be extended to any models available on the internet.

In the next chapter, we will focus on optimizing the ONNX models using ONNX Simplifier and ONNX Runtime libraries. Learning to optimize the models will help us execute these models more efficiently on edge devices.

CHAPTER 4
Model Optimization Using ONNX Simplifier and ONNX Runtime

Introduction

Up till now, we have learned about the ONNX ecosystem and how to derive an ONNX model from a given trained model. In this chapter, we will be focusing on how to optimize an ONNX model using tools like ONNX Simplifier and ONNX Runtime. We will also develop an in-depth understanding about the different types of optimizations applied by these tools and have a look at the impact of these optimizations on the overall execution time of the model.

Structure

We will learn about the following topics in this chapter:

- Overview of Graph Optimizations
- Types of Graph Optimizations
- Tools for Graph Optimization
- Optimizing Models with ONNX Simplifier
- Optimizing Models with ONNX Runtime

Overview of Graph Optimizations

We know that trained models consist of several nodes, where each can perform mathematical or non-mathematical operations. The mathematical operations include Convolution and Sigmoid, whereas non-mathematical operations such as Transpose, Reshape, and Slice are performed over a given tensor.

In the training regime, a model is defined via the code and not nodes, and each operation is defined by a function. In Pytorch, softmax is applied either using **`torch.nn.Softmax()`** or **`torch.nn.function.softmax()`**. When the model is exported to the ONNX model, these layers or functions are converted to corresponding nodes in the ONNX graph. When the model is defined using code for the training purpose, efficient execution is not the sole focus. In fact, the core focus during training is to run the model end-to-end, capture the gradients, and update the weights. Efficient execution becomes the focus when the model is trained and ready for production. There are some redundant nodes that are relevant during the training phase, but they cease to be relevant during the inference time. Thus, the goal of graph optimization is to find out such potential redundancies in the model and get rid of them. These optimizations do not change the model mathematically; hence the output remains unchanged. These optimizations either remove the redundant nodes or fuse together a group of nodes such that the overall execution becomes efficient.

Types of Graph Optimizations

Now that we have a general idea of graph optimizations, let us understand their different types:

- **NoOp Removal:**
    - Nodes like Dropout, that are important during training for regularization, become redundant during inference time. Removing such nodes is mandatory for the inference phase. Another example is the Identity node, which is added to update the output tensor name. Such nodes can also be removed from the graph.
    - Apart from the above, there are other nodes like Concat, Reshape, and Slice that perform tensor manipulation operations. The Concat node concatenates more than one tensor of compatible shapes. But if it has a single input then it will not perform any work. We can get rid of such Concat nodes. Similarly, if the Reshape node performs an operation that results in an output shape identical to the input shape, it becomes irrelevant and can be removed.
    - These nodes are called NoOp nodes as they do not perform any task. Such nodes include Cast, Concat, Expand, Flatten, Pad, Reshape, Split,

and Transpose. We can check their inputs, outputs, and attributes to understand whether they are actually NoOp nodes and get rid of them.

- *Figure* 4.1 shows the example of a hypothetical graph which contains a NoOp Reshape node and a NoOp Dropout node:

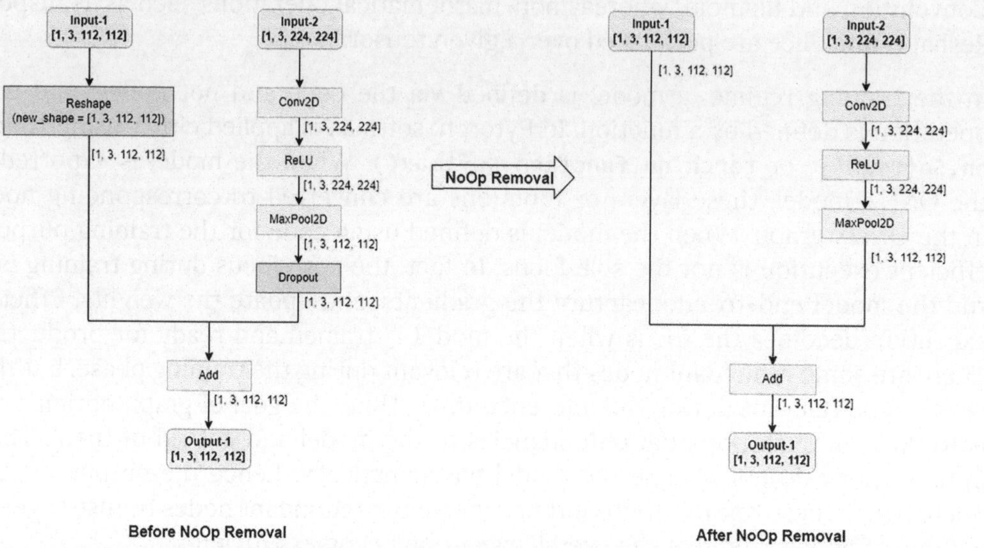

Figure 4.1: *Example of NoOp Removal optimization. In this example the red colored Reshape node and Dropout node are redundant. These are removed in the right side graph*

- **Constant Folding**
  - Constant Folding optimization identifies the nodes which have either constant inputs, or inputs coming from constant foldable nodes. Since the inputs of such nodes are constant and can be known before the execution, this optimization will pre-calculate the output by running ONNX Runtime inference on the model and will replace them with a single constant tensor.
  - *Figure* 4.2 shows how Constant Folding optimization works. In the example, the red-colored nodes are either constant nodes or nodes whose inputs are coming from constant foldable nodes. These can be removed after the optimization phase.

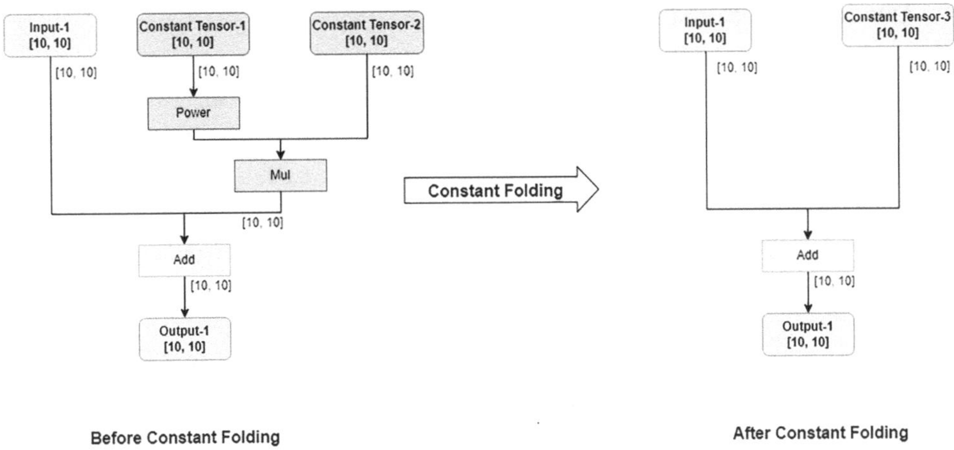

Figure 4.2: *Constant Folding optimization removing constant foldable nodes which are marked as red color. These nodes are replaced by a new constant tensor after constant folding*

- **Consecutive Node Removal**
    - Nodes such as Reshape and Concat can appear in consecutive manner and can be merged into a single node.
    - As shown in *Figure* 4.3, the model contains consecutive Reshape nodes and consecutive Concat nodes. These can be replaced by a single Reshape node and single Concat node, respectively.
    - This optimization can also be applied for nodes such as Transpose, Squeeze, Unsqueeze, and Log Softmax.

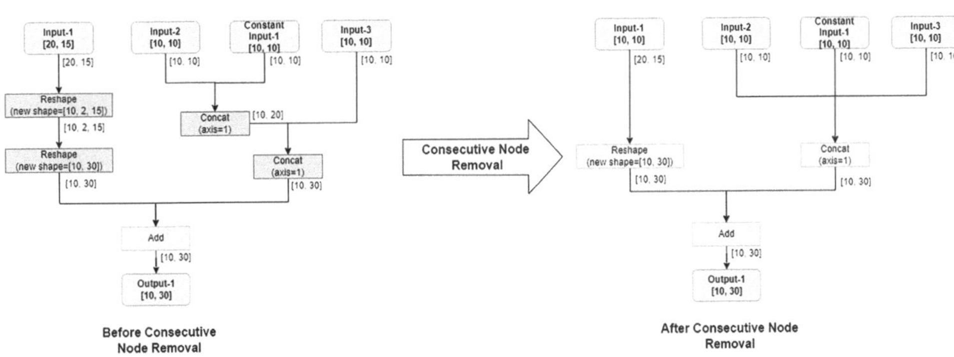

Figure 4.3*: Example showing Consecutive Node Removal optimization. Consecutive Reshape and Consecutive Concat nodes are removed after this optimization*

- **Dead Code Elimination**
    - This optimization gets rid of the nodes which do not contribute to the output of the model by traversing the graph from outputs to input and marking visited nodes. The unvisited nodes are treated as dangling nodes and can be removed.
    - Technically the ONNX models obtained from trained TensorFlow/Pytorch models will not require this optimization. However, other applied optimizations might leave some nodes in a dangling state in the graph, thereby making this optimization pass a requisite.
    - Figure 4.4 showcases the example where the Conv2D and ReLU nodes in red are not contributing to the computation of output-1 tensor. The ReLU node's output is not being used by any other node, which leaves these nodes dangling. Hence, they can be removed using this optimization.
    - This optimization also eliminates unused constant tensors in the graph.

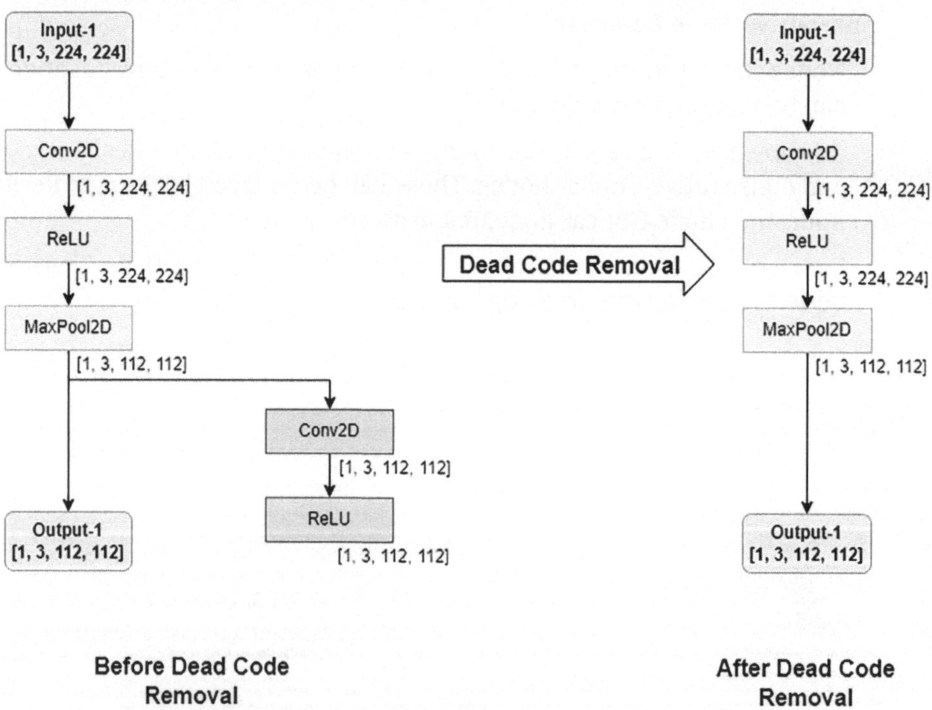

Figure 4.4: *Dead Code Removal optimization removes redundant Conv2d and ReLU nodes which are shown in red color*

- **Operator Fusion**
    - During training, the nodes are executed independently of their neighboring nodes. However, when we want to use the model in production, there are

a few node sequences, which can be fused together to form fewer nodes that will run efficiently.

- Conv2D followed by BatchNorm2D can be fused together to form a new, mathematically equivalent Conv2D node. The proof can be corroborated with *Footnote*[1].
- Another such example is the Matmul node followed by an Add node. Usually, Matmul nodes can be easily converted into Conv2D nodes with a 1x1 kernel shape. The Add node can be made the bias of Conv2D node. Hence, the Matmul+Add node pair can be replaced by a single Conv2D node. This is beneficial when it is executed on hardware, where Conv2D is implemented efficiently.
- *Figure* 4.5 represents an example of operator fusion where Conv2D and BatchNorm2D nodes are fused into a new Conv2D operator.

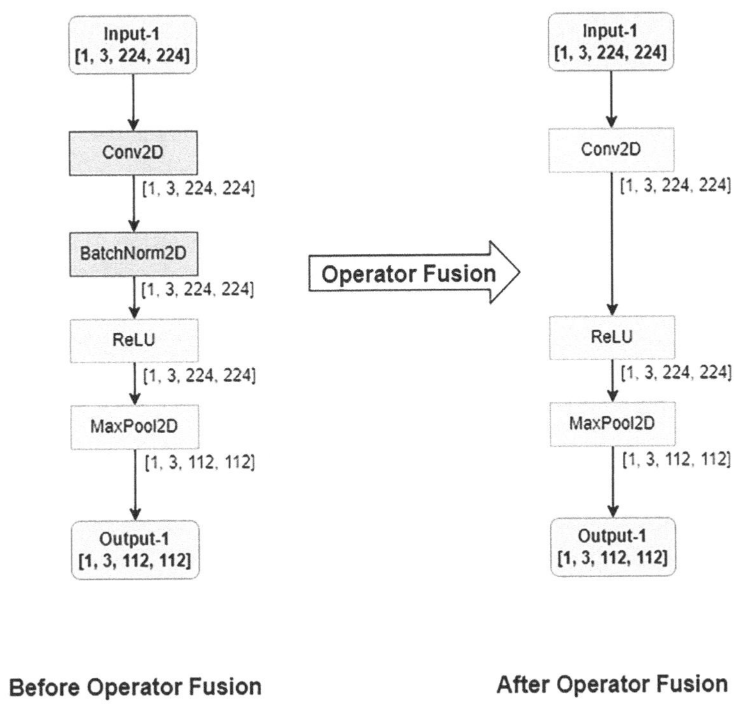

***Figure* 4.5:** *Example showing Convolution and Batchnorm fusion*

- **Duplicate Constant Removal**
  - There are cases where the same constant tensor is defined multiple times in the graph and is used at different places. Since the value of the constant

[1] https://leimao.github.io/blog/Neural-Network-Batch-Normalization-Fusion/
https://treeinthepark.tistory.com/7

tensor is the same, redundant copies can be removed and replaced by new graph connections.

- As shown in *Figure* 4.6, the model has 2 constant tensors with the same values. Both have the shape of **`[10, 10]`** and contain all values as 1s. **`Constant Tensor-2`** can be removed from the graph and its dependent node can use the **`Constant Tensor-1`** as input instead.

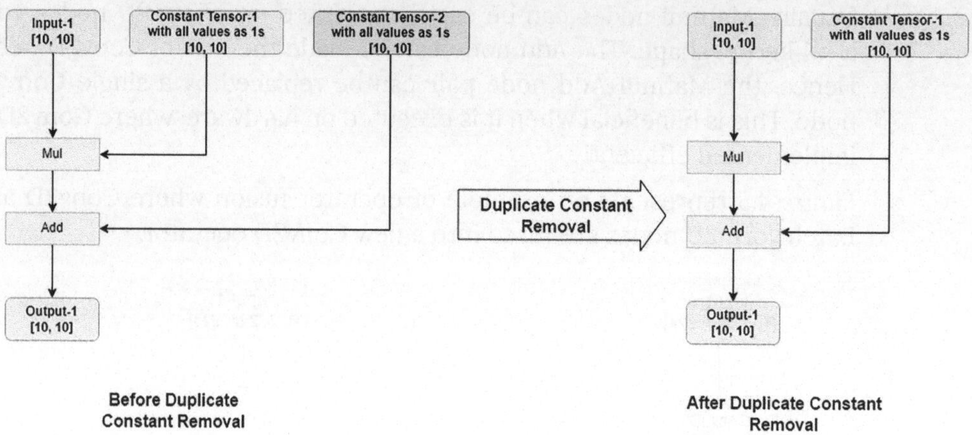

Figure 4.6: *Removal of duplicate constant tensor (red colored) using Duplicate Constant Removal optimization*

- **Shape Node Removal**
  - The Shape node in the ONNX model is used to determine the shape of the input during runtime. But if the shape is already known, the operator can be removed from the graph.
  - *Figure* 4.7 shows an example where **`Input-1`** is followed by a Shape node. Since **`Input-1`**'s shape **`[10, 10]`** is known already, the Shape operator becomes redundant. Hence, it can be replaced by a new **`Constant Tensor-3`** with the value **`[10, 10]`**.

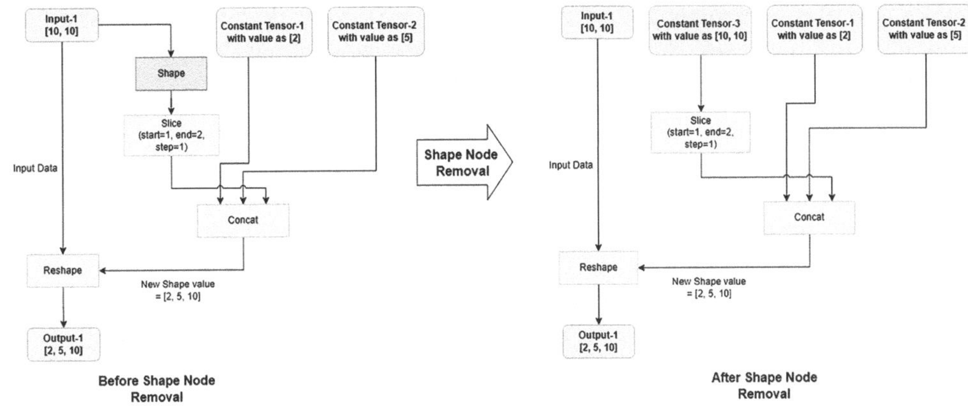

Figure 4.7: *Example of Shape Node Removal optimization*

- **If Node Removal for Constant Condition**
  - There are some ONNX models that contain If nodes in the graph. It has one boolean input and two attributes that contain subgraphs for either condition. If the boolean input is true, then the first attribute's subgraph will be executed, or else, the second attribute's subgraph is executed. This mechanism is helpful when we want dynamic behavior during runtime. However, if the boolean condition is known beforehand, we can replace the If node with corresponding subgraph.
  - In *Figure* 4.8, the If node has the conditional input True. Hence, we can replace If node with the **`cond=True`** subgraph.

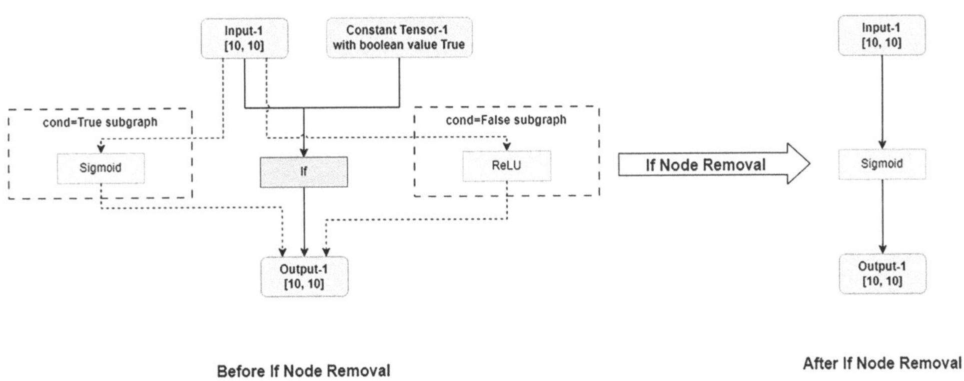

Figure 4.8: *Example of If Node Removal optimization. Conditional input of If node is known which makes If node redundant*

All the aforementioned optimizations are available in almost all the graph optimization toolkits. Now that we understand the different types of graph optimizations, it is important to know how these are applied. Usually, applying one optimization can make it possible to apply other optimizations if they were not applicable earlier. Hence, it is important to apply all these optimizations in an iterative manner. The stopping criteria consists of either arriving at a fixed number of iterations or the unchanged state of the graph after optimization. These optimizations are available in ONNX Optimizer[2] and are applied in an iterative manner by the ONNX Simplifier.

Tools for Graph Optimizations

Since we now understand graph optimizations well, we will now learn about their application. When we want to apply graph optimizations, we might need to traverse the graph, match patterns of specific nodes, remove node connections, and build new nodes and connections. The logic of graph manipulation will be different for each optimization, but high-level operations performed on graphs will be similar across different optimizations. The ONNX ecosystem has tools such as ONNX Simplifier and ONNX Runtime, which internally perform all the mentioned functions. We will learn more about these tools in the following sections:

Optimizing Models with ONNX Simplifier

The ONNX Simplifier is widely used for optimizing ONNX models. While it utilizes the ONNX Optimizer tool for common graph optimizations, the Simplifier offers broader functionality. The ONNX Simplifier can perform constant folding, selectively apply ONNX Optimizer graph optimizations, and perform shape inference on the model. It is equipped with the infrastructure to iteratively apply graph optimizations and constant folding until the graph converges, or a specified number of iterations is achieved.

Now, we will try to learn how to use this tool. Till now, we have been playing around with the ResNet ONNX model. For this purpose, we will be using a different and more complex model than ResNet. We will use the GPT-2 model from HuggingFace's `transformer` library and try to export it to ONNX to use it. The HuggingFace's `transformer` library provides a wide collection of open source models from domains like Natural Language Processing, Computer Vision, and Speech Recognition, which are present in the form of easy-to-use APIs. It allows the user to run these models and fine-tune them based on custom datasets.

Before moving forward, let us learn a bit about the GPT-2 (Generative Pre-trained Transformer 2), which is an advanced AI language model developed by OpenAI and is designed for generating human-like text using a decoder-only Transformer architecture. It follows an autoregressive approach and predicts the next word based on previous context. Since it is trained on a massive dataset of internet text, it can perform simple tasks like text completion, summarization, and translation.

GPT-2 uses the Transformer architecture that was first introduced in the 2017 paper *Attention Is All You Need*[3]. Every Transformer layer consists of self-attention

---

[2] https://github.com/onnx/optimizer/blob/master/onnxoptimizer/pass_registry.h

[3] https://arxiv.org/abs/1706.03762

mechanisms and feedforward layers that allow it to process text efficiently. Unlike bidirectional models such as BERT, GPT-2 uses only the decoder component of the Transformer.

A high-level idea of GPT-2 is illustrated in *Figure* 4.9. For a deeper understanding of transformer architecture and GPT-2 model architecture, readers can refer to Footnote[4] and Footnote[5], respectively.

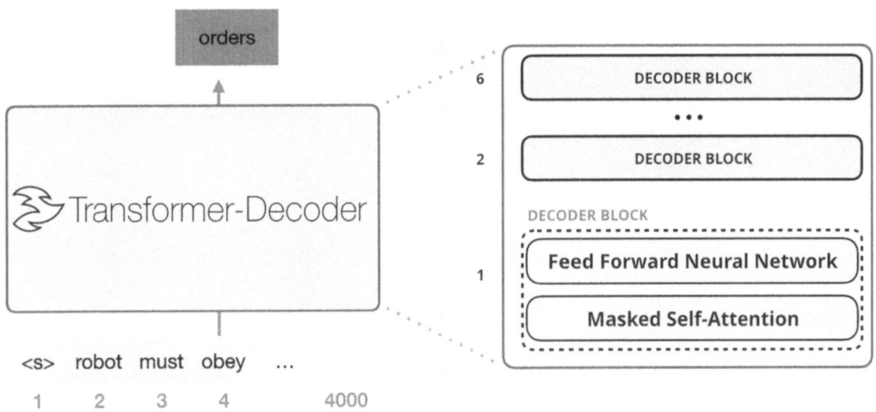

***Figure* 4.9:** *Autoregressive working of GPT-2 model (Source: Footnote[5])*

We will be following the Jupyter Notebook[6] of this chapter. Unlike earlier chapters, we will now focus on the core part of Notebook ignoring the self-explanatory cells. You must note that this notebook may use a significant amount of resources if it is run on a personal laptop with low specifications. In such cases, use Google Colab to run it.

Firstly, loading the GPT-2 model and exporting it is very similar to the steps followed with the ResNet model. The primary difference is that GPT-2 is loaded from the **`Transformer`** library's **`AutoModelForCausalLM`** class. We obtain the pre-trained model by calling **`AutoModelForCausalLM.from_pretrained()`** with the name of the desired GPT-2 model from the HuggingFace hub. The preprocessing phase for these language models is handled by a tokenizer, which is loaded via **`AutoTokenizer.from_pretrained()`** and the same model identifier. To prepare a sample input, we pass a text string to the tokenizer, which converts the words into numerical tokens that can be interpreted by the model. This tokenized input is then fed into the model to generate output tokens that must be decoded back into a string of words to form a human-readable prediction. *Figure* 4.10 shows a code snippet to load the GPT-2 model and run it on a sample input.

[4] https://jalammar.github.io/illustrated-transformer/
[5] https://jalammar.github.io/illustrated-gpt2/
[6] https://github.com/ava-orange-education/Ultimate-ONNX-for-Optimizing-Deep-Learning-Models

```
# Load GPT2 model from HuggingFace: https://huggingface.co/openai-community/gpt2

from transformers import AutoTokenizer, AutoModelForCausalLM

tokenizer = AutoTokenizer.from_pretrained("openai-community/gpt2")
model = AutoModelForCausalLM.from_pretrained("openai-community/gpt2")

# Encode the input text (prompt) into tokens
input_text = "Once upon a time"
input_ids = tokenizer.encode(input_text, return_tensors='pt')
print("Input Ids shape: ", input_ids.shape)

# Generate text using the model
output = model.generate(input_ids, max_length=50, num_return_sequences=1, no_repeat_ngram_size=2)

# Decode the generated tokens back into text
generated_text = tokenizer.decode(output[0], skip_special_tokens=True)

print("--"*30)
print(f"Given input: {input_text}")
print(f"Generated output: {generated_text}")
print("--"*30)
```

Figure 4.10: *Loading of the GPT-2 model from HuggingFace transformer and running inference on the same*

The loaded model can generate output by calling model.generate(). As previously discussed, the GPT-2 model is autoregressive, meaning that it generates one token at a time based on the provided input tokens. The entire output is produced iteratively by feeding the newly generated token, along with the previous inputs to predict the next token. This process repeats for N steps or until the model generates an <eos> (end-of-sentence) token.

The model.generate() function abstracts this iterative inference process, handling incremental inputs internally, and returning the final aggregated result. The GPT-2 model outputs tokenized representations of words, which can later be decoded using tokenizer.decode().

```
------------------------------------------------------------
Given input: Once upon a time
Generated output: Once upon a time, the world was a place of great beauty and great dange
r. The world of the gods was the place where the great gods were born, and where they wer
e to live.

The world that was created was not the same
------------------------------------------------------------
```

Figure 4.11: *Sample output from GPT-2 model's inference*

Figure 4.11 shows a sample input and the corresponding generated output. Note that the output text includes initial words from the input for context - these are not generated by the model but prepended for readability.

Now, let us understand how to export the GPT-2 model into an ONNX model. We have learned that the torch.onnx.export API can be used for this purpose. It takes a PyTorch model object, sample inputs for tracing the computational graph, the output path for the ONNX model, optional input and output names, and a dynamic axes dictionary to generate models with dynamic shapes

Earlier, we used model.generate() and passed the tokenized input tensor to run multiple inferences. However, we still do not know the exact inputs required by the model under the hood. To understand this, we need to examine the source code of the GPT-2 model from Hugging Face's Transformers repository. Since we have used transformers==4.53.2, we can refer to source code[7] to identify the input arguments of the **`forward`** method in the GPT-2 model. These are illustrated in *Figure* 4.12.

As shown in *Figure* 4.12, the **`forward`** function has multiple input arguments. Among these, we have only provided the **`input_ids`** tensor during the **`model.generate()`** call, while the rest of the arguments assumed their default values. A notable argument is **`logits_to_keep`**, which is set to **`0`** by default. Consequently, when exporting the model, the resulting ONNX model will expect two inputs: **`input_ids`** and **`logits_to_keep`**.

```
class GPT2LMHeadModel(GPT2PreTrainedModel, GenerationMixin):

    @auto_docstring
    def forward(
        self,
        input_ids: Optional[torch.LongTensor] = None,
        past_key_values: Optional[tuple[tuple[torch.Tensor]]] = None,
        cache_position: Optional[torch.LongTensor] = None,
        attention_mask: Optional[torch.FloatTensor] = None,
        token_type_ids: Optional[torch.LongTensor] = None,
        position_ids: Optional[torch.LongTensor] = None,
        head_mask: Optional[torch.FloatTensor] = None,
        inputs_embeds: Optional[torch.FloatTensor] = None,
        encoder_hidden_states: Optional[torch.Tensor] = None,
        encoder_attention_mask: Optional[torch.FloatTensor] = None,
        labels: Optional[torch.LongTensor] = None,
        use_cache: Optional[bool] = None,
        output_attentions: Optional[bool] = None,
        output_hidden_states: Optional[bool] = None,
        return_dict: Optional[bool] = None,
        logits_to_keep: Union[int, torch.Tensor] = 0,
        **kwargs,
    ) -> Union[tuple, CausalLMOutputWithCrossAttentions]:
```

Figure 4.12: *Signature of the GPT-2 model's forward method*

[7] https://github.com/huggingface/transformers/blob/37f8b0b53512e6aae0cfd15746c133c1017 83178/src/transformers/models/gpt2/modeling_gpt2.py#L1149

The **`logits_to_keep`** argument is used to filter specific logits for a given token from the input. If we keep the default value (**`0`**), it will be treated as an input in the ONNX model, which is undesirable. Instead, we can pass **`None`** to prevent it from becoming a required input. *Figure* 4.13 demonstrates the code for exporting the GPT-2 model to ONNX, including the use of the **`kwargs`** argument to explicitly set **`logits_to_keep`** to **`None`** during export.

We will be exporting two variants of the model. One variant is with static shaped inputs and the other variant is with dynamic shaped inputs. The dynamic-shaped model will enable us to use it for any shape of input when deployed. However, it has some drawbacks. The dynamically shaped model contains nodes that could have been optimized, but due to the nature of dynamic inputs, these nodes must remain in the model to ensure correct execution during deployment. For exporting models with dynamic shapes, we need to pass **`dynamic_axes`** as an additional argument to the **`torch.onnx.export`** function. The model with static-shaped input and model with dynamic-shaped input can be exported by following code shown in *Figure* 4.13:

```
# Export GPT2 model to ONNX

import os
import torch
os.makedirs("./exported_models/", exist_ok=True)
static_shape_output_path = "./exported_models/gpt2_hf_static_shape.onnx"
dynamic_shape_output_path = "./exported_models/gpt2_hf_dynamic_shape.onnx"

# Export the model to ONNX with static shapes
dummy_static_input_ids = torch.ones([1, 128], dtype=torch.int32)
torch.onnx.export(
    model,
    args=(dummy_static_input_ids,),
    f=static_shape_output_path,
    kwargs={'logits_to_keep': None},
    input_names=["input_ids"],
    output_names=["logits"],
    opset_version=14
)

# Export the model to ONNX with dynamic shapes
torch.onnx.export(
    model,
    args=(input_ids,),
    f=dynamic_shape_output_path,
    kwargs={'logits_to_keep': None},
    input_names=["input_ids"],
    output_names=["logits"],
    # Dynamic axes for batch size and sequence length
    dynamic_axes={"input_ids": {0: "batch_size", 1: "sequence_length"},
                  "logits": {0: "batch_size", 1: "sequence_length"}},
    opset_version=14
)
```

Figure 4.13: *Exporting the GPT-2 model with static input shapes and with dynamic input shapes*

The benefit of having static input shapes is that we know the shapes of inputs and all the intermediate tensors beforehand. It increases the overall scope of the graph optimizations. However, this comes at a cost as for this GPT-2 model, it will expect a single input named "**input_ids**" of shape **["batch", "sequence"]**. If we fix the input shape to **[1, 128]**, then we will need to pad the input of **[1, 100]** with 28 zeros to make it **[1, 128]**. Due to this step, the model will have to perform extra computation. However, this fixed shape is incompatible with the input **[1, 256]**, making it inappropriate. In such cases, we might need to fix the input to the maximum possible sequence length in the production or maximum sequence length as supported by the model.

If the model has dynamic input shapes, then it limits the scope of graph optimizations. We will see this while optimizing both of these models.

Now, in order to optimize these models using ONNX Simplifier, we need to call one simple API "**simplify**" of the **onnxsim** package. *Figure* 4.14 shows the function to optimize the model. For common use cases, the plain usage of API is sufficient. However, there are other optional arguments for the "**simplify**" function that provide us fine-grained control over the applications of optimizations. Readers can refer to ONNX Simplifier's source code[8] for the same.

```
import onnx
from onnxsim import simplify

def optimize_model_using_simplifier(model_path, output_path):
    # Load onnx model
    onnx_model = onnx.load(model_path)

    # Simplify model using Onnx-Simplifier
    simplified_model, status = simplify(onnx_model)

    # Save simplified model
    onnx.save(simplified_model, output_path)
    print(f"Before Nodes: {len(onnx_model.graph.node)}")
    print(f"After Nodes: {len(simplified_model.graph.node)}")
```

***Figure* 4.14:** *Code for optimizing model using ONNX Simplifier*

The above approach works for an in-memory ONNX model, where both the input and output models reside in memory of an existing python process. However, there is an alternative way to optimize the ONNX model using the ONNX Simplifier. We can use the command-line interface of the **onnxsim** package, as shown in the code below, to optimize the model and save the optimized version to a specified location on the disk. The CLI command mentioned as follows takes **input_model.onnx**, optimizes it, and saves it as **output_model.onnx**:

```
python -m onnxsim input_model.onnx output_model.onnx
```

When we optimize both models using the preceding function, we will witness a change in the number of nodes in each of them. *Table* 4.1 shows the change in the number of nodes of these graphs before and after the optimizations were applied.

8 https://github.com/daquexian/onnxsimplifier/blob/master/onnxsim/onnx_simplifier.py#L100

Sr. No.	Model Type	Nodes in Original Model	Nodes in Optimized Model
1	Model with static input	1168	673
2	Model with dynamic input	2766	1435

Table 4.1: *Table showing number of nodes changed in GPT-2 model after ONNX Simplifier optimizations*

From the table, we can notice a visible difference between the number of nodes in the original model with static shapes and the number of nodes in the original model with dynamic shapes. This is because the shapes are resolved during the runtime with the help of dynamic operators such as Shape, Gather, and Slice.

Another noteworthy observation from the table is the change in the number of nodes after optimization. The ONNX Simplifier has reduced the number of nodes by almost half for both of these models. It will be reflected when we run the ONNX Runtime inference and measure the execution time of the model, especially on edge devices where resources are limited.

Optimizing Models with ONNX Runtime

Now, let us perform similar optimizations with the ONNX Runtime tool. The ONNX Runtime tool allows the user to apply graph optimizations when the model is loaded in the ONNX Runtime session. It offers fundamental optimizations that overlap with the ONNX Simplifier tool. In addition to these, it includes other optimizations like Conv+Add fusion, Conv+Mul fusion, transformer-specific optimizations such as GeLU fusion and Attention fusion, as well as layout optimizations. These optimizations are grouped and enabled via different optimization levels of ONNX Runtime. *Table 4.2* offers a detailed explanation of these levels. Readers can learn more about these levels and the corresponding optimizations applied in them through ONNX Runtime documentation[9] and its pass registry implementation[10].

Sr. No.	Optimization Level	Description
1	ORT_DISABLE_ALL	Disables all optimizations
2	ORT_ENABLE_BASIC	Enables basic optimizations such as removal of NoOp such as **`Identity`**, **`Dropout`**, **`Reshape`**, **`Unsqueeze`**, **`Cast`**, fusion of **`Add`**, **`Mul`**, **`BatchNorm`** with **`Conv/MatMul`**, **`LayerNorm`**, **`Gelu`**, Quantized-Dequantized node removal, **`constant folding`**, **`common subexpression elimination`**, and so on

[9] https://onnxruntime.ai/docs/performance/model-optimizations/graph-optimizations.html
[10] https://github.com/microsoft/onnxruntime/blob/754ee21f83518bf127ba481cf1bedf58ee3b5374/onnxruntime/core/optimizer/graph_transformer_utils.cc

3	ORT_ENABLE_EXTENDED	Enables basic and extended optimizations by incorporating optimizations specific to individual backends such as **CUDA** for Nvidia devices, and **ROCm** for AMD devices
4	ORT_ENABLE_ALL	Enables all available optimizations including layout optimizations to change the layout of the input of the nodes by adding or removing a **Transpose** node. This is required when a particular backend has efficient implementation for a given layout. An example of this is **NCHW** input to **NHWC** input conversion. Here **N** is the batch, **C** is the channels, **H** is height and **W** is width

Table 4.2: *Table showing different levels of optimizations in ONNX Runtime*

Having grasped the overall idea of optimizations, let us now try to optimize the GPT-2 model using the ONNX Runtime. *Figure* 4.15 shows the example code to optimize the model using ONNX Runtime.

```
import onnxruntime as rt

def optimize_model_using_ort(model_path, output_path):
    # Load onnx model
    sess_options = rt.SessionOptions()
    sess_options.graph_optimization_level = rt.GraphOptimizationLevel.ORT_ENABLE_ALL

    # Below are the different levels of optimizations in onnxruntime
    # rt.GraphOptimizationLevel.ORT_DISABLE_ALL -> Disables all optimizations
    # rt.GraphOptimizationLevel.ORT_ENABLE_BASIC -> Enables basic optimizations
    # rt.GraphOptimizationLevel.ORT_ENABLE_EXTENDED -> Enables basic and extended optimizations
    # rt.GraphOptimizationLevel.ORT_ENABLE_ALL -> Enables all available optimizations including layout optimizations

    # To enable model serialization after graph optimization set this
    sess_options.optimized_model_filepath = output_path

    session = rt.InferenceSession(model_path, sess_options)

    # No need to run the model. Initializing the session will generate the optimized model

    orig_model = onnx.load(model_path)
    opt_model = onnx.load(output_path)
    print(f"Before Nodes: {len(orig_model.graph.node)}")
    print(f"After Nodes: {len(opt_model.graph.node)}")
```

Figure 4.15: *Code for optimizing model using ONNX Runtime*

The ONNX Runtime optimizes the model when the **session** is initiated. Till now, we have not used the **session_options** argument while creating a session. This argument allows us to tweak the model loading and execution within the session itself. Readers can learn more about it from ONNX Runtime documentation[11]. We need to use the **session_options** flag to provide the graph optimization level and the output path of the optimized model. Once we provide this while creating a session, the optimized model will be saved on the output path.

[11] https://onnxruntime.ai/docs/api/python/api_summary.html#onnxruntime.SessionOptions

We can measure the effectiveness of the optimization by checking the number of nodes in the graph before and after the optimization is applied. *Table* 4.3 demonstrates how well the ONNX Runtime has optimized the models. We can observe that the number of nodes in the optimized model has decreased even further than what the ONNX Simplifier achieved. This is mainly due to transformer architecture specific optimizations present in ONNX Runtime.

Sr. No.	Model Type	Nodes in Original Model	Nodes in Optimized Model
1	Model with static input	1168	365
2	Model with dynamic input	2766	1120

***Table* 4.3:** *Table showing number of nodes changed in GPT-2 model after ONNX Runtime optimizations*

Conclusion

In this chapter, we focused on the graph optimization of the Deep Learning model. We learned about the importance and examples of these graph optimizations in detail. We also experimented with optimizing the GPT-2 model using ONNX Simplifier and ONNX Runtime, and understood the impact of these tools on the model in terms of the number of nodes.

In the next chapter, we will explore additional techniques for improving model efficiency, while diving deeper into quantization and its role in optimizing models. Just like in this chapter, we will experiment with a model by applying quantization, and evaluating its performance.

CHAPTER 5

Model Quantization Using ONNX Runtime

Introduction

So far, we have learned about the ONNX model, how to export it to the ONNX representation, and optimize the ONNX model. Now, we will dive deeper into the quantization part of machine learning. We will understand how to execute the model efficiently by quantizing it, the fundamentals of quantization, types of quantization methods, and the overall process of quantizing models. Later in the chapter, we will gain hands-on experience as we quantize the BERT model on a SQuAD dataset and measure the gains in the model execution.

Structure

This chapter covers the following topics:

- Overview of Quantization
- Example of Quantization
- Overall Process of Quantization
- Types of Quantization
- Benefits and Drawbacks of Quantization
- Quantizing BERT Model
- Quantized Model in ONNX

Overview of Quantization

All machine learning models are usually trained on a **single-precision floating point** number (FP32) or a **half-precision floating point** (FP16) representation. It is useful because during training we would need to calculate gradients, apply the chain rule, and update the weights. Achieving higher precision in training machine learning models can reduce numerical errors, leading to more stable and reliable calculations. This stability can, in turn, help the model converge more effectively during the training process, especially while working on complex or sensitive tasks. Once it is trained, the model can be executed in lower precision, such as in integers with 8-bit representation.

Since matrix multiplication is the major part of Machine Learning model calculation, optimizing multiplication and addition operations can improve the execution significantly. The quantization process makes it possible to execute such operations in lower precision. The integer operations are simpler and faster because they only involve basic bit-wise operations, with no fractions or decimals. On the other hand, **floating-point operations** are more complex because they require managing exponents, mantissas, and rounding, all of which adds extra steps. Modern processors are highly optimized for integer operations, making them faster than floating-point operations, which need more computational resources for accurate calculation. It should be noted that the quantization process quantizes the weights of the model as well as its intermediate tensors. That means the entire model is executed in lower precision.

This conversion results in a loss of precision in the calculations, leading to computational errors when compared to higher-precision computations. This discrepancy, known as quantization noise, can negatively affect the model's accuracy.

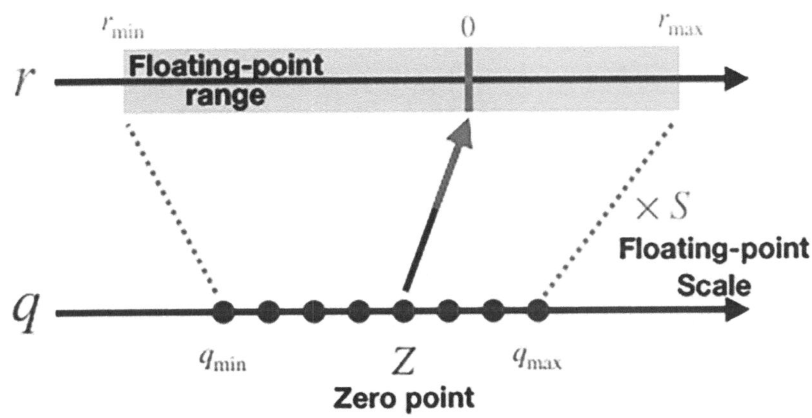

***Figure 5.1:** Mapping of floating point data range into integer data range*

Having understood the idea of reducing precision, we will now look at how it can be done. As shown in *Figure* 5.1, a floating point tensor with range `[r_min, r_max]` can be mapped to a lower precision format `q` with range `[q_min, q_max]` with the help of scaling factor `S` and zero point `Z` on lower precision. All tensors related to each layer/node can be mapped similarly. The range `[r_min, r_max]` for every activation (layer output) can be found by tracking the output of each tensor by running the model through ONNX Runtime with the help of a calibration dataset.

To understand these detailed calculations, let us begin by defining the key parameters. Consider an input tensor with a maximum value r_{max} and a minimum value r_{min}. For lower-precision quantization, we use INT8 as a reference, which has an 8-bit representation. The signed INT8 format covers the range `[-128, 127]`, while the unsigned INT8 range is `[0, 255]`. In contrast, the single-precision floating-point (FP32) representation supports a much wider range, approximately `[-3.4e+38, 3.4e+38]`. However, when the tensor's dynamic range $[r_{min}, r_{max}]$ is tracked, it often occupies only a small fraction of the FP32 or FP16 range.

The values within `[rmin, rmax]` can be mapped to a quantized representable range `[qmin, qmax]` using two key equations: *Equation* (1) describes the de-quantization process which converts the quantized tensor to unquantized tensor, while *Equation* (2) defines the quantization process. A detailed derivation of these mappings can be found in Footnote[1].

$$x = s(x_q - z) \tag{1}$$

$$x_q = \text{clip}\Big(\text{round}\big(\frac{1}{s}x + z\big), \alpha_q, \beta_q\Big) \tag{2}$$

$$s = \frac{r_{\text{max}} - r_{\text{min}}}{q_{\text{max}} - q_{\text{min}}} \tag{3}$$

$$z = \text{round}\Big(\frac{r_{\text{max}}q_{\text{min}} - r_{\text{min}}q_{\text{max}}}{r_{\text{max}} - r_{\text{min}}}\Big) \tag{4}$$

Where:

- **x**: The original floating-point value in range $[r_{min}, r_{max}]$
- x_q: Quantized value of x in range $[q_{min}, q_{max}]$
- **s**: A floating point scaling factor that determines the resolution of the quantization
- **z**: An integer offset used to represent zero in the quantized space
- $\text{clip}(x, \alpha_q, \beta_q)$: defined as

$$\text{clip}(x,\alpha_q,\beta_q) = \begin{cases} \alpha_q \text{ if } x \le \alpha_q \\ x \text{ if } \alpha_q < x < \beta_q \\ \beta_q \text{ if } x \ge \beta_q \end{cases}$$

[1] https://leimao.github.io/article/Neural-Networks-Quantization/

Example of Quantization

Having understood the theory of quantization, let us now quantize a sample tensor of 6 values. In the following example, we have taken an arbitrary tensor **X** with random values:

$$\mathbf{X} = \begin{bmatrix} 0.72 & -1.34 & 2.15 & 0.89 & -0.45 & 1.67 \end{bmatrix}$$

This tensor has a range of **[-1.34, 2.15]**. So, r_{min} **= -1.34** and r_{max} **= 2.15**. Now, we want to map this to the signed INT8 range. Hence, q_{min} **= -128** and q_{max} **= 127**. By using *Equation* (3) and *Equation* (4), we can find the values of scale (**s**) and zero-point (**z**).

$$\begin{aligned} s &= \frac{2.15 - (-1.34)}{127 - (-128)} \\ &= 0.013686 \end{aligned}$$

$$\begin{aligned} z &= \text{round}\left(\frac{2.15 * (-128) - (-1.34) * 127}{2.15 - (-1.34)}\right) \\ &= \text{round}(-30.08) \\ &= -30 \end{aligned}$$

Once we get the values of scale and zero-point, we can use *Equation* (2) to quantize individual values of tensor **X**. We will show a sample quantization calculation for the first value of tensor **X** which is 0.72. The rest of the values have been left for you to complete as an exercise.

$$\begin{aligned} \text{For} \quad x &= 0.72 \\ x_q &= \text{clip}\left(\text{round}\left(\frac{1}{0.013686}0.72 + (-30)\right), -128, 127\right) \\ &= 23 \end{aligned}$$

Similar calculations can be performed for the remaining elements of the tensor **X**. The quantized version of X (**Xq**) will be as follows:

$$\mathbf{X_q} = \begin{bmatrix} 23 & -128 & 127 & 35 & -63 & 92 \end{bmatrix}$$

To check it again, we will convert this quantized tensor Xq into an un-quantized tensor X ($\hat{\mathbf{X}}$). Let us dequantize the first value which is 23 using *Equation* (1):

$$\begin{aligned} \hat{x} &= 0.013686(23 - (-30)) \\ &= 0.725358 \end{aligned}$$

When we do the same for all the other values of ×q, we will get tensor $\hat{\mathbf{X}}$ as shown:

$$\hat{\mathbf{X}} = [0.725358 \quad -1.341228 \quad 2.148702 \quad 0.88959 \quad -0.451638 \quad 1.669692]$$

As we can see, the values in tensor $\hat{\mathbf{X}}$ are not the same as the values of tensor **X**. The difference is shown as tensor δ here:

$$\delta = [-0.005358 \quad 0.001228 \quad 0.001298 \quad 0.00041 \quad 0.001638 \quad 0.000308]$$

This difference is due to quantization. Here, we transformed single-precision floating-point data into integer precision, resulting in the loss of the fine-grained precision inherent to the single-precision floating-point range. This difference is called **quantization noise**, due to which the operations in the model would not produce exact results when they are performed in lower precision.

Overall Quantization Process

Till now, we have learned a lot about quantization and its fundamentals. However, we are yet to look at the big picture. The overall quantization process[2] looks similar to training a model, but there are few differences.

In the quantization process, the weights are static and can be quantized as shown earlier, but quantizing the weights is not sufficient. We want to run individual layers of the model in lower precision. It means the operators such as Convolution and MatMul should also run in lower precision. Instead of floating point multiplication, it should perform integer multiplication. For that, the input of such operators should also be quantized. These inputs and outputs are called **activation**.

In case of weights, we know the min and max from their distribution, which will not change during inference. However, we do not know the range of input values during deployment. Hence, the general practice is to first identify a small, unbiased, and balanced dataset that reflects the distribution like the samples that you might encounter during inference. This dataset is called a **calibration dataset**.

During the quantization process, we will feed the samples from this calibration dataset to the model, while generating and tracking the outputs of each layer. We will capture the histogram of all the values encountered during the process for a given output of a layer. Based on the histogram, we will be able to understand the overall distribution of the value of the output of a particular layer. *Figures* 5.2 and 5.3 show examples of such a distribution for weights and activation of the convolution layer of MobileNetv2, respectively.

[2] https://pytorch.org/blog/quantization-in-practice/

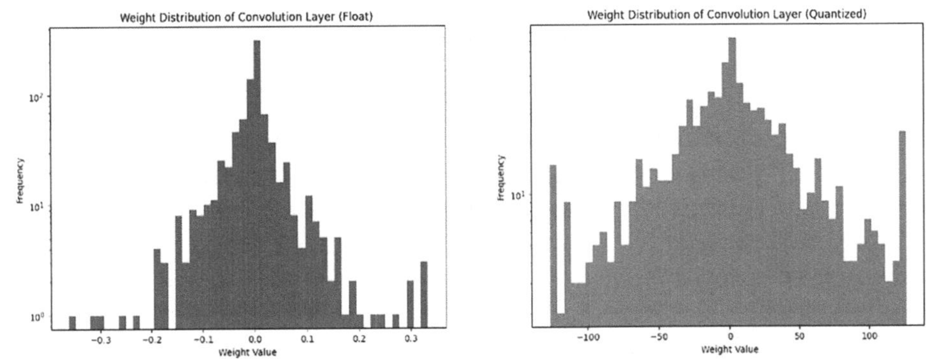

Figure 5.2: *Weight distribution of a convolution layer of MobileNetv2 model in unquantized and quantized range (Source: Footnote[3])*

As shown in *Figure* 5.3, the histogram of activation is mainly centered around 0 in floating point range. It forms a normal distribution. However, there can be cases where the distribution of histograms is completely skewed to either side.

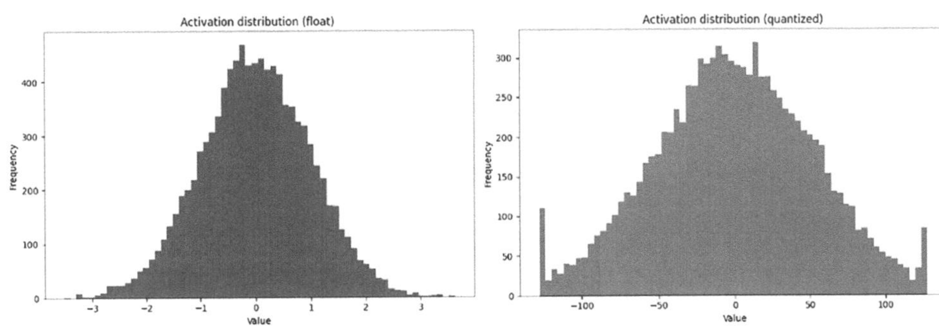

Figure 5.3: *Activation distribution of a convolution layer of MobileNetv2 model in unquantized and quantized range (Source: Footnote[3])*

If the calibration dataset is biased, unbalanced, and does not represent the test time distribution, then the tracked histogram will be different from the histograms of samples encountered at the inference time. Since, we will use this histogram to quantize the float values to integer values, the optimal mapping will not occur if the calibration dataset is biased and unbalanced.

Once we have the histogram distribution of every model activation, we can calculate the scale and zero-point for each activation. We can then quantize the input before feeding it to a particular operator. It will execute the operator in lower precision. The inputs can be quantized by introducing a Quantize node before the operator and the outputs from the layer can be dequantized by introducing a DeQuantize node after

[3] https://www.edge-ai-vision.com/2024/04/quantization-of-convolutional-neural-networks-quantization-analysis/

the operator. As mentioned in ONNX Runtime source code[4], not all the operators can support lower precision execution. In such cases, the preceding node's DeQuantize node will become the parent node of such operator and next node's Quantize node will become its child node. It means that there will not be any Quantize node before and a DeQuantize node after such the operator to allow its execution in higher precision. In case of operators which can work with lower precision, operators in a quantized graph are preceded by a Quantize node and are followed by a DeQuantize node. This means that between two consecutive quantized operators, there exists a pair of DeQuantize (from the first operator) and Quantize (for the next operator) nodes. Since these two operations cancel each other out, the quantized output of the first operator can be directly fed as input to the subsequent operator without intermediate conversions. This is shown in *Figure 5.4*.

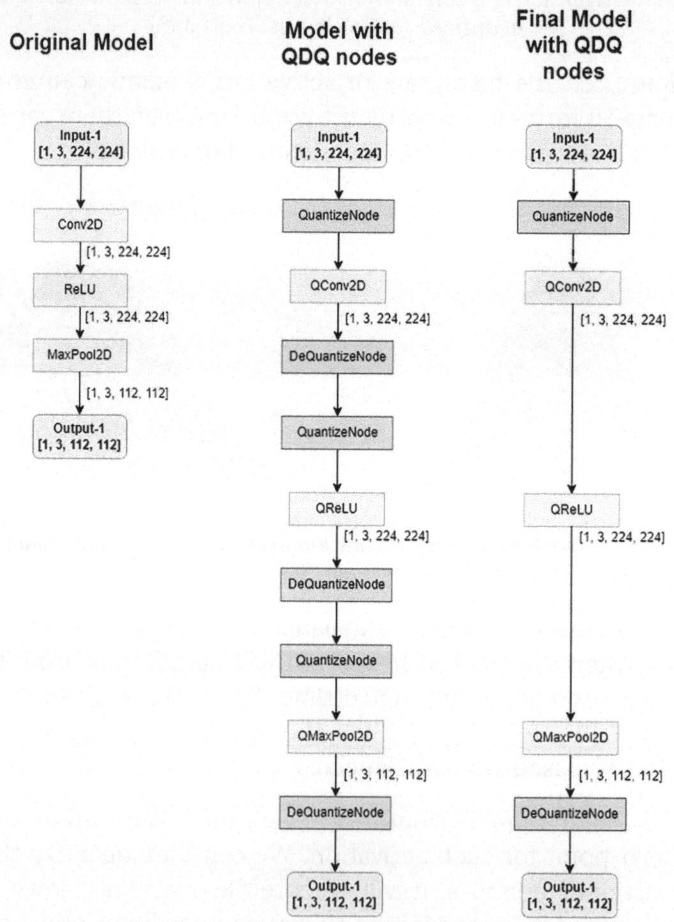

Figure 5.4: *Changes in the model during the quantization process. The model has one Quant and one DeQuant node. Normal operators such as Conv2D are now converted into QConv2D*

[4] https://github.com/microsoft/onnxruntime/blob/main/onnxruntime/python/tools/quantization/registry.py

After removal of redundant Quant-DeQuant nodes, ideally there will be only a single Quant node at the start of the graph and a single DeQuant node at the end of the graph. These are required because the model's input and output will still remain in single floating point precision (FP32). These can be skipped by feeding quantized input and obtaining quantized output as well.

Types of Quantization

Now that we possess a solid understanding of quantization, let us understand more about its different types[5]:

- **Post Training Quantization (PTQ)**
  - As the name suggests, here the model is quantized once it is trained. It does not require retraining the model.
  - For this, a calibration dataset is used to gather the histograms of the activation and weights. Based on that the scale and zero-point are calculated for each activation and weight.
  - For most use cases, PTQ performs well. However, it struggles in scenarios where the model contains sensitive layers (such as Attention Layers), has a non-uniform weight distribution caused by outliers or long-tailed data, or has already been pruned.
- **Quantization Aware Training (QAT)**
  - Quantization Aware Training is a technique where quantization is simulated during the training process. The model is trained with quantization in mind, allowing it to learn to compensate for quantization noise.
  - The training graph of the model is populated with fake quantization nodes, which mimic the behavior of the actual quantization. The activation and weights of the model are quantized and dequantized on the fly during training to simulate the effects.
  - Gradients are calculated using quantized values but the weights are updated in full precision (FP32).
  - This technique is usually preferred when PTQ fails to achieve a particular accuracy threshold.
  - Since the training parameters are adjusted to compensate for quantization noise, such quantized model is more accurate than the PTQ quantized model.
  - QAT can be either performed on the entire dataset if the model is untrained or on the calibration dataset if the model is already trained.

[5] https://newsletter.maartengrootendorst.com/p/a-visual-guide-to-quantization

Apart from these techniques, there are two more worth understanding. These are based on when the histogram is computed and weights and activations are quantized:

- **Static Quantization**
  - In static quantization, the model's weights and activations are quantized before the inference. The histogram for every activation is identified using a calibration dataset and quantized using the same. As the entire model is pre-quantized before the inference, the inference does not have any extra overhead due to quantization. The execution would happen in lower precision.
  - This method works well on edge devices where the resources are limited.
  - Both PTQ and QAT techniques fall under static quantization as activation ranges are pre-computed before inference.
- **Dynamic Quantization**
  - In dynamic quantization, only model weights are quantized ahead of time. The activations are quantized dynamically at the runtime just before executing computations.
  - It is relatively easier to implement as there is no need to get the calibration dataset and calculate histograms of activations. It works well for Transformer based architectures where activation ranges vary significantly.
  - There are cases where it is less accurate as the activations are quantized based on individual inputs encountered at the runtime rather than finite sized calibration dataset. The individual inputs can have outliers and those outliers can significantly influence the values of scale and zero-point. When we determine the scale and zero-point from histogram obtained through calibration dataset, such outliers play a less significant role.
  - Since the activations are quantized at the runtime, there is an extra overhead, which makes Dynamic Quantization slower to execute than static quantized models.

Generally, it is recommended to use dynamic quantization for sequence-based models such as RNN and Transformers and static quantization for CNN based models. Both methods fall under Post Training Quantization (PTQ). If these cannot satisfy the accuracy criteria, then Quantization Aware Training (QAT) can be performed to retrain the model and compensate for lost accuracy. Originally, ONNX Runtime lacked support for quantized operators. During this period, it officially supported Quantization-Aware Training (QAT). However, once the native quantized operator support was introduced, the QAT feature was deprecated in ONNX Runtime. Users are now advised to perform QAT directly in the source framework (PyTorch[6] or TensorFlow) before exporting the model to ONNX.

Besides these methods, there are several range mapping schemes used for mapping floating-point precision to lower precision. These schemes determine how the scale and zero-point are computed and are mentioned as follows:

- **Symmetric Quantization Schema**
  - In this schema, the zero point of the floating point range is mapped to zero point of the integer range. It centers the input range around 0, which eliminates the need for zero-point calculation. Hence, in *Equation (1)*, the value of **z** is taken as 0. This reduces the computational overhead during runtime. The range is calculated as the maximum of the absolute min value and max value of the floating point. This range is mapped to the min and max of the integer range.
  - It works well when the histogram of activations or weights is centered around zero, as seen in *Figure* 5.3. It will not yield improved accuracy when the histogram distribution is heavily skewed to one side of zero. It will also not work well when the range contains only positive or negative activations.
- **Asymmetric (Affine) Quantization Schema**
  - In this schema, the floating point range is mapped to an integer range with adjustable zero-point. The floating point zero is not mapped to integer zero value but to some other value in integer range. The scale and zero-point are calculated using the equations described in previous sections.
  - It is more suitable when the distribution is skewed towards one side of zero as the min of float is mapped to min of integer and max of float is mapped to max of integer.

Figure 5.5 shows examples of symmetric and asymmetric quantization schemas. Here, we have considered a floating-point tensor with a value range of **[-3, 4]**. As shown in the symmetric schema, the **4** value is used as r_{min} and r_{max} both, whereas in the asymmetric schema, **-3** is taken as r_{min} and **4** is taken as r_{max}. Please note that when we use symmetric quantization for integer precision, the integer range is taken as **[-127, 127]** instead of **[-128, 127]**.

[6] https://pytorch.org/blog/quantization-in-practice/

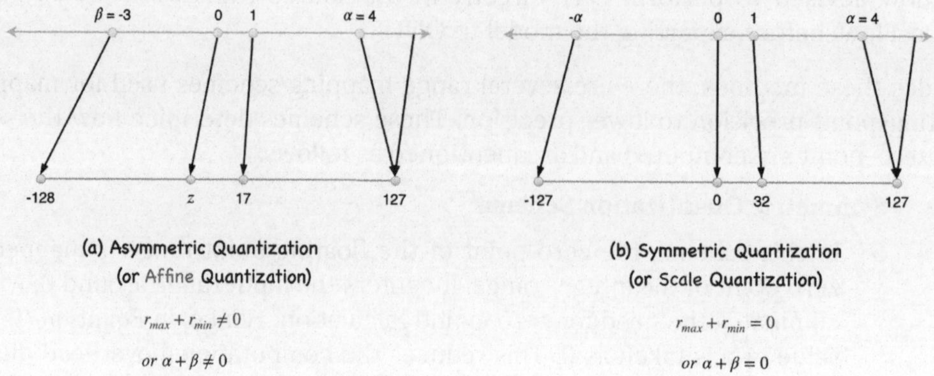

Figure 5.5: *Example showing symmetric and asymmetric quantization schema (Source: Footnote[7])*

Benefits and Drawbacks of Quantization

Till now we have understood all the technical details about quantization. Learning about these fundamental concepts allows us to understand the benefits and drawbacks of quantizing a model which are mentioned as follows:

- **Benefits**
    - As the model's layer/operators are computed in lower precision, the execution of such layers will be faster than their higher precision counterparts. The activations in FP32 will occupy 4 bytes, FP16 will occupy 2 bytes, and INT8 will occupy 1 byte. Hence, the data movement of the lower precision activation will require lesser memory bandwidth. This will result in faster memory access. The arithmetic computation performed on INT8 precision is often faster than FP32 precision. The usual speed up of 3x-4x is obtained for FP32 to INT8 quantization and 1.5x-2x is obtained for FP16 to INT8 precision.
    - The weights of the model are also quantized. Just like in activation, when the weights are also available in FP32 precision, they occupy 4 bytes per parameter. For FP16 weights, it will occupy 2 bytes per parameter. Due to this, when we quantize the model from FP32 to INT8, we will see a model size reduction of around 4x. For FP16 to INT8, we will see a reduction of around 2x. This reduction in model size is favorable for edge computing use cases with limited memory.

[7] https://www.linkedin.com/pulse/fundamentals-quantization-llms-part-3-akash-gautam-vtmhc/

  - Since quantization reduces the model size, larger and accurate models can be deployed on the same edge device, leading to more accurate responses from the model.
  - As the lower precision operations tend to consume lower power, the overall execution of the model becomes energy efficient, which is required for battery-powered devices like drones, smartphones, and IoT devices.
  - Some edge device hardware has a specialized block for INT8 operations. By quantizing the models to INT8, we can utilize such hardware in a better way.
- **Drawbacks**
  - The quantization process lowers the precision of the model's activation and weights, which negatively impacts accuracy. The quantized model's output will not be the same as the unquantized model's output. In some cases, the model's weights are very sensitive to quantization. In such cases, we may need to apply advanced quantization techniques for such models.
  - The quantization process involves selecting an unbiased and representative calibration dataset. Identifying the appropriate size and characteristics of the dataset can be time-consuming. Once the dataset is determined, the quantization process requires running model inference on the dataset and analyzing the histograms of activations and weights, which is another time-intensive step.
  - The performance improvements from quantization are often most noticeable on hardware optimized for low-precision arithmetic (such as Tensor Cores and TPUs). The speedup might be less significant or even negligible on hardware that is not optimized for INT8 or other low-precision formats.
  - Different edge devices support quantized models up to a certain capacity. It may happen that the quantized model may contain some operators, which are not executable in lower precision by the edge devices. In such cases, the performance improvement will not be as significant as one might expect.
  - Quantizing the model is not the best solution for all the tasks. It is useful where the lower precision is less critical, but it is not suitable for the tasks that require high-precision computations, such as scientific simulations or tasks requiring extremely fine-grained numerical accuracy.

Quantizing BERT model

Now we will apply our knowledge by quantizing the BERT model. Before proceeding with it, let us understand a little bit about BERT. BERT (Bidirectional Encoder

Representations from Transformers) is a powerful NLP model developed by Google in 2018. It is designed to understand the meaning of words in a specific context via a bidirectional Transformer architecture, making it highly effective for tasks like text classification, question answering, and understanding languages. *Figure* 5.6 visualizes the BERT architecture and its usage in sequence classification tasks. Readers are encouraged to refer to *Footnote*[8] to learn more about BERT in detail.

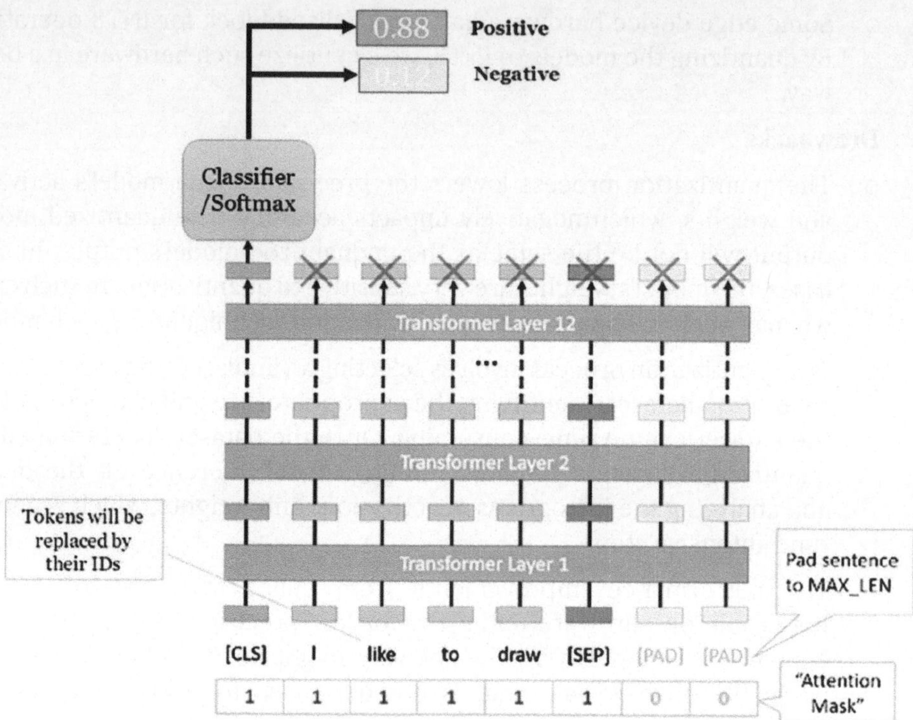

Figure 5.6: *Architecture of BERT model and its application in sequence classification task (Source: Footnote*[9]*)*

In this section, we will utilize the pre-trained BERT model to classify movie reviews as either positive or negative. The model has been trained on the IMDB movie review dataset[10] and can be accessed on the HuggingFace hub[11]. We will be quantizing this model using ONNX Runtime. For this purpose, we will be following Chapter-5 Jupyter Notebook[12]. It is recommended to run this notebook on Google Colab, or a machine with sufficient RAM, as the quantization process is resource-intensive.

[8] https://huggingface.co/blog/bert-101
[9] https://blog.nowhere.co.jp/archives/20210521-29957.html
[10] https://huggingface.co/datasets/stanfordnlp/imdb
[11] https://huggingface.co/fabriceyhc/bert-base-uncased-imdb
[12] https://github.com/ava-orange-education/Ultimate-ONNX-for-Optimizing-Deep-Learning-Models

As a first step, we will be loading the model from HuggingFace and exporting it to the ONNX model. We will be using the BERT model trained on IMDB dataset from "**fabriceyhc/bert-base-uncased-imdb**" model card of HuggingFace. *Figure* 5.7 shows the code snippet to load the model and export it to ONNX using a sample input. This BERT model takes "**input_ids**" and "**attention_mask**" as input and generates "**logits**" as output from the model.

```
# Load IMDb test dataset
dataset = load_dataset("imdb")
test_dataset = dataset["test"]

# Load model and tokenizer
tokenizer = AutoTokenizer.from_pretrained("fabriceyhc/bert-base-uncased-imdb")
model = AutoModelForSequenceClassification.from_pretrained("fabriceyhc/bert-base-uncased-imdb")

# Export model to onnx
dummy_inputs = tokenizer(test_dataset[0]["text"], return_tensors="pt")
onnx_model_path = "./bert_base_uncased_imdb.onnx"

torch.onnx.export(model, (dummy_inputs["input_ids"], dummy_inputs["attention_mask"]),
                  onnx_model_path,
                  input_names=["input_ids", "attention_mask"], output_names=["logits"],
                  dynamic_axes={"input_ids": {0: "batch_size", 1: "sequence"},
                                "attention_mask": {0: "batch_size", 1: "sequence"},
                                "logits": {0: "batch_size"}}
                  )
```

Figure 5.7: *Loading and exporting of BERT model*

Once the model is exported, we will create a calibration dataset, which is usually made from a test dataset, or from samples found when the model is executed in production. Since it is used to quantize the model, we need to ensure that the dataset is free from biases. In the case of the IMDB dataset, the test set contains 12500 samples with negative reviews and 12500 samples with positive reviews. If we sample 1000 reviews and all reviews are negative, then the sampled dataset will become biased as it does not have an equal distribution of positive and negative reviews. Hence, we will randomly pick 500 samples from negative reviews and positive reviews each to construct a calibration dataset. We also need to make sure that the calibration dataset has reviews of all types of sequence lengths, since it is not favorable that it contains only shorter sequences.

For this purpose, we have plotted the histogram of sequence lengths of test dataset and calibration dataset in *Figure* 5.8. The code to obtain the calibration dataset and these histograms are presented in the Jupyter Notebook. These plots show no bias with respect to sequence length. The sequence length distribution of the calibration dataset is similar to that of the test dataset. The peak at value 512 in both histograms is because the BERT model is trained to take a long sequence with 512 tokens only.

Hence, any sequence longer than 512 is truncated to the required length. For this task, we have picked the samples cautiously at random to obtain the calibration dataset, but it will not be easy for other datasets in real-world use cases. In such cases, we may need to study different characteristics of the dataset and sample accordingly.

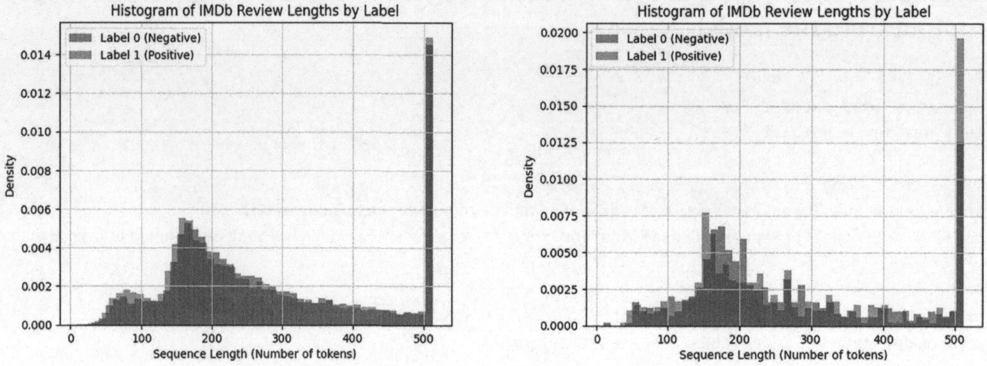

Figure 5.8: *Histogram distribution of sequence lengths of test dataset and calibration dataset. The left image represents the test dataset histogram and the right image represents the calibration dataset histogram*

The next step will be using this calibration dataset to quantize the model. Before starting the quantization process, shape inference and graph optimizations are applied as a general practice. The goal of these steps is to improve the quality of quantization. The ONNX Runtime quantization tool works best when the tensor's shape is known. Graph optimization performs certain operator fusion that makes ONNX Runtime's job easier. Applying graph optimization after the quantization may not be fruitful due to the addition of Quantize and DeQuantize nodes in the graph, which may prevent the fusion of the operators. The ONNX Runtime provides a "**`quant_pre_process`**" API for this purpose. It internally calls ONNX's shape inference API, ONNX Runtime's symbolic shape inference API, and ONNX Runtime's optimizations. This preprocessed model is then used for quantization.

For quantizing the model, ONNX Runtime offers two APIs—one is "**`quantize_static`**" and the other is "**`quantize_dynamic`**". The "**`quantize_static`**" API uses calibration dataset to identify the histograms of all the activations and weights and then calculates the scale and zero point based on it to quantize the model. The "**`quantize_dynamic`**" API does not need the calibration dataset as it inserts DynamicQuantize nodes to calculate scale and zero point to quantize the activations at the runtime.

Figure 5.9 shows how "**`quantize_static`**" API is used. Here, we have fixed the datatype for weights and activations to **`QInt8`** which has a representation range of **`[-128, 127]`**. We can also change this to **`QUInt8`** which has a representation range of **`[0, 255]`**. In *Figure* 5.9, for static quantization we are using **`calibration_data_reader`** argument, which expects a **`CalibrationDataReader`** class's object. This class can be easily created if we have a Pytorch's **`Dataset`** object. The "**`quantize_static`**" API provides detailed options for using various calibration methods, applying channel-wise quantization, and selecting specific nodes for quantization while excluding others. Readers can see ONNX Runtime source code[13] for the same.

```
# Firstly, apply shape inference and onnxruntime model optimization before quantizing the model.
quant_pre_process(onnx_model_path, onnx_model_path_static_quant, skip_symbolic_shape=True)

# Apply static quantization
quantize_static(
    model_input=onnx_model_path_static_quant,           # Input ONNX model
    model_output=onnx_model_path_static_quant,          # Output quantized model
    calibration_data_reader=BertDataReader(),
    weight_type=QuantType.QInt8,        # Quantize weights to int8
    activation_type=QuantType.QInt8,    # Quantize activations to int8
    calibration_providers=["CPUExecutionProvider"]
)
```

Figure 5.9: *Usage of `quantize_static` API to statically quantize model*

Figure 5.10 shows the code to get the **DataLoader** object of Pytorch from the **Dataset** object of Pytorch. In *Figure* 5.10, we need to pass a **Dataset** object, batch size, and number of parallel workers. The **get_dataloader** also defines a collate function. This collate function is required to combine sequences of different lengths in a single batch by adding padding to sequences which are smaller than the largest one in the batch.

```
def get_dataloader(dataset_instance, batch_size=1, num_workers=0):
    # Define collate function to combine sequences of different lengths.
    def collate_batch(sample):
        updated_sample = defaultdict(list)
        for batch in sample:
            for k, v in batch.items():
                if k == "labels":
                    v = v.unsqueeze(dim=0)
                updated_sample[k].append(v)

        for k, v in updated_sample.items():
            updated_sample[k] = pad_sequence(v, batch_first=True)
        return updated_sample

    # Create a DataLoader for batching
    dataloader = DataLoader(
        dataset_instance,
        batch_size=batch_size,
        shuffle=False,
        num_workers=num_workers,
        collate_fn=collate_batch
    )

    return dataloader
```

Figure 5.10: *Sample code to get the `DataLoader` required for BERT model*

[13] https://github.com/microsoft/onnxruntime/blob/977efe4788b2ee24371523b5fa14dd02efcd4942/onnxruntime/python/tools/quantization/quantize.py#L479

Figure 5.11 shows the code to get the **CalibrationDataReader** object required for the calibration process from the **DataLoader** object. In *Figure* 5.11, the **calibration_dataset** variable represents the Pytorch **DataLoader** object. It outputs the Pytorch tensors, which have to be converted to numpy tensors, before using them in ONNX Runtime. It also produces tensors for "**labels**" and "**token_type_ids**" keys, which are redundant for ONNX Runtime inference as only "**input_ids**" and "**attention_mask**" inputs are required. Hence, we are popping the "**labels**" and the "**token_type_ids**" tensors. Readers can refer to Pytorch documentation[14] to understand more about Pytorch's **Datasets** and **DataLoaders**.

```
# Custom data reader for calibration
class BertDataReader(CalibrationDataReader):
    def __init__(self):
        self.data = get_dataloader(calibration_dataset)
        self.enum_data = iter(self.data)

    def get_next(self):
        data = next(self.enum_data, None)
        if data is None:
            return None

        data.pop("token_type_ids")
        data.pop("labels")

        for k, v in data.items():
            data[k] = v.numpy()
        return data

    def rewind(self):
        self.enum_data = iter(self.data)
```

Figure 5.11: *Sample code for calibration data reader required for BERT quantization*

Now, let us use dynamic quantization, where the model's layers are quantized during the runtime based on the given input. *Figure* 5.12 shows a code example to dynamically quantize the model using ONNX Runtime's "**quantize_dynamic**" API. Please note that unlike "**quantize_static**", the "**quantize_dynamic**" will not require you to pass a calibration dataset. For dynamic quantization, we only need to quantize weights. Hence, here we are only passing the **weight_type** parameter and setting its value to **QInt8** precision. The activation of the models is quantized at the runtime. The "**quantize_dynamic**" API also provides fine-grained control over options like the quantization method, nodes to quantize, and nodes to exclude. Readers can refer to ONNX Runtime source code[15] for the same.

[14] https://pytorch.org/tutorials/beginner/basics/data_tutorial.html

[15] https://github.com/microsoft/onnxruntime/blob/977efe4788b2ee24371523b5fa14dd02efcd4942/onnxruntime/python/tools/quantization/quantize.py#L794

```
# Firstly, apply shape inference and onnxruntime model optimization before quantizing the model.
quant_pre_process(onnx_model_path, onnx_model_path_dynamic_quant, skip_symbolic_shape=True)

# Apply dynamic quantization
quantized_model = quantize_dynamic(
    model_input=onnx_model_path_dynamic_quant,        # Input ONNX model
    model_output=onnx_model_path_dynamic_quant,       # Output quantized model
    weight_type=QuantType.QInt8     # Quantize only weights to int8, activations will be quantize during runtime
)
```

Figure 5.12: *Usage of* `quantize_dynamic` *API to dynamically quantize model*

Once we get the quantized model, we can measure its accuracy on a test dataset and compare it against the original model's accuracy on the test set. To keep the execution short, we have used a calibration dataset in the Jupyter Notebook to measure the accuracy as it contains only 1,000 samples compared to the test dataset, which contains 25,000 samples. *Figure* 5.13 shows the comparison of the accuracy of the original model, static quantized model, and dynamic quantized model. To quicken the execution, we have obtained these numbers for the calibration dataset instead of the test dataset. In practice, we should be using a test dataset to measure the impact of quantization on accuracy. However, these numbers will give us a fair idea on how well the quantized model performs during production.

As illustrated in *Figure* 5.13, the accuracy for the static quantized model is poor, compared to the original model. This might be because of the quantization parameters selected during the process. Readers can play with different options provided by the API to understand how each of these options affect the model's accuracy. Readers can change "**`calibrate_method`**" from MinMax (default) to Entropy, or enable **`per_channel`** quantization to define individual scales and zero-points for each channel separately. There is an "**`extra_options`**" in the API, which can also be explored for the same. In this use case, the dynamic quantized model has the same accuracy as the unquantized model. But this behavior is not true for all the models. Like static quantization, there is scope to play around with the different options offered by the "**`quantize_dynamic`**" API.

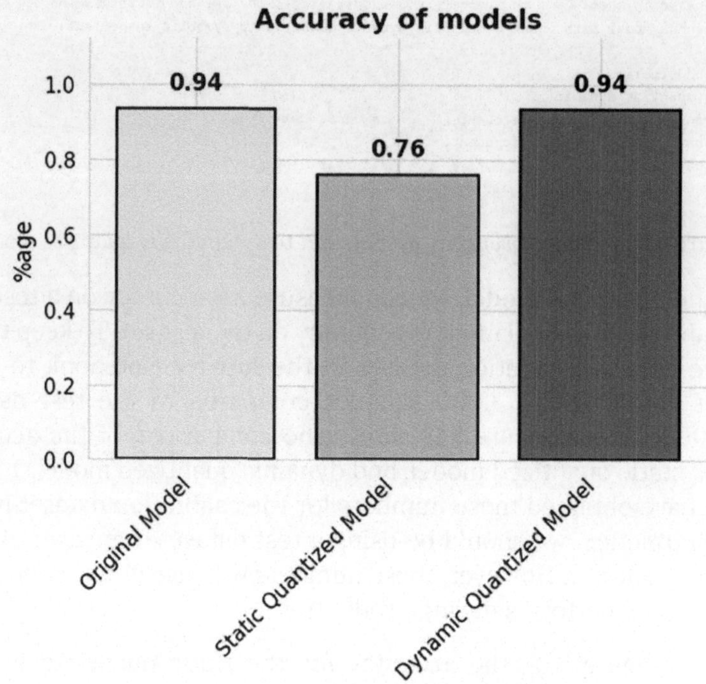

Figure 5.13: *Accuracy comparison between original model, static quantized model and dynamic quantized model on calibration dataset*

Figure 5.14 shows a comparison of the execution time of original model, static quantized model, and dynamic quantized model. From the *Figure* 5.14, it is evident that the dynamically quantized model runs faster than the original model despite the quantization being performed at the run time. It is also visible that the execution of the static quantized model execution is poorer than the original one.

These numbers are obtained on a consumer grade machine with the "`AMD Ryzen 5 5600H`" processor. These numbers may vary based on different hardware and will be completely different if we use GPUs. These numbers and their relative improvements will also differ for edge devices such as Raspberry Pi. While modern CPUs and GPUs demonstrate superior performance with dynamic quantization due to their computational throughput and optimized execution, edge devices with constrained compute resources and limited memory bandwidth will show better results with static quantization. Hence, it is always advisable to get the numbers for the hardware on which the model is to be deployed.

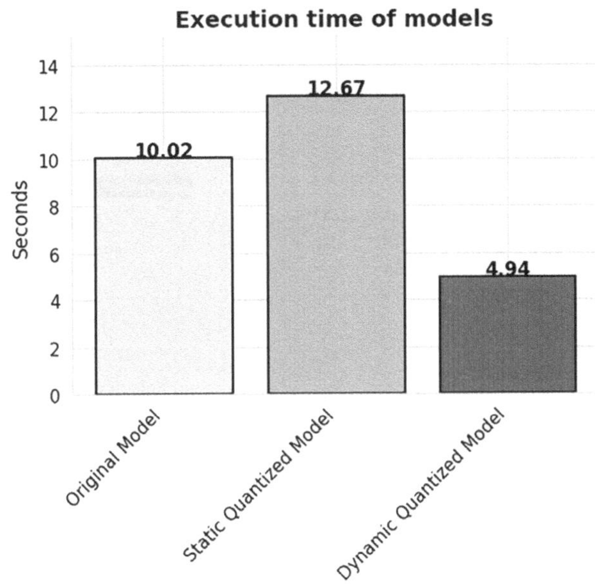

Figure 5.14: *Execution speed comparison between original model, static quantized model and dynamic quantized model on random 10 samples of [16, 512] input*

Quantized Model in ONNX

The ONNX Runtime tool can accept quantized models from various sources, such as Pytorch/TensorFlow frameworks, from Quantization Aware Training (QAT), or ONNX Runtime's quantization APIs. ONNX Runtime can take two formats[16], namely, Operator-oriented and Tensor-oriented (QDQ-based). In the Operator-oriented representation, all the quantized operators have their own ONNX definitions, such as **`QlinearConv`** and **`MatMulInteger`**. Meanwhile, the Tensor-oriented representation inserts **`DeQuantizeLinear(QuantizeLinear(tensor))`** between the original operators to simulate the quantization and dequantization process. In static quantization, the **`QuantizeLinear`** and **`DeQuantizeLinear`** operators carry the quantization parameters. In dynamic quantization, a **`ComputeQuantizationParameters`** FunctionProto is inserted to calculate quantization parameters during runtime. *Figure* 5.15 shows both representations.

[16] https://iot-robotics.github.io/ONNXRuntime/docs/performance/quantization.html

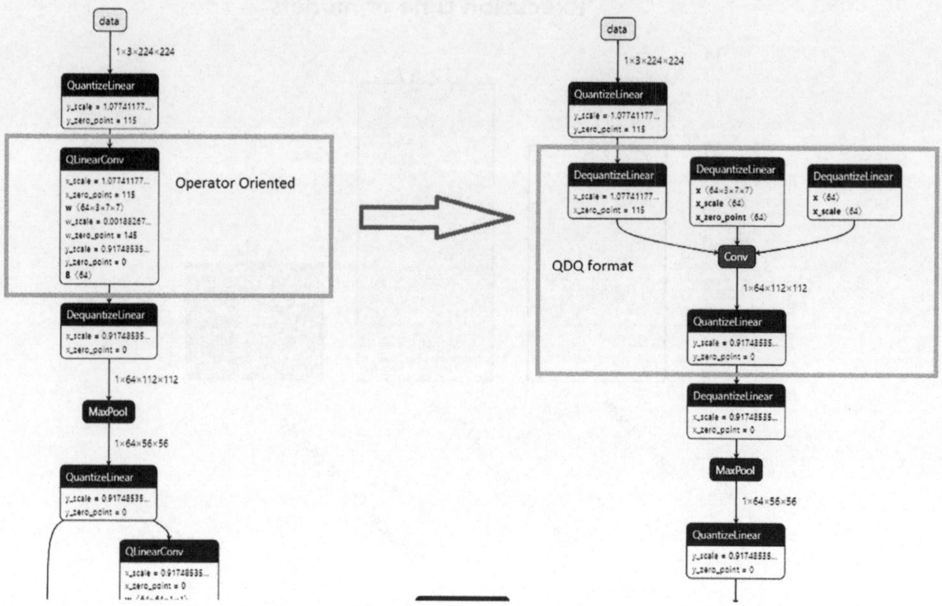

Figure 5.15: ONNX's *quantized model representation. Left one is Quantized operator based representation and the right one is QDQ format based representation*

Let us visualize the models we have quantized. *Figure* 5.16 and *Figure* 5.17 show the visualization of statically quantized model and dynamically quantized model, respectively. By default, the "**quantize_static**" API will develop QDQ representation of the model. Once we get the quantized model, we can apply ONNX Runtime optimizations on it. After the optimizations, the **Quantize**, **MatMul** and **DeQuantize** node chains are converted into a single **QLinearMatMul** node as shown in *Figure* 5.16. Standalone **Quantize** and **DeQuantize** nodes are present in the model as well and are required when the inputs of the operator, such as Add, have two different scales.

Similarly, in *Figure* 5.17 the quantized model has operators such as **DynamicQuantizeMatMul**, instead of **MatMul**. These are added during the quantization process. When executed, they will quantize the input and compute the **MatMul** operation in lower precision (INT8) and then dequantize the output for the next operator. Please note that the weights of these operators are already quantized during the process.

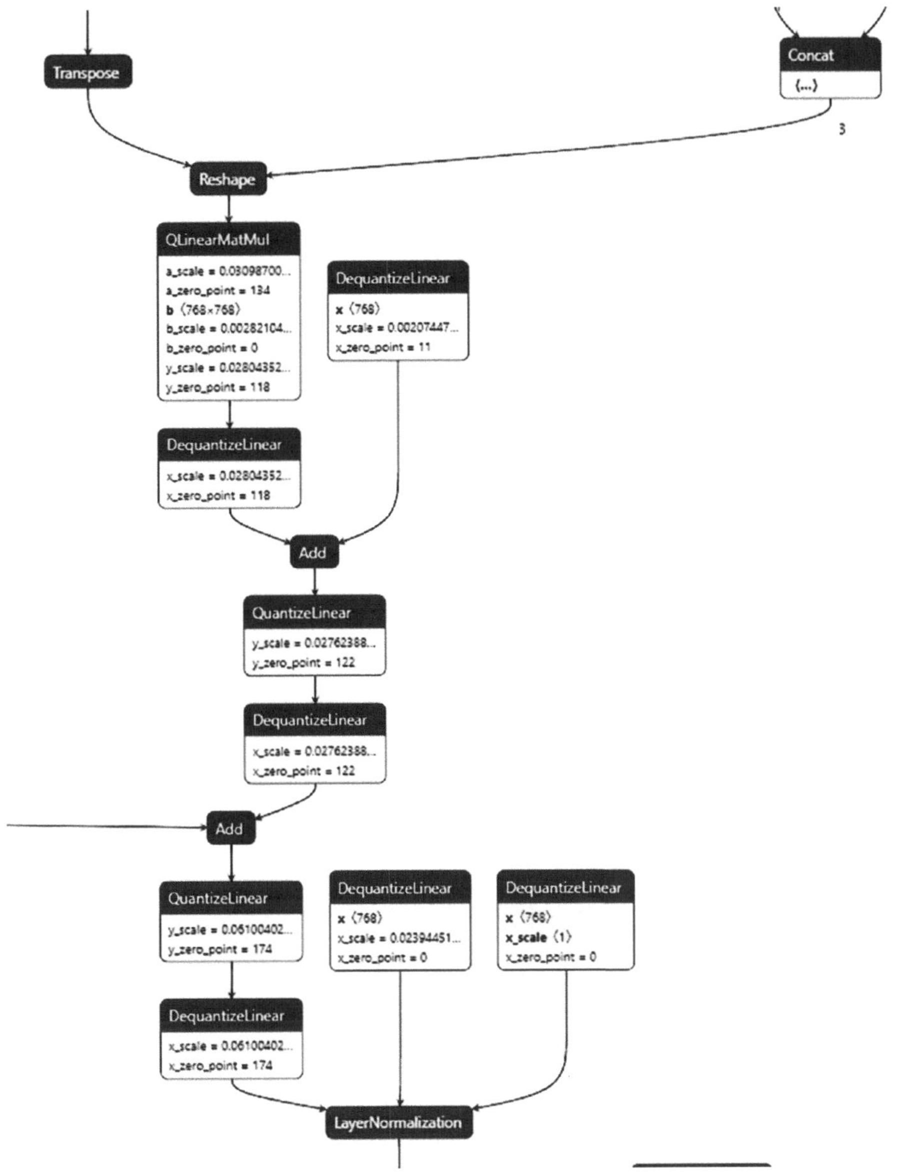

Figure 5.16: *Visualization of static quantized model*

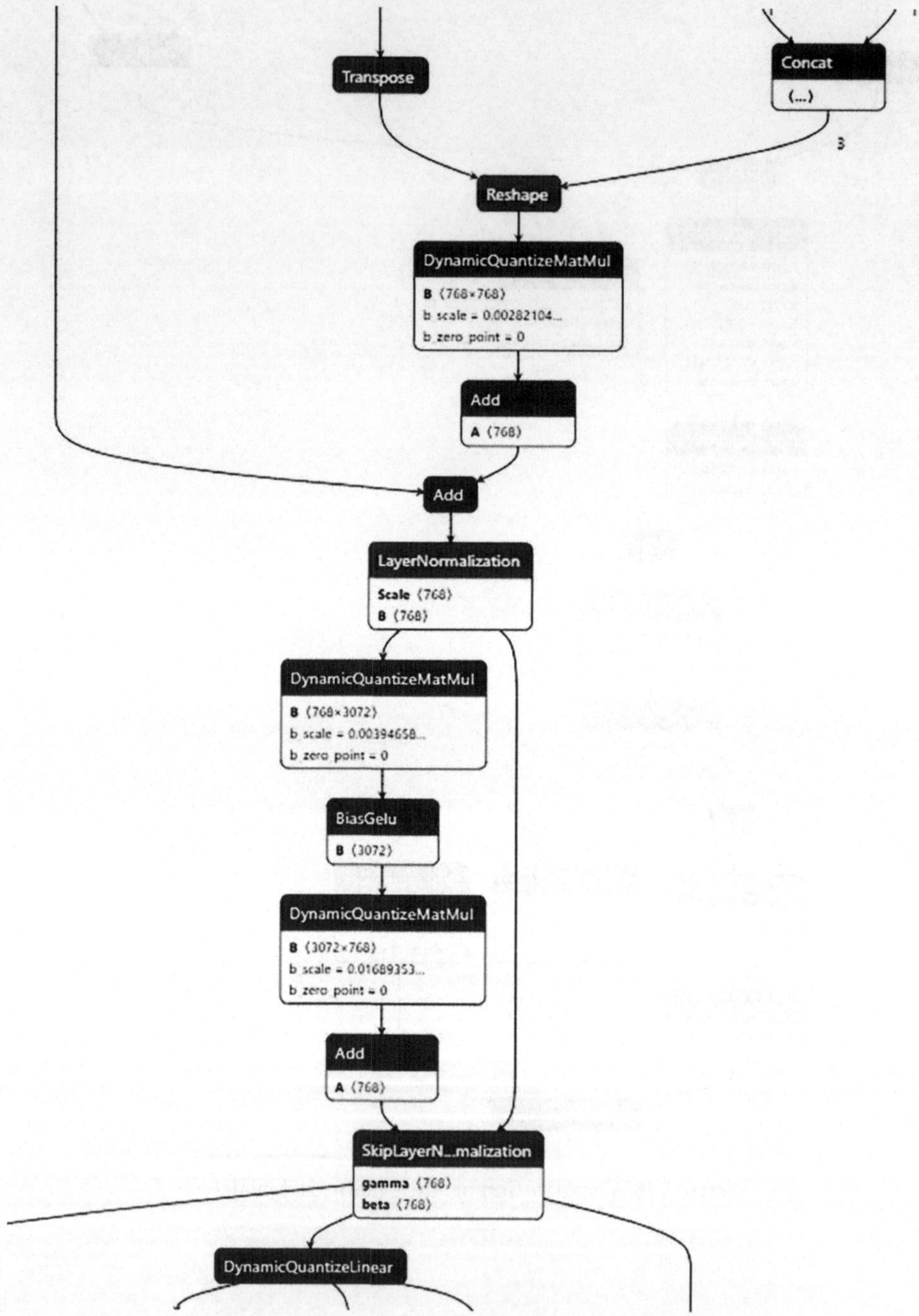

Figure 5.17: *Visualization of dynamic quantized model*

Conclusion

In this chapter, we learned about the theory of quantization, laying a solid foundation for this pivotal concept. To reinforce our knowledge, we explored a concrete example of quantization, while examining the broader process and various quantization techniques, methods, and schemas. We gained insight into the advantages and limitations of quantization, and tested our knowledge by experimenting with the BERT model. Through both static and dynamic quantization, we assessed the model's performance by measuring accuracy and execution speed.

In the next chapter, we will shift focus to pruning, which is another powerful technique for enhancing model performance in edge deployment scenarios. We will explore the intricacies of pruning methods, and observe how they are applied in practice to further optimize model efficiency.

CHAPTER 6

Model Pruning in Pytorch and Exporting to ONNX

Introduction

So far, we have learned how to optimize the execution of ONNX graphs with the help of graph optimizations and quantization. In this chapter, we will learn about Model Pruning, which can improve the execution of the models on edge devices. We will learn how this technique helps in achieving faster execution of the models. We will also know about different types of pruning techniques and try to apply them on a ResNet model using the Pytorch framework.

Structure

This chapter covers the following topics:

- Overview of Pruning
- Types of Pruning
- Pruning Strategies
- Pruning Using Pytorch
- Unstructured Pruning of ResNet50
- Structured Pruning of ResNet50

Overview of Pruning

Recent deep learning models often have billions of parameters that help them solve complex tasks. These parameters also help them consume terabytes or petabytes of data during training without over fitting. Due to their size, such models are difficult to put into production, where limited resources are available. Due to the high parameter count, the model has redundant parameters which can be identified and removed before deploying the model in production. The technique to identify redundant parameters from the model is called **Pruning**.

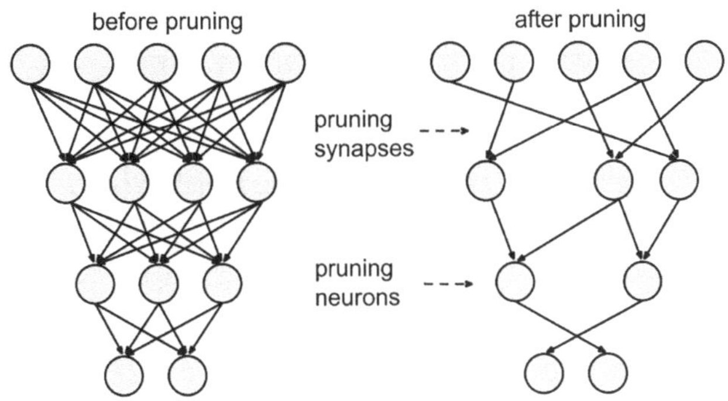

Figure 6.1: *Intuitive idea of model pruning (Source: Footnote[1])*

Pruning has been proven to shrink the size of the model and make it sparse by eliminating the neurons that do not contribute much to the output of the model. Much like quantization, reducing the number of parameters also has a side effect. Since the model has been trained with certain parameters, the neurons that were dependent on these parameters now receive zero input whenever they are removed. As a result, the outputs of subsequent neurons are altered, creating a cascading effect that impacts the model's accuracy. *Figure*-6.1 further illustrates how pruning works.

Model pruning offers both advantages and disadvantages. One of the main drawbacks, as mentioned, is its potential impact on the model's accuracy. The extent of this impact depends on factors such as the pruning ratio (percentage weights which are pruned), the model's architecture, and the level of redundancy within it. For instance, in a shallow network, there is limited opportunity to prune less important weights. However, in a model with billions of parameters, there is much greater potential for effective pruning. Besides this, the computational cost of pruning must also be taken into account. Gradient-based methods, for instance, require extra training cycles. The process of ranking weights or neurons by magnitude, gradient sensitivity, or importance scores adds on to the computational overhead. As the model size grows, this cost becomes increasingly significant.

The pruned model typically has fewer parameters, resulting in faster execution. This is particularly beneficial for edge device applications where resources are limited. The performance improvement depends on factors such as the pruning method used, the pruning ratio applied, and hardware support for sparse kernels. A higher pruning ratio can lead to better execution on specific hardware.

[1] https://medium.com/@souvik.paul01/pruning-in-deep-learning-models-1067a19acd89

Types of Pruning

Now that we have an idea about pruning, let us try to understand different types of pruning techniques available to prune the model. These techniques are classified based on how they remove the less important weights from the model:

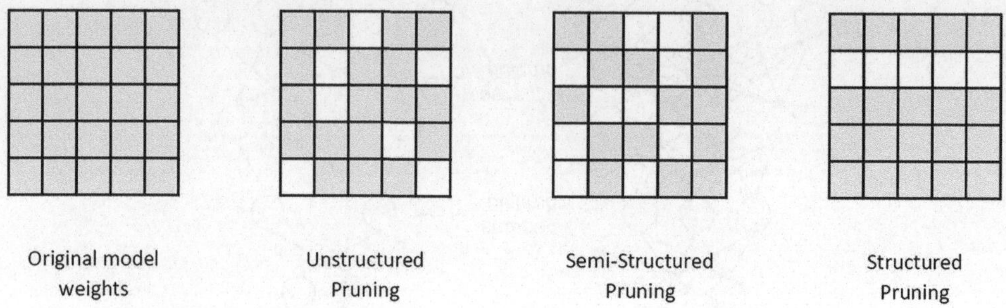

Figure 6.2: *Types of pruning and their effects on the model's weights*

- **Unstructured Pruning**
    - In Unstructured Pruning, individual parameters (weights or connections) are selectively removed (for example, based on magnitude), resulting in irregular sparsity while preserving the model's original architecture. This process involves applying a binary mask to the weights, which filters out certain weights before using the remaining ones with the input. The goal is to identify a mask that zeroes out the less important weights, which have a negligible impact on the model's output or accuracy.
    - As a result of removing less important weights (for example, via magnitude-based pruning), the weight matrix becomes sparse, resulting in a sparse model. However, the number of channels or the rows/columns in the weight matrix remains unchanged, so the model's size does not decrease.
    - The performance improvement comes from specialized kernels that can efficiently handle sparse matrices. However, support for these kernels varies across different hardware platforms and deployment libraries, making the technique less effective on a wide range of devices.
- **Structured Pruning**
    - In Structured Pruning, weights are pruned in a way to create a specific structure, affecting entire rows or columns of the weight matrix. Since this approach alters the structure of the weight matrix, it also changes the matrix's shape, which in turn alters the model's size.
    - When the weight matrix of one layer is modified, it changes the output shape of that layer, making it incompatible with the next layer. As a result, the next layer, which also has weights that need to be pruned, must be adjusted in a similar way to maintain compatibility with the previous layer.

- Unlike unstructured pruning, where individual less important weights are removed, structured pruning removes entire rows or columns, leading to a more significant impact. As a result, specialized methods must be explored and carefully evaluated to achieve the best pruned model.
- Structured pruning involves removing entire channels, rows, attention heads in transformers, or even entire layers. Unlike unstructured pruning, it does not rely on specialized hardware or software support, allowing for direct acceleration of the model.

- **Semi-Structured Pruning**
  - Semi-structured pruning is a middle ground between unstructured and structured pruning. It removes weights in a way that still allows efficient computation on modern hardware while achieving significant model compression.
  - Unlike unstructured pruning, which removes individual weights selectively (for example, by magnitude) and creates irregular sparsity (inefficient on dense hardware), and structured pruning, which removes entire filters or neurons (which may be too aggressive), semi-structured pruning balances both approaches by targeting coarse-grained groups of weights.
  - Typically, the semi-structured pruning is described using N:M structured sparsity, where out of every M consecutive weights, only N are retained.

All these different granularities of pruning and their effect on the weight matrix are demonstrated in *Figure*-6.2, along with an example (look at the third figure) of 3:5 structured sparsity.

Pruning Strategies

Pruning can be applied at different stages of the model's life cycle. The following strategies can be described based on when pruning is performed:

- **One-Shot Pruning**
  - As the name implies, this technique involves pruning in a single step after the model is fully trained. Depending on the amount of accuracy loss, the pruned model may require fine-tuning.
- **Iterative Pruning**
  - In this method, the model is pruned in small increments, followed by fine-tuning to recover any accuracy lost due to pruning. This process is repeated over multiple iterations. It allows for gradual pruning, often resulting in a more robustly pruned model by the end of the process.

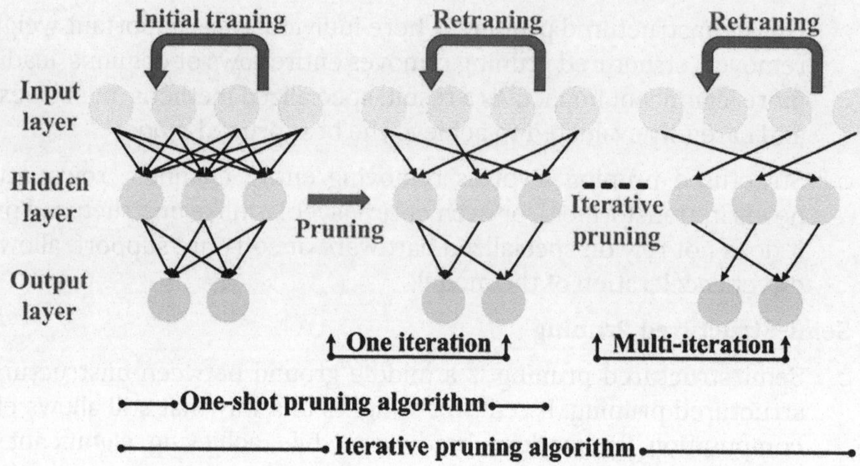

Figure 6.3: *Example showing how one-shot and iterative pruning are applied (Source: Footnote*[2]*)*

Pruning techniques can be categorized based on how they identify less important weights. Here's a high-level overview of each method, as the detailed explanations and implementations are beyond the scope of this book.

- **Magnitude-Based Pruning**
  - In magnitude-based pruning, weights with the smallest magnitudes are selected for removal. This can be done using a threshold value: if a weight's value is below a certain threshold, it is pruned in unstructured pruning. For structured pruning, the L1 or L2 norm of the rows or columns of weights is calculated and those below a threshold are removed.
- **Gradient-Based Pruning**
  - This technique prunes weights that contribute the least to the loss function and have the smallest gradient values. They can be tracked over the training process, or second-order derivatives can be used to evaluate how sensitive a weight is to the loss function. While being more accurate than magnitude-based pruning, gradient-based pruning requires additional computations and is more expensive for large models.
- **Taylor Series Pruning**
  - In Taylor series pruning, a first-order Taylor expansion is used to estimate the effect of weight removal on the loss function. Since this method considers both the weight value and its gradient, it is more precise than simple magnitude-based pruning. However, it is computationally more expensive.

[2] https://www.linkedin.com/pulse/traditional-pruning-methods-impact-model-size-speed-ayoub-kirouane/

- **Activation-Based Pruning**
    - This approach focuses on activations and identifies weights responsible for generating low activations across multiple inputs. It retains only those weights that produce high activations. This method works particularly well with CNN-based architectures, but requires tracking activations during forward passes across multiple iterations, thereby making it costlier.
- **Variance-Based Pruning**
    - Variance-based pruning removes weights that show low variance in their activations. If a neuron's output doesn't change significantly across different inputs, it is considered redundant. This method helps eliminate weights that do not contribute to varied inputs. However, it requires statistical analysis of activations across the training data.

Pruning Using Pytorch

So far, we have utilized ONNX and its ecosystem to experiment with graph optimizations and model inference. However, when it comes to model pruning, ONNX does not provide built-in APIs like PyTorch, but can store sparse models exported from PyTorch, and ONNX Runtime can utilize sparsity on supported hardware. Most open-source pruning algorithms are available in PyTorch. Here, we demonstrate pruning in PyTorch, then convert the pruned model to ONNX to complete the end-to-end workflow.

At the time of writing of this chapter, the latest available version of PyTorch was 2.6.0. This version natively supports the pruning algorithms listed below. Since pruning is an active area of research, various approaches to it are available within the open-source community. Readers interested in exploring the pruning domain further can investigate these options. For the purpose of this chapter, we will focus on PyTorch's APIs and how they are used. As shown in *Table 6.1*, PyTorch provides APIs for both unstructured and structured pruning, which are detailed in the table. These APIs can be found in the "`torch.nn.utils.prune`" module of Pytorch[3].

Sr. No.	API (Under torch.nn.utils.prune)	Description
1	random_unstructured	Prunes weights randomly.
2	l1_unstructured	Prunes weights which have the lowest L1-norm
3	random_structured	Prunes weights by removing random channels along the specific dimension
4	ln_structured	Prunes weights by removing channels with the lowest Ln-Norm along the specified dimension

[3] https://pytorch.org/docs/stable/nn.html

5	global_unstructured	Prunes the entire model based on the provided pruning method

Table 6.1: *Table showing Pytorch pruning APIs and their pruning logic*

To understand pruning in more detail, we will use a ResNet50 model and train it on the relatively simple Cats vs. Dogs dataset[4]. After training, we will apply the "**`torch.nn.utils.prune.l1_unstructured`**" and "**`torch.nn.utils.prune.ln_structured`**" APIs to perform unstructured and structured pruning respectively on the model while observing the effects of pruning. Additionally, we will try to recover losses in accuracy by retraining the pruned model. For this, readers are encouraged to follow the Jupyter Notebook provided for this chapter[5]. This notebook requires PyTorch with CUDA support, as we will use GPUs to train the original model and retrain the pruned model. For faster execution, readers should run the code on GPU-enabled devices or Google Colab with GPU runtime.

To maintain the focus on pruning in the following section, we will skip the model training process (though readers can refer to the Chapter-7 code walkthrough to understand this aspect), which can be easily followed in the Jupyter notebook. The "Cat vs. Dog" problem is a basic classification task, where an image is classified as either a cat or a dog. We have chosen this dataset and the large ResNet50 model intentionally to highlight the redundancy of the model's parameters for this relatively simple task, especially when compared to the more complex ImageNet task that the model was originally trained on. The following sections assume that a ResNet50 model has already been trained on the Cats vs. Dogs task. In one execution of the Jupyter notebook, the model achieved an accuracy of **95.39%** on the test set after training for 3 epochs. This will serve as the baseline for comparing the accuracy of the pruned model.

Unstructured Pruning of ResNet50

As mentioned in the previous section, we will use the "**`torch.nn.utils.prune.l1_unstructured`**" API[6] to perform unstructured pruning on the ResNet50 model. This API can be applied to any layer with trainable parameters, such as the weights and biases in Convolution layers.

In this case, we will apply pruning only to the weights of all Convolution layers in the model. Biases are typically not pruned, as they carry important information that helps the network shift activations, improving learning, especially when inputs do not naturally align with the desired output. Removing or pruning biases can negatively

[4] https://huggingface.co/datasets/microsoft/cats_vs_dogs

[5] https://github.com/ava-orange-education/Ultimate-ONNX-for-Optimizing-Deep-Learning-Models

[6] https://pytorch.org/docs/stable/generated/torch.nn.utils.prune.l1_unstructured.html#torch.nn.utils.prune.l1_unstructured

impact the model's performance. Moreover, the performance gains from removing biases are negligible compared to pruning weights, as biases are relatively few.

When the "**torch.nn.utils.prune.l1_unstructured**" API is applied to a parameter, the original parameter is renamed to **<parameter_name>_orig**, and a new buffer tensor, **<parameter_name>_mask**, is created. This mask buffer is a binary tensor, where 0s indicate the pruned weights. To obtain the pruned weights, the **<parameter_name>_mask** must be multiplied with the **<parameter_name>_orig** weights. These pruned weights are then used in the model. Once the pruning is complete, the "**torch.nn.utils.prune.remove**" API is used to remove the "**_orig**" and "**_mask**" buffers, replacing them with a **<parameter_name>** buffer that contains the product of the two. *Figure* 6.4 illustrates the application of these APIs to prune all the convolution layers in the ResNet50 model.

```
# We will apply unstructured pruning to all the convolution layer weights.

def apply_unstructured_pruning(model, prune_ratio=0.2):
    for name, module in model.named_modules():
        if isinstance(module, torch.nn.Conv2d):
            prune.l1_unstructured(module, name='weight', amount=prune_ratio)

    return model

def update_model_post_pruning(model):
    # To remove pruning reparameterization and store permanently
    for name, module in model.named_modules():
        if isinstance(module, torch.nn.Conv2d):
            prune.remove(module, 'weight')

    return model
```

Figure 6.4: *Pytorch API example for unstructured pruning*

In the Jupyter notebook, we are pruning **40%** of the weights across all convolution layers, resulting in an overall model sparsity of **39.95%**. Despite removing **40%** of the weights, the model's accuracy has barely been affected, dropping from **95.39%** to **95.11%**, a minimal decrease of just **0.28%**. This demonstrates the redundancy in the model and reinforces the notion that the model is highly parameterized for a simple task like Cats vs. Dogs. Since the impact on accuracy is minimal, there is no need to retrain the model after pruning. In this case, we are dealing with a simple use case, so retraining is not necessary. However, in real-world scenarios, pruning at this level could significantly affect the accuracy, in which case retraining might be required.

Next, we visualize the weights of the first convolution layer in **layer1**, both before and after pruning. *Figure* 6.5 illustrates a portion of the original weights, the corresponding pruning mask, and the pruned weights. It also shows the shape of the weights before and after pruning. As mentioned earlier, unstructured pruning does not alter the shape of the weights. As seen in *Figure* 6.5, the weight matrix after unstructured pruning contains zeros.

```
Weights before pruning
tensor([[[[-0.0064]],

         [[ 0.0312]],

         [[-0.0454]]],


        [[[ 0.1461]],

         [[-0.0112]],

         [[ 0.0454]]],


        [[[-0.0481]],

         [[-0.0449]],

         [[-0.0237]]]])

Shape of the weight before pruning
torch.Size([64, 64, 1, 1])
```

```
Weight mask for unstructured pruning
tensor([[[[0.]],

         [[1.]],

         [[1.]]],


        [[[1.]],

         [[0.]],

         [[1.]]],


        [[[1.]],

         [[1.]],

         [[1.]]]], device='cuda:0')
```

```
Weights after unstructured pruning
tensor([[[[-0.0000]],

         [[ 0.0312]],

         [[-0.0454]]],


        [[[ 0.1461]],

         [[-0.0000]],

         [[ 0.0454]]],


        [[[-0.0481]],

         [[-0.0449]],

         [[-0.0237]]]], device='cuda:0')

Shape of the weight after pruning
torch.Size([64, 64, 1, 1])
```

Figure 6.5: *A part of original weights, prune mask and pruned weights after unstructured pruning*

Now that the model has been pruned, let us export it to ONNX and visualize it. The ONNX export process is similar to what we've done in previous chapters of the book. *Figure* 6.6 shows the pruned model. As observed, one of the weights of the model is selected, and its properties indicate that it has **40%** sparsity. Additionally, we can see that some of the weights have been set to 0.

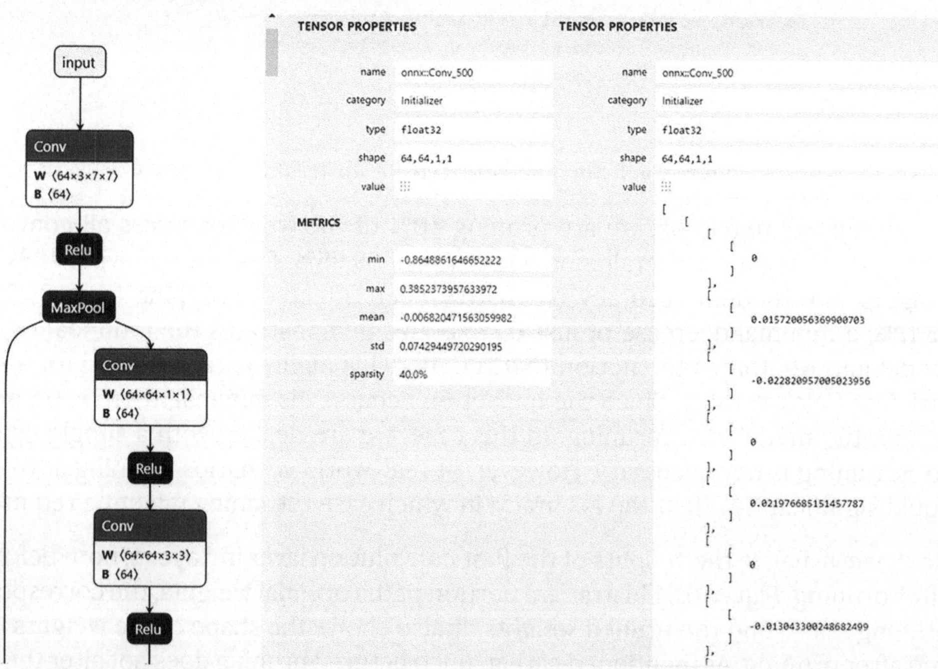

Figure 6.6: *ONNX visualization of model pruned using unstructured pruning*

Structured Pruning of ResNet50

Similar to unstructured pruning, we will use the "**torch.nn.utils.prune.ln_structured**" API for structured pruning. However, unlike unstructured pruning, structured pruning cannot be applied to individual layers in isolation. As mentioned earlier, structured pruning alters the output shapes of the pruned layer, which can make the output incompatible with the subsequent layer. Therefore, structured pruning must be applied in pairs of layers. Specifically, the output channels of one layer and the input channels of the next layer must be pruned together, using the same pruning ratio. *Figure* 6.7 illustrates the use of the structured pruning API.

In the case of structured pruning, we are passing two additional parameters: "**n**" and "**dim**". The "**dim**" parameter specifies the dimension to be pruned, while the "**n**" parameter indicates the type of norm used to compute the importance of each channel. Detailed information on the various types of norms is available in Pytorch documentation[7]. For beginners, n=1 can be used to rank the channels to prune based on the sum of their absolute values across the specified dimension. For more details on the API, refer to Pytorch documentation[8].

```
def prune_weights(name, module, prune_ratio, channel_mask, in_channel=True):
    dim = 1 if in_channel else 0
    # ln_structured will identify redundant input or output channels from the weights.
    prune.ln_structured(module, name="weight", amount=prune_ratio, n=1, dim=dim)
    update_remaining_channels(name, module, channel_mask, in_channel)
```

Figure 6.7: *Pytorch API example for structured pruning*

Just like in unstructured pruning, a binary mask is generated here as well to represent the channels to be pruned and those to be kept. When pruning the output channels of a Convolution, this mask can also be applied to filter out the biases of the Convolution layer, along with the scale and offset values of dependent layers like BatchNorm, as they share the same dimensionality as the Convolution layer's output. Based on the mask, we can filter and update the weights, replacing the existing Convolution, BatchNorm, or Linear layers with their pruned counterparts.

Unlike the previous unstructured pruning example where we pruned the weights of all the Convolution layers, here we will only prune the last block of the ResNet model (**layer4**) and the FC layer. We will prune **10%** of the weights in these layers during every iteration. The reasoning behind pruning the last layers is that, typically, CNN-based models like ResNet have more generic features in the earlier layers, while the later layers contain task-specific features. Pruning these task-specific layers is less likely to affect the fundamental learning of the model. Readers can

[7] https://pytorch.org/docs/stable/generated/torch.linalg.norm.html#torch.linalg.norm

[8] https://pytorch.org/docs/stable/generated/torch.nn.utils.prune.LnStructured.html#torch.nn.utils.prune.LnStructured

experiment further by pruning all layers of the model to observe how pruning impacts accuracy.

Since we are removing entire channels from the model, there will be a more significant impact on accuracy. As shown in *Table 6.2*, pruning the last layer block and FC layer reduces the overall parameter count by **11.06%**, and the accuracy drops from **95.39%** to **79.50%**, which is considerable. To recover this loss in accuracy, we will train the pruned model for one epoch, improving the accuracy from **79.50%** to **92.18%**. After this, we will prune the same selected layers again, removing **10%** of the available weights. We will then check the accuracy and retrain the model to recover the lost accuracy. Since this is a simpler task, we will observe that retraining the pruned model for one epoch results in a noticeable improvement. After three iterations of pruning, the pruned model has **27.65%** fewer parameters, with the accuracy dropping from **95.39%** to **94.40%**. This reduction of just **1.01%** is negligible compared to the reduction in parameters. Specifically, for the ResNet50 model, the total parameters are reduced from **23,485,568** to **16,990,908**. This illustrates the typical iterative pruning workflow.

As we concluded in the unstructured pruning case, we can see here that the model is highly overparameterized for simpler tasks like Cats v/s Dogs classification. Please note that due to the randomness in training samples and weight initializations, the results can vary. However, the process can be made reproducible by setting a random seed, which readers can explore later.

Iteration	Before Pruning		After Pruning		
	Overall %age pruning	**Accuracy**	**Overall %age pruning**	**Post Pruning Accuracy**	**Post Retraining Accuracy**
1	0%	95.39%	11.06%	79.50%	92.18%
2	11.06%	92.18%	20.13%	49.62%	94.77%
3	20.13%	94.77%	27.65%	49.62%	94.40%

Table 6.2: *Table displaying the percentage of pruned parameters and accuracy across various iterations of iterative pruning*

Figure 6.8 displays a portion of the weights from the first Convolution layer of the **`layer4`** block, both before and after pruning. As shown, the values have been replaced with new values, indicating that some channels have been removed. The figure also illustrates the shape of the weights before and after pruning. The weights are represented in the format of **`[out_channels, in_channels, kernel_height, kernel_width]`**. It is evident that the output channels of this Convolution layer have decreased from **512** to **373**, making the shape of the weights as **`[373, 1024, 3, 3]`** instead of the original shape of **`[512, 1024, 3, 3]`**. Consequently, the input channels of the next layer in the model have also been updated from **512** to **373**. Since we are pruning the output channels of the next layer as well, the shape of the weights for this layer will now be `[373, 373, 3, 3]` instead of the original shape of `[512, 512, 3, 3]`.

```
Weights before pruning
tensor([[[[-2.4183e-03]],

         [[ 1.6129e-02]],

         [[ 1.1725e-02]]],


        [[[ 4.3987e-02]],

         [[ 3.0392e-02]],

         [[ 1.8671e-02]]],


        [[[-3.4788e-02]],

         [[ 3.7122e-03]],

         [[ 1.9509e-05]]]])

Shape of the weight layer4.conv1 in pruning model
torch.Size([512, 1024, 1, 1])
```

```
Weights after structured pruning
tensor([[[[-0.0286]],

         [[-0.0179]],

         [[ 0.0131]]],


        [[[-0.0385]],

         [[ 0.0290]],

         [[-0.0172]]],


        [[[ 0.0439]],

         [[-0.0122]],

         [[-0.0087]]]], device='cuda:0')

Shape of the weight layer4.conv1 in pruned model
torch.Size([373, 1024, 1, 1])

Shape of the weight layer4.conv2 in pruned model
torch.Size([373, 373, 3, 3])
```

Figure 6.8: *A part of original weights and pruned weights after structured pruning*

Figure 6.9 presents a comparison of the ResNet50 model before and after pruning, with the `layer4` block highlighted in purple. As observed, the dimensionality of the weights in the purple block has been reduced proportionally. For instance, **512** has been reduced to **373** and **2048** has been reduced to **1493**. This is a result of applying iterative pruning with the same pruning ratio across all layers of the block. Readers can experiment with different pruning ratios for each layer, as well as try various retraining epochs and iterative pruning iterations to achieve an optimal balance between the number of pruned parameters and model performance.

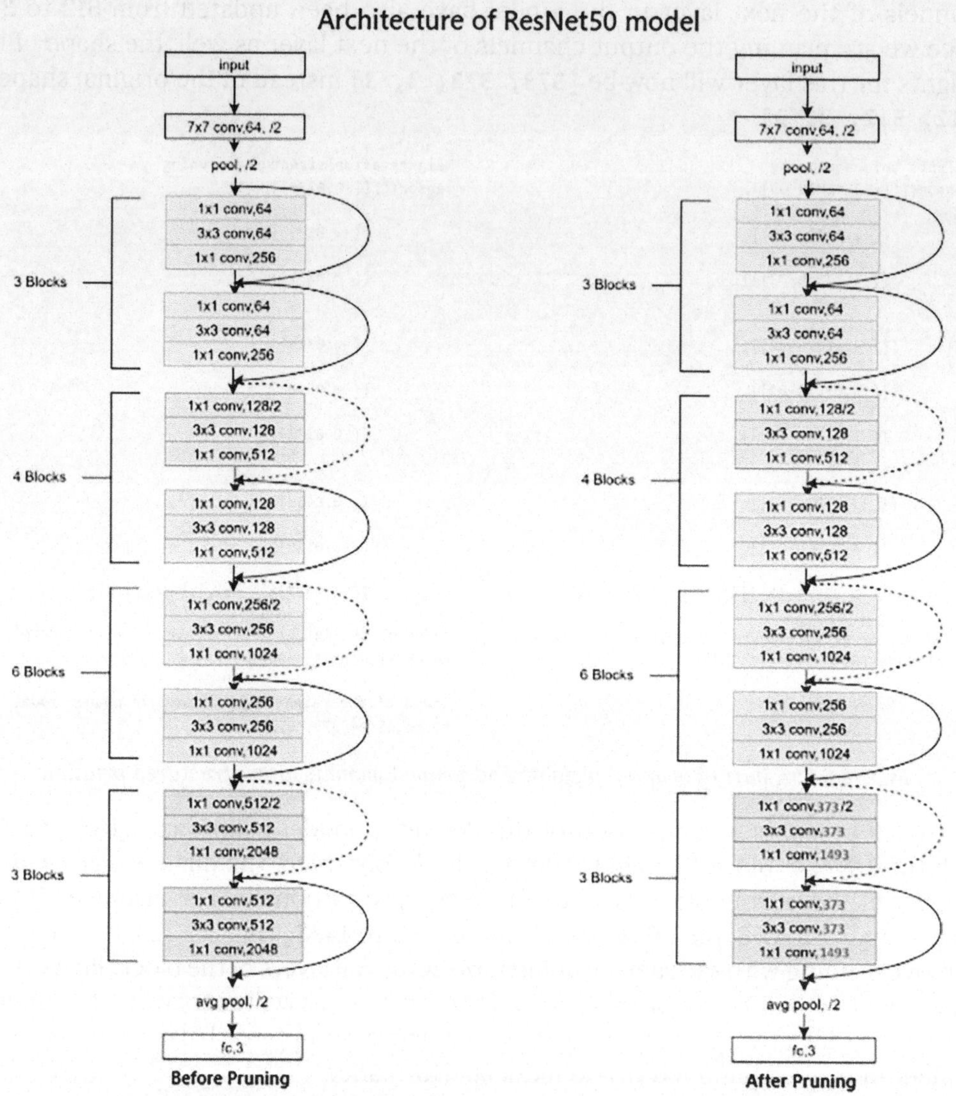

Figure 6.9: *ResNet50 model before and after structured pruning*

Let us now export the pruned model to ONNX and visualize it in a more interactive way. *Figure* 6.10 displays the first Convolution layer of the **layer4** block. As shown, the weights are dense rather than sparse, in contrast to what we observe with unstructured pruning. As a result, the reduction in the number of output channels is clearly visible. Additionally, we can see that some weights remain unchanged when we compare these weights to the original model, while others have been removed during the process. Readers can also examine the subsequent layers of the **layer4** block and the final FC layer to gain a deeper understanding of how pruning has altered the model's structure.

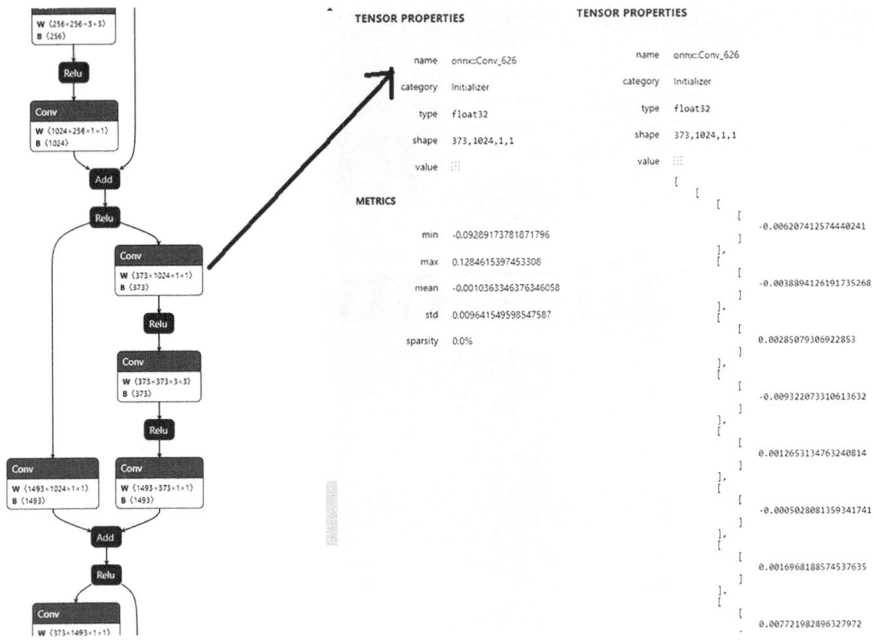

Figure 6.10: ONNX *visualization of model pruned using structured pruning*

Conclusion

In this chapter, we explored the pruning technique for model compression. We discussed how pruning improves model efficiency, the various types of pruning methods, and different pruning strategies. We also examined pruning support in the PyTorch framework. Later, we applied both unstructured and structured pruning to a ResNet50 model trained on the Cats vs. Dogs dataset. Finally, we exported the pruned models to ONNX and visualized them.

The next chapter will introduce you to creating efficient models through knowledge distillation. We will explore various knowledge distillation methods and their underlying algorithms. Using ResNet models as our example, we will demonstrate how knowledge distillation helps achieve both efficiency and accuracy in model representations.

CHAPTER 7
Knowledge Distillation for Edge AI

Introduction

So far, we have explored ONNX models, their optimizations, as well as techniques like quantization and pruning. In this chapter, we will learn a technique called knowledge distillation, which is used to develop smaller, efficient and accurate models required for edge deployment. Using ResNet as an example, we will demonstrate how knowledge distillation can be used to create such compact models. Additionally, we will export the distilled model to ONNX for deployment, ensuring compatibility with edge devices. Finally, we will discuss future advancements and potential research directions in knowledge distillation.

Structure

This chapter covers the following topics.

- Overview of Knowledge Distillation
- Knowledge Distillation Techniques Based on Information Flow
- Knowledge Distillation Techniques Based on Teacher
- Knowledge Distillation Algorithms
- Architectural Decisions in Knowledge Distillation
- Example of Knowledge Distillation in Pytorch
- Exporting Distilled Model to ONNX

Overview of Knowledge Distillation

Traditionally, machine learning models are trained on labeled datasets in supervised learning and unlabeled datasets in unsupervised learning. In supervised learning, the model learns the probability distribution of the labels based on the given inputs. Knowledge distillation is a technique typically used in conjunction with supervised learning.

In knowledge distillation, two models are involved: a pre-trained larger model called the teacher model and a smaller model called the student model. The student model is trained using both supervised learning objectives (based on ground-truth labels) and output signals from the teacher model. Specifically, the student is trained to mimic the teacher's output distribution while the teacher model remains frozen (its weights are not updated). This process effectively transfers learned knowledge from the teacher to the student, hence the term knowledge distillation. *Figure* 7.1 illustrates the overall concept.

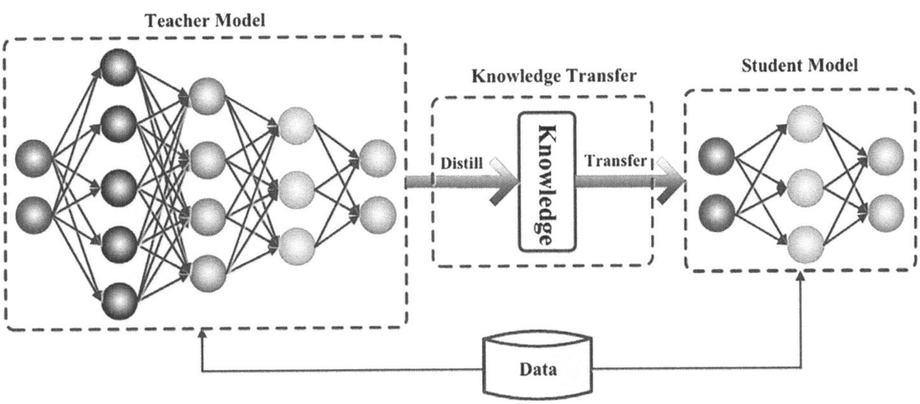

Figure 7.1: *Overview of the knowledge distillation process (Source: Footnote[1])*

This framework has proven transformative across AI domains. In computer vision, distillation enables efficient deployment of models for tasks like image classification and object detection, while specialized applications (for example, cross-resolution face recognition) leverage teacher-student architectures to bridge capability gaps. For NLP, distillation is indispensable for compressing massive language models–DistilBERT, for instance, achieves 60% faster inference while retaining 97% of BERT's accuracy. Another notable example is Meta's LLaMA models[2], where the 1B and 3B student models were distilled from larger 8B and 70B teacher models. The distillation process used the teachers' logits as token-level targets during pre-training and combined them with pruning to create efficient and capable models. Similarly, speech systems like Amazon Alexa employ distillation to train robust acoustic models with limited labeled data.

[1] https://arxiv.org/abs/2006.05525
[2] https://ai.meta.com/blog/llama-3-2-connect-2024-vision-edge-mobile-devices/

By transferring knowledge across architectures and modalities, distillation delivers compact, high-performance models tailored for real-world deployment.

The first practical application of this technique was demonstrated by Hinton et al.[3] for a classification task. Their approach involved aligning the probability distributions of the teacher and student logits alongside the supervised training objective. Both models are fed the same input, producing probability distributions over the target classes. The student is trained using two loss components as shown in *Equation* (1):

- **Cross-entropy loss** $\mathcal{L}_{CE}$ between the student's logits and the true labels
- **Kullback-Leibler (KL) divergence loss** $\mathcal{L}_{distill}$ between the teacher's and student's temperature-softened probabilities. *Equation* (2) shows the same

$$\mathcal{L}_{overall} = \alpha \frac{1}{T^2} \mathcal{L}_{distill} + (1 - \alpha)\mathcal{L}_{CE} \tag{1}$$

$$\mathcal{L}_{distill} = \frac{1}{m} \sum_{i}^{m} D_{KL}(P(x_i) \| Q(x_i)) \tag{2}$$

where,

$$Q(x_i) = \frac{e^{z_i/T}}{\sum_j e^{z_j/T}} \qquad P(x_i) = \frac{e^{y_i/T}}{\sum_j e^{y_j/T}} \tag{3}$$

$$\begin{aligned} D_{KL}(P \| Q) &= \sum_j P_j(x_i) \log \frac{P_j(x_i)}{Q_j(x_i)} \\ &= \sum_i P_j(x_i) \log P_j(x_i) - \sum_i P_j(x_i) \log Q_j(x_i) \end{aligned} \tag{4}$$

Temperature softening is applied using *Equation* (3), where `P(x`$_i$`)` and `Q(x`$_i$`)` represent the output probabilities of the teacher and student, respectively, for a sample `x`$_i$. In Equation (3), `P = [p₁, p₂, …, pk]` (where `k` is the number of classes), the same applies to `Q`. Here, `Z` and `Y` are the unscaled logits, and `T` is a temperature parameter. A value of `T=1` applies a standard softmax, while higher values produce a smoother probability distribution. This smoothing prevents the student from overfitting to the teacher's sharp predictions (just like one-hot encoded labels) and acts as a regularization mechanism. *Figure* 7.2 shows the effect of temperature value on the probability distribution. Higher temperature value has a higher smoothening effect on the probability distribution.

[3] https://arxiv.org/abs/1503.02531

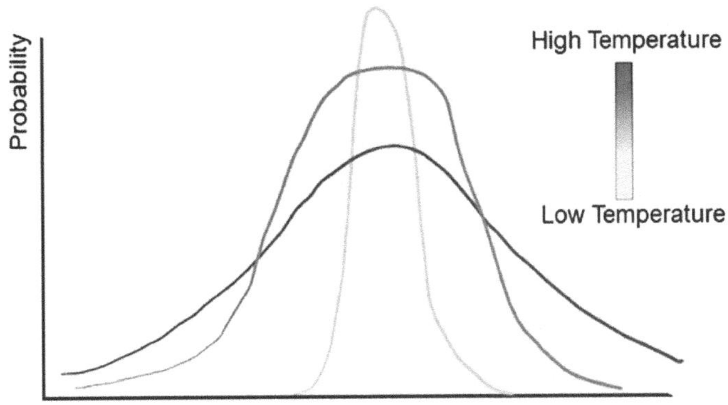

Figure 7.2: *Effect of temperature on probability distribution*

Knowledge Distillation Techniques Based on Information Flow

The approach we described earlier represents just one type of Knowledge Distillation (KD). Various KD methods exist and are differentiated by where the distillation signal originates within the teacher model.

Response-Based Distillation

This method trains the student model using the teacher's output predictions. Our earlier example falls into this category. As the most widely adopted KD technique in deep learning, it is applicable to both classification and regression tasks due to its straightforward implementation. However, response-based distillation has its limitations. It only transfers knowledge from the teacher's final outputs without capturing its internal representations. Consequently, it may be insufficient for tasks requiring complex feature extraction or decision-making. *Figure* 7.3 illustrates this approach.

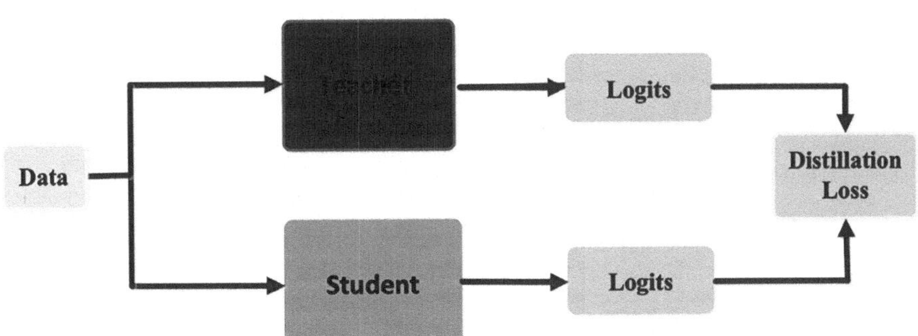

Figure 7.3: *Response-based distillation* (Source: Footnote[1])

Feature-Based Distillation

Unlike response-based methods, this approach utilizes internal features from the teacher's intermediate layers to train the student. Feature alignment between models is achieved through KL divergence loss. Since the teacher and student often have different parameter sizes, a linear layer is typically added to transform the teacher's features to match the student's dimensionality. While more powerful, this method increases computational overhead as it needs to extract internal representations during every iteration. *Figure* 7.4 demonstrates this technique.

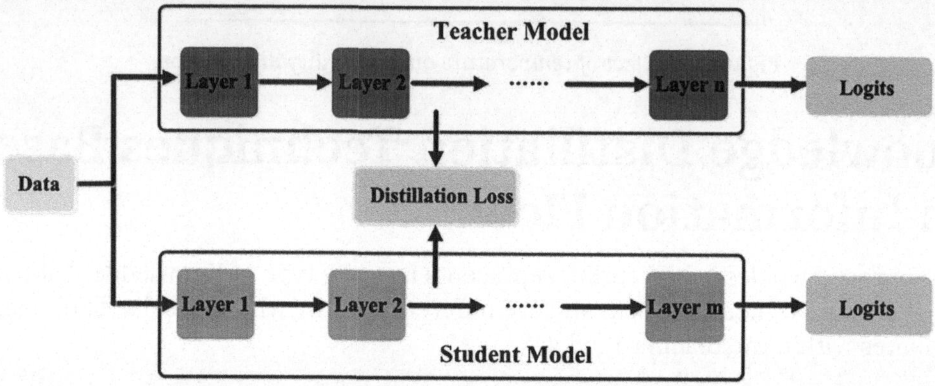

Figure 7.4: *Feature-based distillation (Source: Footnote[1])*

Relation-Based Distillation

This method focuses on teaching the student the relationships between inputs and outputs rather than direct predictions or features. The teacher first generates relationship matrices or tensors that capture input-output dependencies. The student then learns to replicate these relationships by minimizing the difference between its own outputs and the teacher's reference matrices. The key advantage is that the student model learns more robust, generalized relationships than it could discover independently, as it inherits the teacher's learned patterns. However, generating these relationship matrices can be computationally intensive, particularly for large datasets. Additionally, this approach may not suit tasks where input-output relationships are ambiguous or difficult to encode mathematically. *Figure* 7.5 shows how this method is implemented.

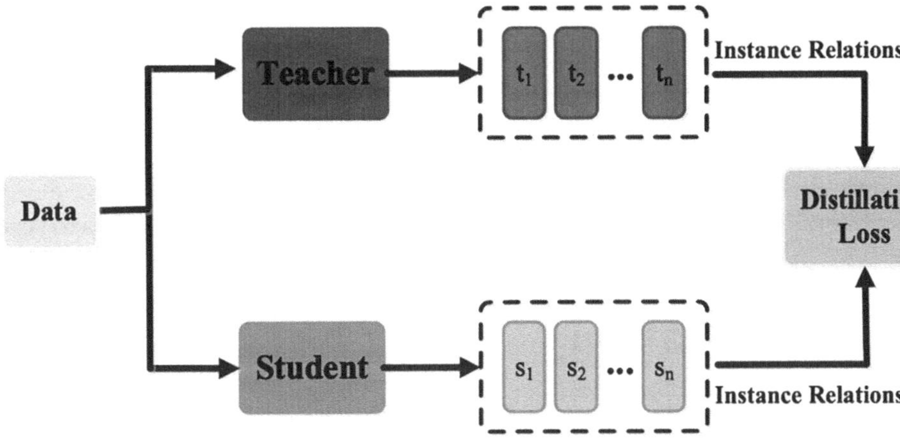

Figure 7.5: *Relation-based distillation (Source: Footnote[1])*

Knowledge Distillation Techniques Based on Teacher

Knowledge distillation techniques can also be categorized based on whether the teacher model is updated during the distillation process. *Figure* 7.6 shows three different categories of distillation methods based on this.

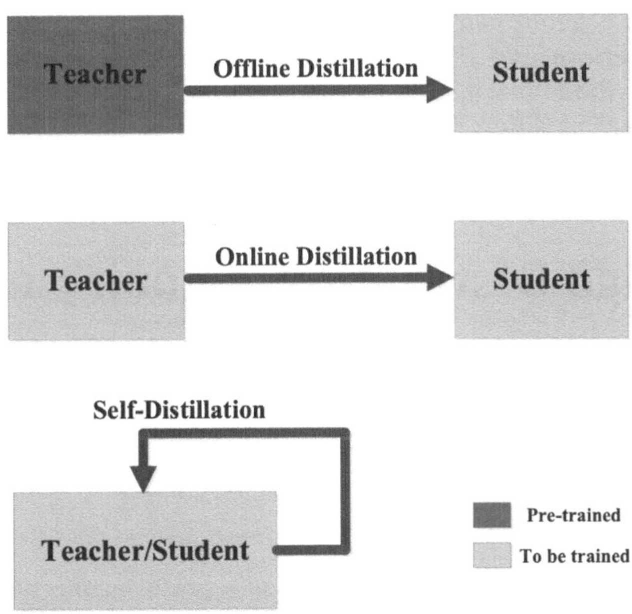

Figure 7.6: *Knowledge distillation categorization based on teacher model's training (Source: Footnote[1])*

Offline Distillation

In offline distillation, the teacher network is pre-trained and then frozen. During student training, the teacher model remains fixed and is not updated. This approach, used in Hinton et al.'s original work and many subsequent studies, focuses primarily on improving knowledge transfer mechanisms rather than teacher architecture design. It enables effective knowledge transfer from high-performing teacher models to student models.

Online Distillation

Online knowledge distillation (also called dynamic or continual distillation) transfers knowledge sequentially as new data arrives. Both teacher and student models are trained simultaneously, with the teacher continuously updating based on new information. The student learns from the teacher's evolving outputs in real-time through a feedback loop where student performance informs teacher updates. This approach is particularly valuable for non-stationary or streaming data, such as in natural language processing applications where data distributions change over time.

Self Distillation

Conventional distillation methods (offline and online) face two key challenges: student accuracy depends heavily on teacher selection, and students often cannot match teacher performance. Self-distillation addresses these issues by using the same network as both teacher and student. Shallow classifiers are attached to intermediate layers at different depths, with deeper classifiers guiding shallower ones during training using divergence-based loss for outputs and L2 loss for features. These auxiliary classifiers are removed during inference.

Knowledge Distillation Algorithms

In this section, we will examine several prominent algorithms used for knowledge distillation. These algorithms facilitate efficient knowledge acquisition by student models, resulting in enhanced performance while reducing model complexity. Let us explore each method in detail.

Adversarial Distillation

Adversarial distillation improves student model's performance by having it learn from both original data and samples specifically designed to challenge the teacher model. The process involves first training the teacher normally, then training the student using an adversarial network that generates samples the teacher finds difficult to classify. These adversarial examples are created by carefully perturbing original inputs to maximize teacher confusion while remaining semantically similar. The student learns to correctly classify these teacher-challenging samples, gaining improved robustness and generalization beyond standard distillation methods.

Multi-Teacher Distillation

Multi-teacher distillation trains a student model using multiple teachers, combining their diverse knowledge for better performance. First, each teacher trains independently on the dataset. The student then learns from all teachers' outputs simultaneously, gaining richer features from their combined perspectives. This approach reduces bias and improves robustness compared to single-teacher distillation. However, loading all teachers in memory during training is resource-intensive, making it challenging for large-scale models like modern billion-parameter language networks. *Figure* 7.7 illustrates the framework.

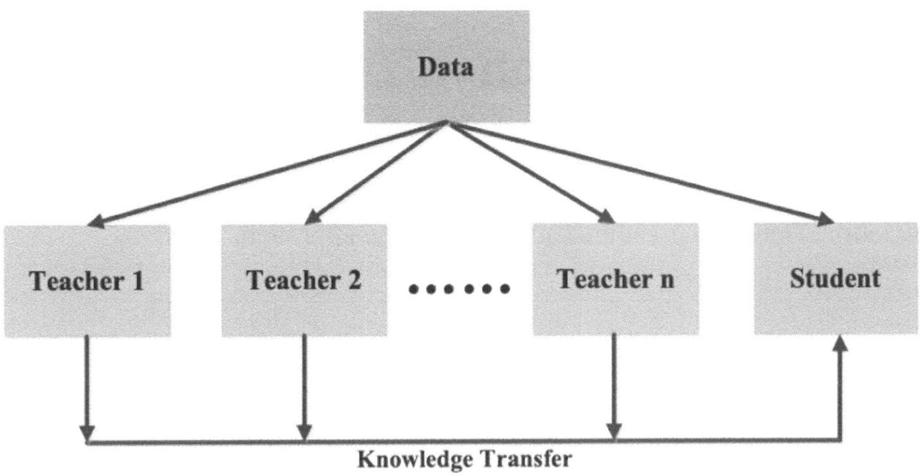

Figure 7.7: *Multi-teacher distillation* (Source: Footnote[1])

Cross-Modal Distillation

Figure 7.8 demonstrates the cross-modal distillation approach, where knowledge is transferred between different input modalities. This becomes necessary when training data or labels are unavailable for certain modalities during model development.

This technique is particularly useful for visual applications. For instance, a teacher model trained on labeled images can distill knowledge to a student processing unlabeled optical flow, text, or audio data. The student learns supervised features derived from the teacher's image-based knowledge, enabling applications like visual question answering and image captioning.

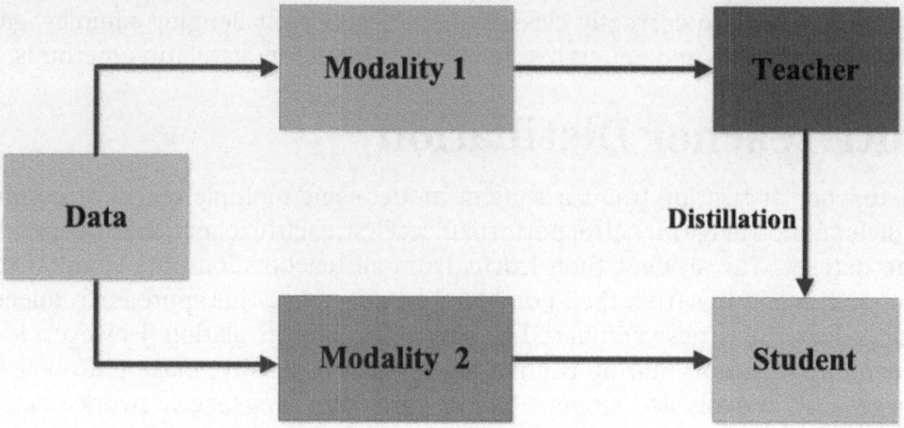

Figure 7.8: *Cross-modal distillation (Source: Footnote[1])*

Quantized Distillation

Quantized distillation employs a high-precision teacher model (typically 32-bit floating point) to train a low-precision student network (often 8-bit). The student learns from the teacher's precise output signals while maintaining efficient quantization. *Figure* 7.9 presents this quantization approach.

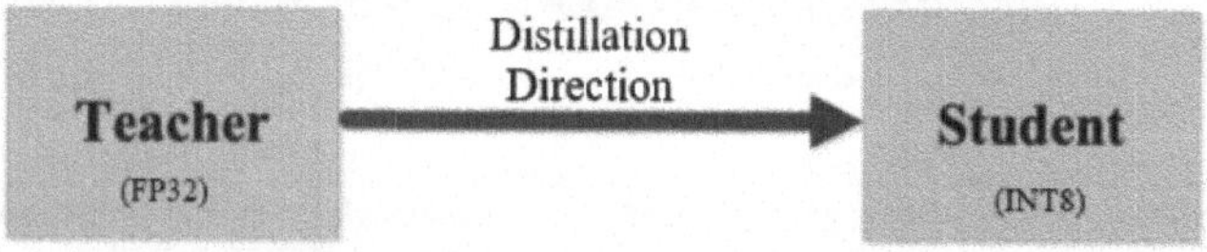

Figure 7.9: *Quantized distillation (Source: Footnote[1])*

Architectural Decisions in Knowledge Distillation

The design of student-teacher architectures plays a pivotal role in effective knowledge transfer. A fundamental challenge arises from the inherent capacity gap between the complex teacher model and its simpler student counterpart. Strategic architectural choices can bridge this gap by optimizing how knowledge flows from teacher to student.

Knowledge transfer from deep neural networks presents unique challenges due to their depth and breadth. Common architectural approaches for the student model include the following:

- A compressed version of the teacher architecture with:
  - Fewer layers and reduced neurons per layer
  - For CNNs: Heuristic reduction of output channels across layers
  - For transformers: Decreased model dimensions (d_model), attention heads, or hidden representations in feed-forward layers
- A quantized variant of the teacher model
- A smaller pruned variant of the original model used as student model and original model as teacher model
- A compact network employing efficient base operations
- A smaller model with optimized global architecture
- An architecture using edge-device-compatible activation functions (particularly useful when original model components lack hardware support)
- In some cases, maintaining identical architecture to the teacher

Beyond these approaches, emerging techniques like neural architecture search offer promising ways to automatically derive optimal student architectures based on provided constraints (for example, size and latency), often specifically tailored to efficiently learn from a given teacher model.

Example of Knowledge Distillation in Pytorch

Now that we have explored the concept of knowledge distillation, we will proceed with its implementation. In this section, we will use ResNet18 as the teacher model and ResNet10 as the student model. First, we will train both models independently using supervised learning with labeled data. For consistency, we will employ the same dataset as in the previous chapter, the Cats vs. Dogs dataset[4]. Readers are encouraged to follow along using the Jupyter notebook provided for this chapter[5].

The training pipeline involves defining a data loading mechanism, initializing the models, setting up optimizers and learning rate schedulers, and implementing training and testing loops. We will use PyTorch for this exercise. To ensure efficient execution, it is recommended to run the code on GPU-enabled hardware, or Google Colab with GPU support.

[4] https://huggingface.co/datasets/microsoft/cats_vs_dogs
[5] https://github.com/ava-orange-education/Ultimate-ONNX-for-Optimizing-Deep-Learning-Models

The Cats vs. Dogs dataset comprises 23,410 images, evenly split between cats and dogs. The objective is binary classification, predicting whether an image contains a cat or a dog. In PyTorch, training requires a **DataLoader** object, which processes data through a **Dataset** class. The **Dataset** class handles data loading from disk, applies necessary preprocessing, and formats the data for model input. Since we are using ResNet18 with pre-trained ImageNet weights, we will preprocess the images according to ImageNet standards.

```
# Setup Dataset object for training

class CatDogDataset(torch.utils.data.Dataset):
    # Load dataset from Hugging Face
    dataset = load_dataset("microsoft/cats_vs_dogs")

    # Split dataset into train and test sets
    train_size = int(0.8 * len(dataset["train"]))
    test_size = len(dataset["train"]) - train_size
    train_dataset, test_dataset = random_split(
        dataset["train"], [train_size, test_size]
    )

    def __init__(self, is_train=True):
        if is_train:
            self.ds = self.__class__.train_dataset
            self.transform_fn = self.transforms()
        else:
            self.ds = self.__class__.test_dataset
            self.transform_fn = self.transforms()

    def transforms(self):
        transform = transforms.Compose(
            [
                T.Resize((224, 224)),
                T.Lambda(
                    lambda img: img.convert("RGB") if img.mode != "RGB" else img
                ),  # Convert grayscale to RGB
                T.ToTensor(),
                T.Normalize(
                    mean=[0.485, 0.456, 0.406], std=[0.229, 0.224, 0.225]
                ),  # ImageNet normalization
            ]
        )
        return transform

    def __len__(self):
        return len(self.ds)

    def __getitem__(self, idx):
        example = self.ds[idx]
        img = example["image"]
        example.pop("image")
        example["images"] = self.transform_fn(img)
        example["labels"] = torch.tensor(example["labels"], dtype=torch.long)
        return example
```

Figure 7.10: *Cats vs. Dogs dataset class*

To create a custom **Dataset** class, we inherit from **torch.utils.data.Dataset** and implement the **__len__** and **__getitem__** methods. The **__len__** method returns the dataset size, while **__getitem__** retrieves and preprocesses the i-th sample. *Figure* 7.10 illustrates the **Dataset** class used in this exercise. As shown, the class loads the dataset and splits it into an 80-20 train-test ratio. The **is_train** flag in the class constructor allows switching between training and test data. The class also defines a series of transforms: resizing images to **224x224** pixels, converting them to PyTorch tensors, scaling pixel values to **[0, 1]**, and applying ImageNet normalization. The **__getitem__** method returns a dictionary with keys for the processed image and its corresponding label, where 0 represents a cat and 1 represents a dog. These labels are already present in the loaded dataset.

```
class Trainer:
    def __init__(
        self,
        model,
        train_dataset,
        test_dataset,
        batch_size,
        num_workers,
        num_epochs,
        lr,
        device,
        model_name,
    ):
        self.batch_size = batch_size
        self.num_workers = num_workers
        self.num_epochs = num_epochs
        self.lr = lr
        self.device = device
        self.model_name = model_name

        self.train_loader = DataLoader(
            train_dataset, batch_size=batch_size, shuffle=True, num_workers=num_workers
        )
        self.test_loader = DataLoader(
            test_dataset, batch_size=batch_size, num_workers=num_workers
        )
        self.model = model
        print(summary(model, input_size=(1, 3, 224, 224)))
        self.model = self.model.to(self.device)
```

Figure 7.11: *Trainer class with __init__ method*

Let us define a **Trainer** class to encapsulate all training-related components. This class uses supervised learning with labeled data to train the model. It includes three key methods: **__init__**, **fit**, and **test**. *Figure* 7.11 illustrates the **__init__** method of the **Trainer** class. The constructor takes a PyTorch model object, training and test dataset objects, and other necessary training arguments. The dataset object we created earlier is used to instantiate a **DataLoader**, which shuffles the data, prepares batches for training, and pre-fetches them for efficient GPU execution. Additionally, the model is moved to a specific device (GPU in our case) via **`model.to(device)`**.

```
def fit(self):
    # Loss and optimizer
    criterion = nn.CrossEntropyLoss()
    optimizer = optim.Adam(self.model.parameters(), lr=self.lr)

    # Training Loop
    train_acc_list = []
    test_acc_list = []
    for epoch in range(self.num_epochs):
        self.model.train()
        total_loss = 0
        correct = 0
        total = 0
        for batch in tqdm(self.train_loader):
            images, labels = (
                batch["images"].to(self.device),
                batch["labels"].to(self.device),
            )
            optimizer.zero_grad()
            outputs = self.model(images)
            loss = criterion(outputs, labels)
            loss.backward()
            optimizer.step()
            total_loss += loss.item()
            _, predicted = outputs.max(1)
            correct += predicted.eq(labels).sum().item()
            total += labels.size(0)

        train_acc = (correct / total) * 100
        train_acc_list.append(train_acc)
        print(
            f"Epoch {epoch + 1}/{self.num_epochs}, "
            f"Loss: {total_loss / len(self.train_loader)}, "
            f"Accuracy: {train_acc:.2f}%"
        )

        # Test Loop
        test_acc = self.test()
        test_acc_list.append(test_acc)
        print(f"Test Accuracy: {test_acc:.2f}%")

    # Save Model
    torch.save(
        self.model.state_dict(),
        f"{self.model_name.replace('.', '_').replace('/', '_')}.pth",
    )
    return train_acc_list, test_acc_list
```

Figure 7.12: *fit method of Trainer class*

Figure 7.12 presents the **fit** method of the **Trainer** class. This method defines the loss function and optimizer, then iterates over the **DataLoader** to process batches of input data. Each full pass through the dataset constitutes one epoch, and multiple epochs are executed based on user configuration. During each epoch, the model processes the entire training dataset, followed by the test dataset to evaluate performance on unseen data. For every batch, cross-entropy loss is computed, gradients are backpropagated, and weights are updated. The model remains in training mode (**model.train()**) throughout this process. During testing, the **test()** method internally switches the model to the evaluation mode (**model.eval()**). Once training completes, the model's parameters are saved to the disk for future use.

```
def test(self):
    # Test loop
    self.model.to(self.device)
    self.model.eval()
    correct = 0
    total = 0
    with torch.no_grad():
        for batch in tqdm(self.test_loader):
            images, labels = (
                batch["images"].to(self.device),
                batch["labels"].to(self.device),
            )
            outputs = self.model(images)
            _, predicted = outputs.max(1)
            correct += predicted.eq(labels).sum().item()
            total += labels.size(0)
    acc = correct / total * 100
    return acc
```

Figure 7.13: *`test` method of Trainer class*

Figure 7.13 depicts the **test** method, which iterates over the test **DataLoader** and measures accuracy on unseen data. This provides insight into how well the model generalizes. At the start of the function, **model.eval()** is called to switch the model into evaluation mode, disabling operations like dropout and batch normalization that are only active during training.

Figure 7.14 shows the initialization of the training and test datasets, which are passed to the **Trainer** constructor, along with the definition of key hyperparameters.

```
# Setup dataset

train_dataset = CatDogDataset(is_train=True)
test_dataset = CatDogDataset(is_train=False)
```

```
# Define Hyperparameters

NUM_CLASSES = 2
BATCH_SIZE = 32
LR = 1e-3
EPOCHS = 10
NUM_WORKERS = 4  # Adjust based on CPU cores
DEVICE = torch.device("cuda" if torch.cuda.is_available() else "cpu")
```

Figure 7.14: *Setting of datasets and defining training hyper parameters*

```
# Setup ResNet18 classifier model
class ResNet18Classifier(nn.Module):
    def __init__(self, num_classes=2, ckpt_path=None):
        super(ResNet18Classifier, self).__init__()

        # Load pretrained resnet18
        self.model = models.resnet18(pretrained=True)

        # Update the last FC layer for 2 class classification problem
        self.model.fc = nn.Linear(self.model.fc.in_features, num_classes)

        # Load the checkpoint if it is provided.
        if ckpt_path is not None:
            if not os.path.isfile(ckpt_path):
                raise FileNotFoundError(f"File not present at: {ckpt_path}.")
            self.model.load_state_dict(torch.load(ckpt_path))

    def forward(self, images):
        logits = self.model(images)
        return logits
```

```
# Train ResNet18 model on Cats v/s Dogs dataset. This model will be considered as teacher model.

MODEL_NAME = "resnet18_cats_dogs_normal"
base_model = ResNet18Classifier(num_classes=NUM_CLASSES, ckpt_path=None).to(DEVICE)

base_trainer = Trainer(
    base_model, train_dataset, test_dataset, BATCH_SIZE, NUM_WORKERS,
    EPOCHS, LR, DEVICE, MODEL_NAME
)
train_acc_list_r18, test_acc_list_r18 = base_trainer.fit()
```

Figure 7.15: *ResNet18 model definition and training of the same*

With the **`Trainer`** class and **`DataLoader`** in place, we can now define and train the model. *Figure* 7.15 demonstrates the implementation of a ResNet18 model by subclassing **`torch.nn.Module`**. The model is loaded from the **`torchvision`** library with pre-trained ImageNet weights, and its final fully-connected layer is modified to predict two classes instead of the original 1,000. The **`forward`** method processes input images and generates logits for these two classes, which the **`Trainer`** uses to compute loss. The latter part of *Figure* 7.15 shows how all components are integrated. The **`ResNet18Classifier`** defines the model, the **`Trainer`** is instantiated with the model, datasets, and hyperparameters, and the training begins by calling the **`fit`** method. After 10 epochs, the model achieves training and test accuracies of **`98.21%`** and **`96.50%`**, respectively.

```
# Setup ResNet10 classifier model
from torchvision.models.resnet import _resnet, BasicBlock

class ResNet10Classifier(nn.Module):
    def __init__(self, num_classes=2, ckpt_path=None):
        super(ResNet10Classifier, self).__init__()

        # Define resnet10 based on torchvision definition
        self.model = _resnet(BasicBlock, [1, 1, 1, 1], None, False)

        # Update the last FC layer for 2 class classification problem
        self.model.fc = nn.Linear(self.model.fc.in_features, num_classes)

        # Load the checkpoint if it is provided.
        if ckpt_path is not None:
            if not os.path.isfile(ckpt_path):
                raise FileNotFoundError(f"File not present at: {ckpt_path}.")
            self.model.load_state_dict(torch.load(ckpt_path))

    def forward(self, images):
        logits = self.model(images)
        return logits

# Train ResNet10 model on Cats v/s Dogs dataset on plain cross entropy loss.
# That means based on only labeled data.
base_model = ResNet10Classifier(num_classes=NUM_CLASSES).to(DEVICE)

MODEL_NAME = "resnet10_cats_dogs_normal"
base_trainer = Trainer(
    base_model, train_dataset, test_dataset, BATCH_SIZE, NUM_WORKERS,
    EPOCHS, LR, DEVICE, MODEL_NAME
)
train_acc_list_r10, test_acc_list_r10 = base_trainer.fit()
```

Figure 7.16: *ResNet10 model definition and training of the same*

Similarly, we can define and train a ResNet10 model under the same settings. *Figure 7.16* provides the corresponding code. Since ResNet10 is not a standard architecture and lacks pre-trained weights, we can construct it using configurable ResNet building blocks. After 10 epochs, it achieves training and test accuracies of **97.13%** and **90.56%**. While this performance is lower than ResNet18, it is reasonable as ResNet10 has approximately **56%** fewer parameters.

```
class KDTrainer:
    def __init__(self, teacher_model, student_model, train_dataset, test_dataset, batch_size, num_workers,
                 num_epochs, lr, device, student_model_name):
        self.batch_size = batch_size
        self.num_workers = num_workers
        self.num_epochs = num_epochs
        self.lr = lr
        self.device = device
        self.student_model_name = student_model_name

        self.train_loader = DataLoader(
            train_dataset, batch_size=batch_size, shuffle=True, num_workers=num_workers
        )
        self.test_loader = DataLoader(
            test_dataset, batch_size=batch_size, num_workers=num_workers
        )
        self.teacher_model = teacher_model
        self.student_model = student_model
        print("Teacher model summary:")
        print(summary(self.teacher_model, input_size=(1, 3, 224, 224)))
        print("Student model summary:")
        print(summary(self.student_model, input_size=(1, 3, 224, 224)))

        self.teacher_model = self.teacher_model.to(self.device)
        self.student_model = self.student_model.to(self.device)

    def distillation_loss(self, student_logits, teacher_logits, labels, T, alpha):
        # KL Div Loss between student's logits and teacher's logits.
        soft_loss = nn.KLDivLoss(reduction='batchmean')(
                        F.log_softmax(student_logits/T, dim=1),
                        F.softmax(teacher_logits/T, dim=1)) * (T * T)

        # Cross entropy loss between student's prediction and ground truth labels.
        hard_loss = F.cross_entropy(student_logits, labels)
        return alpha * soft_loss + (1. - alpha) * hard_loss
```

Figure 7.17: *KDTrainer class for knowledge distillation training*

Now that we have trained the ResNet18 and ResNet10 models using supervised learning, let us explore how knowledge distillation can improve the accuracy of the smaller ResNet10 model.

Similar to the earlier **Trainer** class, we will define a new **KDTrainer** class that uses a teacher model and a student model. This class keeps the teacher model frozen and trains the student model using both labeled data for supervised learning and teacher-generated signals for knowledge distillation. The dataloading process and training loop remain largely unchanged, with the key difference being the use of two models and an updated loss function.

```
def fit(self, T=5.0, alpha=0.5):
    # Optimizer
    optimizer = optim.Adam(self.student_model.parameters(), lr=self.lr)

    # Keep the teacher model frozen
    self.teacher_model.eval()

    # Training Loop
    train_acc_list = []
    test_acc_list = []
    for epoch in range(self.num_epochs):
        self.student_model.train()
        total_loss = 0
        correct = 0
        total = 0
        for batch in tqdm(self.train_loader):
            images, labels = batch["images"].to(self.device), batch["labels"].to(self.device)
            optimizer.zero_grad()

            student_logits = self.student_model(images)
            with torch.no_grad():
                teacher_logits = self.teacher_model(images)

            loss = self.distillation_loss(student_logits, teacher_logits, labels, T, alpha)
            loss.backward()
            optimizer.step()
            total_loss += loss.item()
            _, predicted = student_logits.max(1)
            correct += predicted.eq(labels).sum().item()
            total += labels.size(0)

        train_acc = (correct/total)*100
        train_acc_list.append(train_acc)
        print(f"Epoch {epoch+1}/{self.num_epochs}, "
              f"Loss: {total_loss/len(self.train_loader)}, "
              f"Accuracy: {train_acc:.2f}%")

        test_acc = self.test()
        test_acc_list.append(test_acc)
        print(f"Test Accuracy: {test_acc:.2f}%")

    # Save Model
    torch.save(self.student_model.state_dict(),
               f"{self.student_model_name.replace('.', '_').replace('/', '_')}.pth")
    return train_acc_list, test_acc_list
```

Figure 7.18: *fit method of KDTrainer class*

Figure 7.17 displays the **`KDTrainer`** class implementation, including the **`__init__`** and **`distillation_loss`** methods. Unlike the previous **`Trainer`** class, the constructor now accepts both teacher and student models, while the rest of the initialization remains consistent. The **`distillation_loss`** method takes **`student_logits, teacher_logits`**, and **`labels`** as inputs. The KL divergence loss is computed between the student and teacher logits based on *Equation (4)*. The temperature parameter **`T`** scales the logits before applying **`softmax`** to the teacher outputs and **`log_softmax`** to the student outputs, as required by the **KLDivLoss** function. The final loss is a weighted sum of cross-entropy loss and KL divergence loss, with alpha controlling their respective contributions.

Figure 7.18 illustrates the **fit** method of the **KDTrainer** class. Here, the teacher model is set to evaluation mode, while the student model remains in training mode. The training loop processes batches from the dataloader, computing logits from both models for each batch. These logits, along with the labels, temperature T, and weighting factor alpha, are used to calculate the distillation loss. Gradients are derived from this loss and applied only to the student model during backpropagation. The remaining logic, including the **test** function, mirrors that of the original **Trainer** class.

```
# Train ResNet10 model on Cats v/s Dogs dataset using supervised learning training
# and knowledge distillation training using ResNet18.
teacher_model = ResNet18Classifier(num_classes=NUM_CLASSES, ckpt_path=None).to(DEVICE)
student_model = ResNet10Classifier(num_classes=NUM_CLASSES).to(DEVICE)

# Load the pretrained weights to the teacher model
teacher_model.load_state_dict(torch.load("./resnet18_cats_dogs_normal.pth"))

DISTILL_EPOCHS = 10
STUDENT_MODEL_NAME = "resnet10_cats_dogs_kd"
kd_trainer = KDTrainer(
    teacher_model, student_model, train_dataset, test_dataset, BATCH_SIZE, NUM_WORKERS,
    DISTILL_EPOCHS, LR, DEVICE, STUDENT_MODEL_NAME
)
train_acc_list_r10_kd, test_acc_list_r10_kd = kd_trainer.fit()
```

Figure 7.19: *Knowledge distillation training of ResNet10 model*

Figure 7.19 shows the initialization of the teacher and student models. After initializing the teacher model, we load the pretrained weights obtained from training the ResNet18 model through supervised learning. The student model is initialized randomly. The **KDTrainer** is then instantiated with both models, dataset objects, and training parameters. After 10 epochs of training, the distilled student model achieves **96.89%** training accuracy and **92.65%** test accuracy.

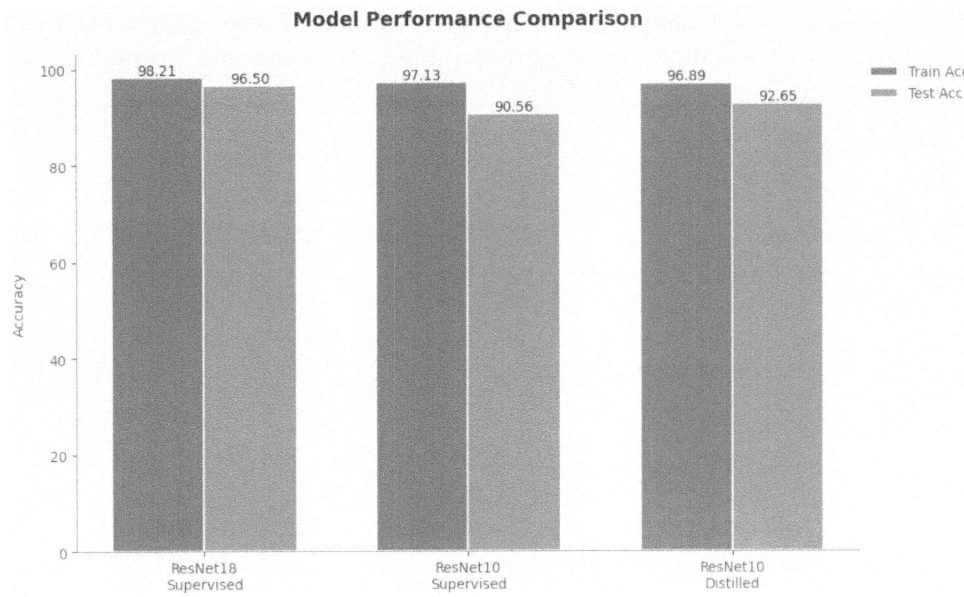

Figure 7.20: *Comparison of results*

Figure 7.20 compares the performance of the supervised ResNet18, the supervised ResNet10, and the distilled ResNet10. The results show a **2.09%** test accuracy improvement for the distilled ResNet10 over its purely supervised counterpart, demonstrating the effectiveness of knowledge distillation. Notably, while the ResNet18 has **11,177,538** parameters and the ResNet10 has just **4,906,818**, the distilled ResNet10 achieves competitive accuracy relative to the supervised ResNet18. This means we attain comparable performance with **56%** fewer parameters, making the distilled model significantly more efficient. Such efficiency is particularly valuable for deployment on edge devices, where resource constraints demand lightweight yet accurate models.

It is worth noting that this example represents a basic implementation of knowledge distillation. Real-world applications may require experimentation with different distillation techniques and loss functions. For further exploration, readers can refer to the survey paper on knowledge distillation cited in *Footnote*[1].

Exporting Distilled Model to ONNX

Having demonstrated the superior performance of the distilled ResNet10 model compared to its supervised counterpart, we can now proceed to export this model to ONNX format for deployment purposes. The export process follows the same straightforward approach we implemented in previous chapters. *Figure* 7.21 illustrates the **export_to_onnx** utility function, which handles model conversion while supporting dynamic batch sizes. This function saves the distilled ResNet10 model in ONNX format at the specified file path. The exported model remains fully compatible with standard tools. It can be executed using ONNX Runtime or visualized through Netron. Readers are encouraged to examine the exported model structure and properties as an additional exercise.

```
# Helper utility to export the model

def export_to_onnx(model, output_path):
    # Dummy input tensor for ONNX export
    dummy_input = torch.randn(1, 3, 224, 224)
    model.to("cpu")

    # Export the pruned model to ONNX
    torch.onnx.export(
        model, dummy_input, output_path,
        input_names=["input"], output_names=["output"],
        dynamic_axes={"input": {0: "batch_size"}, "output": {0: "batch_size"}},
        opset_version=11
    )

    print(f"Model has been exported to {output_path}")
```

```
# Export the distilled ResNet10 model

student_model_onnx_path = "./resnet10_cats_vs_dogs_distilled.onnx"
export_to_onnx(student_model, student_model_onnx_path)
```

Figure 7.21: ONNX *export of distilled ResNet10 model*

Conclusion

This chapter provided a comprehensive exploration of knowledge distillation, covering various techniques, algorithms, and associated architectural considerations. Given its significance for efficient edge deployment, we adopted a practical approach by implementing the technique using PyTorch with ResNet18 and ResNet10 models. Through this hands-on experience, we gained valuable insights into the effectiveness of knowledge distillation in model optimization.

In the next chapter, we will focus on deploying models on edge devices. We will start by exploring the Raspberry Pi as a candidate edge device and setting up the environment for deployment. Then, we will run a model on the Raspberry Pi to get hands-on experience with deploying models on edge devices.

CHAPTER 8
Deploying ONNX Models on Edge Devices

Introduction

So far, we have explored ONNX models, their optimizations, and techniques such as quantization, pruning and knowledge distillation. In this chapter, we will shift our focus to deploying these models on edge devices. Specifically, we will focus on deploying a model on the Raspberry Pi 3 as one example of an edge device. Additionally, we will walk through the process of setting up the Raspberry Pi 3 for edge deployment.

Structure

This chapter covers the following topics:

- Overview of Edge Devices
- Overview of Raspberry Pi
- Initial setup of Raspberry Pi
- Building ONNX Runtime
- Overview of ONNX Runtime C++ APIs
- End-to-End Inference Example

Overview of Edge Devices

In the first chapter, we explored edge devices, their use cases, benefits, and challenges. In this section, we will dive deeper into the concept of edge computing and its evolving role in AI-driven applications. While edge devices have been in use for some time, advancements in AI have significantly impacted the edge device market. Modern edge devices are now equipped with AI-specific processing cores, enabling dedicated and efficient AI computations.

There are various types of edge devices designed for different applications, including wearable devices, industrial-grade solutions, drones, and more. Below, we discuss some of the most commonly available edge devices used for AI model deployment.

- Nvidia Jetson[1]
  - Nvidia offers an extensive product lineup catering to different edge computing requirements, delivering AI performance ranging from 0.5 TOPS (Tera Operations Per Second) to 275 TOPS, with the Jetson AGX Orin at the upper end of this range.
    - The Jetson Nano, which was launched in 2019, provides 0.5 TOPS of AI performance with 128 CUDA cores, which are Nvidia's proprietary processing units for AI workloads, similar to CPU cores. It operates at a power consumption of approximately 5W, making it suitable for low-power edge AI applications. It was later upgraded to the Jetson Orin Nano, launched in 2022, which significantly increased performance to 34 TOPS with 512 CUDA cores at a power range of 5 to 20W. This upgrade was meant to adapt to the growing demands of edge compute requirements.
- Raspberry Pi[2]
  - Raspberry Pi is a compact yet powerful single-board computer featuring multiple connectivity options such as Bluetooth, Wi-Fi, USB, HDMI, and Ethernet. Due to its versatility, it is widely used in edge computing, IoT, AI, robotics, and embedded systems.
    - **Raspberry Pi 4:** Offers 0.1 to 0.4 TOPS of compute capability
    - **Raspberry Pi 5:** Provides 0.5 to 1 TOPS of AI performance
    - **Expandable AI Performance:** The modularity of Raspberry Pi allows integration with dedicated accelerators like the Hailo AI accelerator, which can boost AI performance up to 26 TOPS
- Google Coral[3]
  - Google Coral is a single-board computer similar in form factor to Raspberry Pi, but it is specifically designed for AI applications. Unlike Raspberry Pi, which is a general-purpose computing platform, Coral features the Edge TPU (Tensor Processing Unit), a dedicated AI accelerator optimized for

[1] https://www.nvidia.com/en-us/autonomous-machines/embedded-systems/jetson-orin/
[2] https://www.raspberrypi.com/news/raspberry-pi-ai-hat/
[3] https://coral.ai/products/

machine learning inference, making it significantly more efficient for AI workloads.

- **Key Strength:** Its power efficiency, delivering 4 TOPS of performance at just 2W, making it ideal for power-sensitive edge AI use cases
- **Expandable AI Capabilities:** Also available as an accelerator module that can be attached to a Raspberry Pi to enhance its AI processing power

- Intel Neural Compute Stick[4] (NCS) 2
    - The Intel NCS2 is a USB-based AI accelerator designed for low-power AI inference on edge devices such as Raspberry Pi, laptops, and embedded systems.
        - **Performance:** Provides 1 to 2 TOPS of AI compute power at around 2.5W
        - **Use Case:** Suitable for AI applications that require efficient inference processing with minimal power consumption
- Consumer-Grade Edge AI Devices
    - Beyond dedicated AI accelerators, modern consumer-grade devices are increasingly equipped with on-device AI capabilities:
        - iPhone 16 Pro (A18 Pro Chip): Delivers 35 TOPS of AI performance[5].
        - Samsung Galaxy S24 (Snapdragon 8 Gen 3 Chip): Provides up to 34 TOPS[5].
        - Laptops with Dedicated NPUs: The latest consumer laptops now feature dedicated Neural Processing Units (NPUs) capable of delivering up to 40 TOPS for AI workloads. Notable examples include laptops powered by Intel Core Ultra processors, AMD Ryzen AI processors, Qualcomm's Snapdragon processors and Apple's M-series chips, all of which integrate specialized AI acceleration for enhanced performance[6].
- Industry-grade System on Chip (SoC)[7]
    - Several System on Chips (SoCs) in the market are specifically designed for edge AI applications, offering AI processing capabilities in the range of 5 to 10 TOPs (Tera Operations Per Second). These chips are equipped with a dedicated Neural Processing Unit (NPU) to efficiently handle AI workloads such as machine learning inference and data processing. They are ideally

[4] https://venturebeat.com/business/intels-neural-compute-stick-2-is-8-times-faster-than-its-predecessor/

[5] https://www.cpu-monkey.com/en/cpu_benchmark-ai_benchmark

[6] https://www.techpowerup.com/320933/microsoft-copilot-to-run-locally-on-ai-pcs-with-at-least-40-tops-of-npu-performance

[7] https://www.rock-chips.com/a/en/products/

suited for edge devices like drones, robotics, surveillance cameras, and other IoT applications where real-time AI processing is critical.

When selecting an edge device for AI applications, several critical factors must be considered. AI performance, measured in TOPS (Tera Operations Per Second), directly impacts the device's ability to handle real-time inference. Power consumption is another key factor, especially for battery-operated and energy-efficient applications. The configuration of the CPU, GPU, and NPU plays a crucial role in processing AI workloads efficiently, while memory capacity determines the maximum model size that can be deployed. Additionally, some devices feature dedicated AI hardware, such as NPUs, GPUs, and SoCs to enhance AI computation beyond traditional CPU-based processing.

Overview of Raspberry Pi

Raspberry Pi is a series of small, affordable, single-board computers developed by the Raspberry Pi Foundation. Originally designed to promote computer science education, it has since evolved into a powerful platform for a wide range of applications like edge computing, IoT, AI, robotics, and embedded systems. Due to its compact size, versatility, and extensive community support, Raspberry Pi is widely used in both educational and industrial settings.

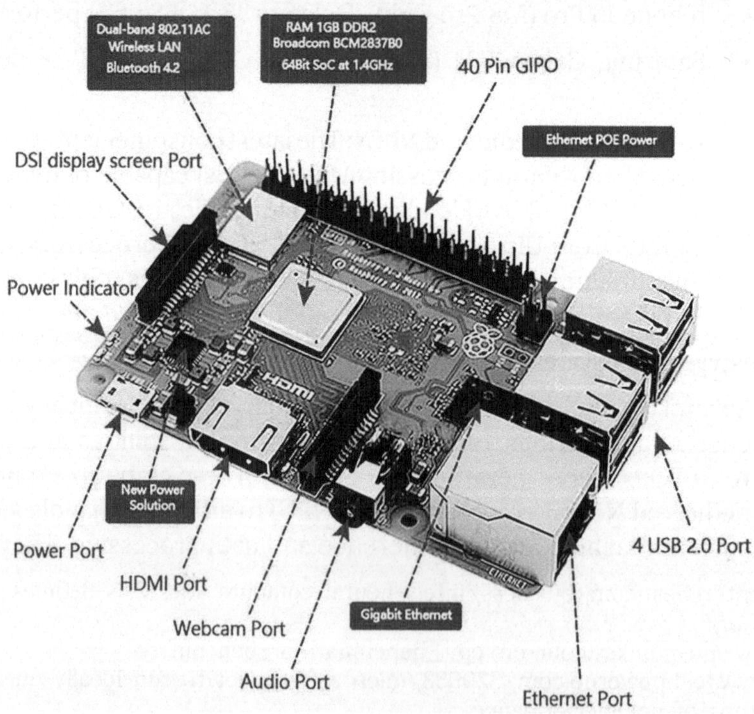

Figure 8.1: *Overview of RaspberryPi 3B+ board and its components*

Figure 8.1 illustrates the various components of a Raspberry Pi board, including the processor, memory, connectivity ports, and GPIO pins, providing a clear understanding of its architecture and expansion capabilities. *Table* 8.1 shows the specifications of different Raspberry Pi versions, ranging from version 3 to version 5.

In this chapter, we will use the Raspberry Pi 3B+ as an example of an edge device and explore how to deploy a model on it. Readers can choose any of the edge devices mentioned above, or try the latest version of Raspberry Pi. The concepts we cover for the Raspberry Pi 3B+ will also be applied to other edge devices.

Model	Processor	Memory	GPU	Connectivity	Compute Performance
Raspberry Pi 3	Broadcom BCM2837, Quad-core Cortex-A53 @ 1.2 GHz	1GB LPDDR2 RAM	Broadcom VideoCore IV	Wi-Fi (802.11n), Bluetooth 4.1, Ethernet	Suitable for lightweight AI workloads and IoT applications
Raspberry Pi 4	Broadcom BCM2711, Quad-core Cortex-A72 @ 1.5 GHz	2GB, 4GB, or 8GB LPDDR4 RAM	Broadcom VideoCore VI	Dual-band Wi-Fi (802.11ac), Bluetooth 5.0, Gigabit Ethernet, USB 3.0	0.1 to 0.4 TOPS
Raspberry Pi 5	Broadcom BCM2712, Quad-core Cortex-A76 @ 2.4 GHz	4GB or 8GB LPDDR4X RAM	VideoCore VII	Wi-Fi 6, Bluetooth 5.2, PCIe expansion for AI accelerators	0.5 to 1 TOPS

Table 8.1: *Table showing specifications of different versions of Raspberry Pi*

Initial Setup of Raspberry Pi

This section focuses on setting up the Raspberry Pi 3B+ from the unboxing stage. If you're already familiar with the process or are using a different edge device, you may skip this section.

To set up the Raspberry Pi, we will need a microSD card with sufficient storage. A 32 GB or 64 GB microSD card will work well for this purpose. The Raspberry Pi provides an Imager tool that allows you to install Raspberry Pi OS onto the card. Raspberry Pi OS is a Linux-based operating system specifically developed for the device. Once the OS is installed, insert the microSD card into the Raspberry Pi and connect to the power supply.

Please note that Raspberry Pi does not come with a monitor, keyboard, or mouse. These peripherals are required for the initial setup. Upon booting up the device, you will be greeted with a desktop environment, similar to that of a Windows or Linux-based OS. These are the basic steps for setting up the Raspberry Pi and more detailed instructions can be found in the official Raspberry Pi documentation[8].

Building ONNX Runtime

In contrast to the previous chapters where we used Python APIs for executing models in ONNX Runtime, this chapter focuses on using its C++ interface. While Python APIs simplify experimentation, they come at the expense of performance. However, the final application may not necessarily be written or deployed in Python. It can be developed with C++ or Java. In some cases, an existing application written in C++ may require model integration done via the C++ interface.

An example of this can be found in video streaming scenarios, where video decoding takes place on the edge device using device-specific APIs. The decoded video frame is then passed to the model for further processing, typically via the C++ interface. Therefore, model execution must also occur through C++ APIs.

Additionally, in certain cases, the model's preprocessing and post-processing steps can be more efficient when implemented in C++, rather than Python due to the lower-level nature of C++. For instance, post-processing tasks in object detection models or language models is often more efficient when it is executed in C++.

Unlike Python, where ONNX Runtime can be accessed via a simple "`pip install`" the C++ interface requires building ONNX Runtime specifically for the target hardware. Fortunately, ONNX Runtime provides prebuilt binaries[9] for Linux, supporting both aarch64 and x64 configurations. It also offers macOS binaries for arm64 and x86_64 configurations. For Windows OS also, binaries are provided for x64 and x86 configuration. For other configurations, users will need to build the library themselves, following the provided instructions. In our case, if we want to deploy the model on a Raspberry Pi, which uses an arm64 architecture, we will need to build ONNX Runtime specifically for this platform.

The build process requires the g++ compiler for the target system's architecture. In our case, since we want to build for an ARM64-based Raspberry Pi device, we would typically need to compile the ONNX Runtime source code directly on that hardware. However, due to the limited resources of the Raspberry Pi, the build process can take an excessive amount of time. To avoid this, we can use an x86 or x64-based system with sufficient resources and install an ARM64 cross-compiler. This allows us to generate executables for the ARM64 architecture from the x86 or x64 host system. Alternatively, we can use a Docker image configured for ARM64 on the x86 or x64 host system to perform the build inside the container, and then transfer the compiled binaries to the Raspberry Pi.

[8] https://www.raspberrypi.com/documentation/computers/getting-started.html
[9] https://github.com/microsoft/onnxruntime/releases

We will utilize the second approach, which involves using a Docker container configured for the arm64/v8 architecture, identical to the configuration of a Raspberry Pi. This Docker setup can emulate the ARM64 architecture on an x86 or x64 system, enabling us to take advantage of more powerful x86/x64 machines. Readers can follow the steps outlined in *Footnote*[10] to build the ONNX Runtime library for Raspberry Pi. However, please be aware that the build process on a typical consumer-grade laptop or PC may take approximately 10 to 12 hours. For those who wish to skip the build process, pre-built ONNX Runtime binaries for Raspberry Pi are available for download in *Footnote*[11].

Overview of ONNX Runtime C++ APIs

Using ONNX Runtime with its C++ APIs is quite similar to working with its Python interface. The overall process is essentially the same, involving loading the model into a session, providing input data, running the session, and generating the output.

```
Ort::Env env(ORT_LOGGING_LEVEL_WARNING, "ONNXRuntimeTest");
Ort::SessionOptions session_options;
session_options.AppendExecutionProvider_CPU(1);
// Use 1 thread for CPU execution (for example)

// For GPU, you would use the following:
// session_options.AppendExecutionProvider_CUDA(0);
Ort::Session session(env, model_path.c_str(), session_options);
```

The code snippet above demonstrates how to initialize an ONNX Runtime inference session. Similar to the Python API, we pass the model path and session options to create an object of **`Session`** class. However, in C++, an additional object of the **`"Env"`** class is required. This object manages the logging state for all other ONNX Runtime components and must be created before any ONNX Runtime functionality can be used. It is also important to note that execution providers, such as CPU and GPU, can be enabled through session options. The necessary header files must also be imported for proper setup.

```
// Get the number of input tensors
size_t num_inputs = onnx_session.GetInputCount();

// Get the number of output tensors
size_t num_outputs = onnx_session.GetOutputCount();

// Get the zeroth input name
const char* input_name = onnx_session.GetInputName(0, env);
```

[10] https://github.com/ava-orange-education/Ultimate-ONNX-for-Optimizing-Deep-Learning-Models/blob/main/Chapter-8/ort_build/build_commands.txt

[11] https://github.com/ava-orange-education/Ultimate-ONNX-for-Optimizing-Deep-Learning-Models/releases/tag/v1.22.0

```
// Get the zeroth input tensor's type information
TypeInfo input_type_info = onnx_session.GetInputTypeInfo(0);
TensorInfo input_tensor_info = input_type_info.GetTensorType
AndShapeInfo();

// Get the shape of the zeroth input tensor
std::vector<int64_t> input_shape = input_tensor_info.GetShape();

// Get the dtype of the zeroth input tensor
auto input_data_type = input_tensor_info.GetElementType();
cout << "Input " << i << " data type: " << input_data_type <<
endl;

// Create input tensor
Ort::MemoryInfo memory_info = Ort::MemoryInfo::CreateCpu
(OrtArenaAllocator, OrtMemTypeDefault);
Ort::Value input_tensor = Ort::Value::CreateTensor<float>
(memory_info, input_tensor_values.data(), input_tensor_values.
size(), input_shape.data(), input_shape.size());
```

The above snippet demonstrates how to gather information about the inputs and outputs of a model using the session. This allows us to understand the number of inputs and outputs, their data types, and shapes. This information is crucial for developing an end-to-end application that can work with models having different types of inputs and outputs. In the Python implementation, we initialize a NumPy object and use it to run the inference by passing it to the session. However, in C++, we must create an **Ort::Value** object, which requires an **Ort::MemoryInfo** object, the data to populate the tensor, the size of the data, the tensor's shape, and its rank. The **Ort::MemoryInfo::CreateCpu** method is used to allocate memory for the CPU execution provider.

```
// Run inference
std::vector<const char*> input_names = {...};
std::vector<const char*> output_names = {...};
std::vector<Ort::Value> output_tensors = session.Run
(Ort::RunOptions{nullptr}, input_names.data(), &input_tensor, 1,
output_names.data(), 1);
```

Unlike the Python APIs, to run the inference session in C++, we need to pass a vector containing the names of the inputs, the input tensor data, the number of inputs, a vector of output names, and the number of outputs. The **session.Run** method will then return a vector of **Ort::Value** objects, each corresponding to one of the model's outputs.

```
// Print top-1 predicted class index
float* output_data = output_tensors[0].GetTensorMutable
Data<float>();
```

To retrieve the raw data from an **`Ort::Value`** object, we can call **`GetTensorMutableData`**, specifying the output's data type as a templated argument.

In the next section, we will use these APIs to load a sample model, run a simple inference, and obtain the model's outputs. Readers can explore additional useful APIs as needed from ONNX Runtime C++ documentation[12].

End-to-End Inference Example

In this section, we will run the ResNet50 model using ONNX Runtime's C++ APIs. The process involves loading the image, resizing and preprocessing it, loading the model, feeding the preprocessed image to the inference session, obtaining the outputs, and decoding them. Readers can follow along with the Jupyter notebook provided for this chapter[13].

In the Python examples from earlier chapters, we used the Pillow module to load the image and the torchvision library for image preprocessing. In C++, we will use a header-only library called STB[14] to load and preprocess the image. *Figure* 8.2 provides a code example for loading the image in RGB format using the STB library. The image is loaded in a **`[height, width, channels]`** format. It is important to note that the ResNet50 model expects the image in a **`[batch, channels, height, width]`** format. Since ResNet50 is trained on the ImageNet dataset with a **`[224, 224]`** image size, we will resize the image to this resolution. Then, we will normalize the image by dividing all pixel values by 255, subtracting the ImageNet mean from each channel, and then dividing by the ImageNet standard deviation for each channel. The processed image will be stored in the "**`inputTensorValues`**" buffer in the **`[batch, channels, height, width]`** format.

[12] https://onnxruntime.ai/docs/api/c/namespace_ort.html

[13] https://github.com/ava-orange-education/Ultimate-ONNX-for-Optimizing-Deep-Learning-Models

[14] https://github.com/nothings/stb/tree/master

```
// ImageNet mean and std values
const float mean[] = {0.485f, 0.456f, 0.406f};
const float std_dev[] = {0.229f, 0.224f, 0.225f};

void preprocessImage(const std::string& imagePath, std::vector<float>& inputTensorValues) {
    int width, height, channels;
    unsigned char* img = stbi_load(imagePath.c_str(), &width, &height, &channels, 3); // Load as RGB

    if (!img) {
        throw std::runtime_error("Failed to load image: " + imagePath);
    }

    int target_width = 224, target_height = 224;
    std::vector<unsigned char> resized_img(target_width * target_height * 3);

    // Resize image to 224x224
    stbir_resize_uint8_linear(img, width, height, 0,
                              resized_img.data(), target_width, target_height, 0, STBIR_RGB);

    // Convert to normalized float format (CHW layout)
    for (int c = 0; c < 3; c++) {  // Loop over channels
        for (int h = 0; h < target_height; h++) {
            for (int w = 0; w < target_width; w++) {
                int idx = (h * target_width + w) * 3 + c;  // HWC index
                inputTensorValues[c * target_width * target_height + h * target_width + w] =
                    ((float)resized_img[idx] / 255.0f - mean[c]) / std_dev[c];  // Normalize & Standardize
            }
        }
    }

    stbi_image_free(img);
}
```

Figure 8.2: *Figure showing code to load and preprocess image for ResNet50 model*

Figure 8.3 presents a complete example that loads the model, preprocesses the image, runs the model, and generates the outputs. In this example, we are utilizing the ONNX Runtime C++ APIs, as discussed earlier. First, we allocate an input buffer and populate it with the pre-processed image data using the **`preprocessImage`** function. This buffer is then passed to the **`session.Run`** method to produce a vector of **`Ort::Value`** objects, representing the output tensors.

Since ResNet50 is trained on the ImageNet dataset, it will output 1000 class logits. When we apply softmax activation over the logits, it will produce 1000 class probabilities. However, for this example, we do not apply softmax as we are interested in finding the maximum value from the logits to achieve the same result. When this code is executed with the provided image of a "cat, the predicted class index will be 282, which maps to the "tiger cat" class in the ImageNet class mapping[15].

[15] https://gist.github.com/yrevar/942d3a0ac09ec9e5eb3a

```
int main() {
    int model_height = 224;
    int model_width = 224;
    int num_channels = 3;
    std::string model_path = "./data/resnet50-v2-7.onnx";
    std::string img_path = "./data/cat.jpg";

    try {
        Ort::Env env(ORT_LOGGING_LEVEL_WARNING, "ONNXRuntimeTest");
        Ort::SessionOptions session_options;

        // Load ResNet50 model
        Ort::Session session(env, model_path.c_str(), session_options);
        Ort::AllocatorWithDefaultOptions allocator;

        // Get input details
        auto input_name = session.GetInputNameAllocated(0, allocator);
        std::vector<int64_t> input_shape = {1, num_channels, model_height, model_width}; // Batch size 1

        // Preprocess image
        std::vector<float> input_tensor_values(num_channels * model_height * model_width, 0.0f);
        preprocessImage(img_path, input_tensor_values);

        // Create input tensor
        Ort::MemoryInfo memory_info = Ort::MemoryInfo::CreateCpu(OrtArenaAllocator, OrtMemTypeDefault);
        Ort::Value input_tensor = Ort::Value::CreateTensor<float>(memory_info, input_tensor_values.data(),
                        input_tensor_values.size(), input_shape.data(), input_shape.size());

        // Run inference
        std::vector<const char*> input_names = {input_name.get()};
        auto output_name = session.GetOutputNameAllocated(0, allocator);
        std::vector<const char*> output_names = {output_name.get()};
        std::vector<Ort::Value> output_tensors = session.Run(Ort::RunOptions{nullptr}, input_names.data(),
                                                   &input_tensor, 1, output_names.data(), 1);

        // Print top-1 predicted class index
        float* output_data = output_tensors[0].GetTensorMutableData<float>();

        int predicted_class = std::max_element(output_data, output_data + 1000) - output_data;
        std::cout << "Predicted Class: " << predicted_class << std::endl;

    } catch (const Ort::Exception& e) {
        std::cerr << "Error: " << e.what() << std::endl;
        return -1;
    }

    return 0;
}
```

Figure 8.3: *Figure showing code to load and execute ResNet50 model in ONNX Runtime using C++ APIs*

We can compile the code using the following commands. These commands are intended for Linux-based operating systems as they use the g++ compiler, which is pre-installed on most Linux systems. An equivalent command should work on Windows. Note that C++ version 14 or higher is required. In the command, the path after **-I** specifies the ONNX Runtime include directory and the STB library include directory. The path after **-L** indicates the location of the compiled ONNX Runtime binaries. The **-lonnxruntime** flag tells the linker to look for the shared library **libonnxruntime.so** in the directories specified by the **-L** flag, which will be dynamically linked during the build process.

```
g++ -std=c++14 -I./onnxruntime-linux-x64-1.21.0/include -I./stb/
-L./onnxruntime-linux-x64-1.21.0/lib -o resnet_inference resnet_
inference.cpp -lonnxruntime
```

This C++ code serves as a foundational example that readers can build upon. It can be extended to create a more generic solution for loading models and inputs via the command line. The preprocessing of inputs and post-processing of outputs can be customized according to the model's specific requirements.

When this C++ code was executed on the Raspberry Pi, it took 2.57080 seconds to complete. The time taken only reflects the duration of the ONNX Runtime session execution. The time spent on loading the image, preprocessing inputs, and post-processing outputs is not included here. This is because in a real-world scenario, video frames will be streamed continuously, and there will be no need to load the image from a file. To focus on the core execution of the model, we are only measuring the session execution time. Table 8.2 presents the execution times for different variants of the ResNet50 model. These variants are available in the ONNX Model Zoo[16].

Sr. No.	Model	Execution time
1	ResNet50 - FP32	2.57080 sec
2	ResNet50 - INT8	1.16976 sec

Table 8.2: *Execution time for ResNet50 model variant on Raspberry Pi 3B+*

As shown in *Table* 8.2, the INT8 model executes twice as fast as the FP32 model. However, this performance is still not sufficient, as the Raspberry Pi 3B+, in its current form, is too slow for the given use case. To address this, we have several options. One approach is to use smaller models, such as ResNet18, or to create a more compact model by applying techniques like pruning and knowledge distillation. Afterward, we can quantize the smaller model for better efficiency. Another potential solution is to upgrade to a Raspberry Pi 5, as it offers significantly more powerful specifications compared to the Raspberry Pi 3, which was launched in 2018 and may not be well-suited for modern deep learning tasks. The Raspberry Pi 5, as previously mentioned, could greatly improve model execution speeds.

Additionally, we could train a new model or fine-tune the existing one with a reduced input resolution. For instance, the model we executed above used an input image resolution of `[224, 224]`. By downscaling this to `[112, 112]`, we could reduce the computational load, though it may come at the cost of accuracy. If this trade-off is acceptable, it provides a valid alternative. Furthermore, while we've built the ONNX Runtime binaries to use the CPU Execution Provider, there are other execution

[16] https://github.com/pustar/onnx_models_zoo/tree/main/vision/classification/resnet

providers, such as the ACL Execution Provider[17] and the ArmNN Execution Provider[18], specifically designed for ARM-based systems. These providers leverage ARM architecture-specific hardware optimizations, which could potentially offer greater efficiency than the standard CPU Execution Provider.

The same approach applies when working with ONNX Runtime C++ APIs across different edge devices or using edge device specific APIs to run the model. The overall process remains consistent: loading inputs, preprocessing them, loading the model, allocating input buffers, running the model, and decoding the outputs. The primary difference will lie in the APIs provided by the edge device or the libraries used, but the core flow will stay the same.

In edge computing, one of the most common scenarios involves processing video streams in real time. Unlike working with a single image frame, real-world applications typically deal with incoming video streams that arrive at a fixed frame rate, commonly measured in frames per second (FPS). To maintain synchronization with the video feed, it is crucial that the model's inference processing happens within a time frame that matches the FPS of the incoming data. For example, if the video feed is at 30 FPS, the edge device must process each frame in 33 milliseconds or less to keep up.

The incoming video feed in edge computing is frequently compressed to minimize data size and reduce bandwidth requirements. Common compression formats include H.264, which is widely used for video streaming. Before these compressed frames can be passed to the model for inference, they must first undergo decoding to restore the original visual information. Once decoded and processed by the model, the outputs (such as analytics, insights, or visual data) are either saved or displayed, depending on the application's needs.

This workflow is not limited to video. Similar principles apply when dealing with audio signals or sensor data from microphones, machinery, or other devices. In these cases, the incoming data must also be processed in real time, ensuring that the system's processing capability aligns with the rate at which the data is arriving.

A fundamental challenge in edge computing is ensuring that the model's processing rate aligns with the incoming data rate. For example, if a system receives data at 60 FPS, but the edge device can only process it at 20 FPS, it will effectively miss 2 out of every 3 frames. This may or may not be acceptable depending on the use case.

For instance, in an application where the scene does not change rapidly, such as monitoring vehicles crossing an intersection, a processing rate of 20 FPS might be sufficient to capture the necessary information. However, in safety-critical applications, such as self-driving cars, where real-time decision-making is crucial, it

---

17 https://onnxruntime.ai/docs/execution-providers/community-maintained/ACL-ExecutionProvider.html

18 https://onnxruntime.ai/docs/execution-providers/community-maintained/ArmNN-ExecutionProvider.html

is essential to process frames at a much higher rate—ideally 55 FPS or even 60 FPS—to ensure that the system can respond accurately and swiftly to dynamic situations.

Conclusion

In this chapter, we explored various edge devices available on the market, focusing on their computational capabilities. We took an in-depth look at the Raspberry Pi as a prominent example of an edge device, examining its setup and learning how to build the ONNX Runtime library for it. Additionally, we explored the ONNX Runtime C++ APIs and demonstrated running a ResNet model end-to-end using C++.

In the upcoming chapters, we will delve into models from different domains and apply the concepts we have learned in a comprehensive, end-to-end manner. In the next chapter, we will specifically focus on deploying the YOLOv12 model on edge devices, starting with the export process and moving towards the execution on the device.

CHAPTER 9

End to End Execution of YOLOv12

Introduction

In the previous chapters, we explored various aspects of ONNX models and their optimizations in a modular fashion. Now, it is time to bring everything together and apply the concepts and techniques we have learned so far in a practical, end-to-end workflow. Our focus in this chapter will be on the YOLOv12 object detection model. We will walk through the process of exporting the model to ONNX format, optimizing it, and applying quantization techniques.

Structure

This chapter covers the following topics:

- Overview of Object Detection Task
- Overview of YOLOv12 Model
- Exporting to ONNX Model
- Quantizing ONNX Model
- Model Performance Debugging

Overview of Object Detection Task

In the field of computer vision, object detection plays a crucial role. Unlike image classification where an entire image is assigned a single label, object detection involves locating and categorizing multiple objects within an image. Technically, an object detection model outputs the coordinates of the bounding boxes surrounding the detected objects and their corresponding class labels. *Figure* 9.1 illustrates an example of such an output, where objects like a dog, bicycle, and truck are accurately marked with rectangular boxes and their respective labels.

Figure 9.1: *Image showing the output of object detection model (Source: Footnote[1])*

Object detection combines two fundamental tasks: regression and classification. The regression task predicts continuous variables, which in this case refer to the coordinates of bounding boxes within the image space. Meanwhile, the classification task assigns each detected object to a predefined category, such as "dog", "car", or "person".

Object detection models have a wide range of real-world applications. During the COVID-19 pandemic, they were employed to detect whether individuals were wearing face masks or not. They are also used in facial recognition systems for automated attendance marking. Large-scale surveillance systems leverage object detection to monitor human activity and traffic flow. In agriculture, these models help identify plant diseases and pests, while in manufacturing, they detect defective products on assembly lines. One of the most advanced applications is in autonomous vehicles, where object detection models analyze the car's surroundings to ensure safe navigation.

Object detection has seen rapid advancements, with numerous models emerging over time. The journey began with classical machine learning approaches like HOG (Histogram of Oriented Gradients) features and Haar Cascade detectors. However, the rise of deep learning revolutionized the field and led to the emergence of more

[1] https://www.inspiritai.com/blogs/ai-student-blog/object-detection-the-yolo-algorithm-in-ai

sophisticated models such as RCNN (Region-based Convolutional Neural Network), YOLO (You Only Look Once), and SSD (Single Shot Detector).

In the early days of deep learning-based object detection, models were primarily divided into two categories. The first category consisted of two-stage detectors like the RCNN family[2], which operated through a sequential process. These systems first generated numerous region proposals like potential bounding boxes that contained objects, before separately classifying and refining each candidate region. While this approach was highly accurate, it came with a significant complexity. The need to combine and train multiple sub-models, along with complicated operations like RoIAlign, made these architectures cumbersome. Furthermore, their intricate design posed challenges for deployment on edge devices with limited resources.

The second category comprised single-stage detectors, including YOLO[3] and SSD[4], which took a more streamlined approach. These models unified the detection process, predicting both bounding boxes and class labels in a single forward pass. Although early single-stage detectors traded accuracy for speed, their efficiency made them ideal for real-time applications. Over time, continuous improvements in model architecture and training techniques narrowed the performance gap between single-stage and two-stage detectors. Today, most state-of-the-art object detection systems are based on single-stage architectures, achieving both high precision and real-time processing capabilities.

Overview of YOLOv12 Model

The YOLO (You Only Look Once) family of models has a rich and extensive history. It began with the first version, a CNN-based architecture that processed images in a single forward pass. Over time, the approach evolved to detect objects at different scales using multi-scale feature extractors, which generate bounding box predictions and class probabilities across key regions in an image. These predictions are refined using anchor boxes as reference points, converting raw outputs into interpretable detections.

Since YOLO produces thousands of candidate boxes per image, only a few are relevant. The Non-Maximum Suppression (NMS)[5] algorithm filters redundant predictions, keeping only the most confident detections.

---

[2] RCNN paper: https://arxiv.org/abs/1311.2524
Faster-RCNN paper: https://arxiv.org/abs/1506.01497
Overview of RCNN family of models: https://lilianweng.github.io/posts/2017-12-31-object-recognition-part-3/

[3] YOLO paper: https://arxiv.org/abs/1506.02640
YOLOv3 paper: https://arxiv.org/abs/1804.02767

[4] SSD paper: https://arxiv.org/abs/1512.02325

[5] https://learnopencv.com/non-maximum-suppression-theory-and-implementation-in-pytorch/

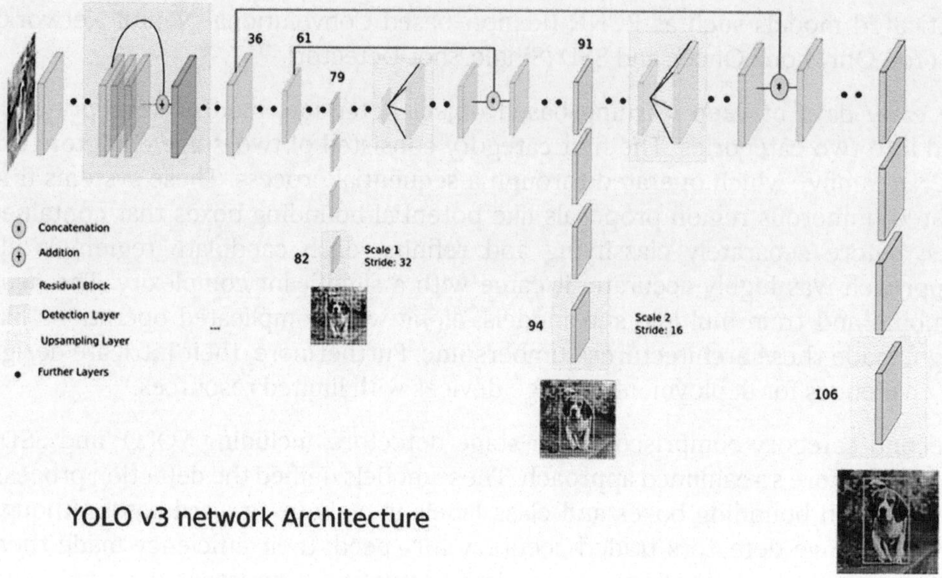

Figure 9.2: *Architecture of YOLOv3 (Source: Footnote[6])*

Every iteration of YOLO introduced innovations in architecture, loss functions, backbone networks, and anchor processing techniques. These improvements addressed prior limitations, resulting in more accurate models. Each iteration of YOLO offers multiple variants with different parameter counts and accuracy levels, which makes them adaptable for various edge device applications. A complete discussion of all the YOLO variants is beyond the scope of this book, but readers are encouraged to explore the blog[7] for a detailed history. *Figure* 9.2 illustrates a high-level overview of the YOLOv3 architecture.

In this chapter, we use YOLOv12 as our object detection model and demonstrate its end-to-end deployment in the ONNX runtime. Unlike earlier versions, YOLOv12 incorporates attention mechanisms, enhancing detection accuracy. The YOLOv12 model is available in five distinct variants (YOLOv12n, s, m, l, and x), each offering different parameter counts and accuracy levels to accommodate varying hardware capabilities. For our purposes, we select YOLOv12n—the smallest and fastest variant—optimized for deployment on edge devices like the Raspberry Pi. With just 2.5 million parameters and requiring only 6.0 GFLOPs when processing standard `[640, 640]` resolution images, this lightweight variant delivers decent efficiency for resource-constrained environments.

---

6 https://dev.to/afrozchakure/all-you-need-to-know-about-yolo-v3-you-only-look-once-e4m

7 https://blog.roboflow.com/guide-to-yolo-models/

The core principle of YOLOv12 is very similar to what we saw earlier for YOLOv3. The processing pipeline begins with feature extractors analyzing the input image to generate raw detection outputs (feature maps). These are decoded using box-scaling techniques and processed by NMS to generate final predictions. Typically trained on the COCO dataset (80 classes), YOLOv12 outputs 8,400 boxes per `[640, 640]` image. Each box includes 4 coordinates (top-left and bottom-right coordinates) and 80 class probabilities, totaling 84 values per box. The NMS algorithm filters these predictions, retaining only the most confident detections. *Figure* 9.3 presents an architectural overview of the YOLOv12 model, illustrating its key components and their interconnections.

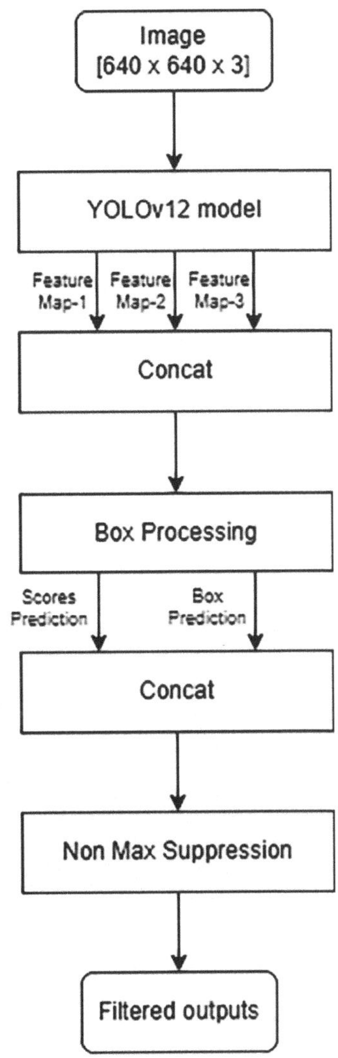

Figure 9.3: *YOLOv12 model overview*

Exporting to ONNX Model

In this and following sections, we will work with the chapter's accompanying Jupyter Notebook[8]. The official YOLOv12 repository[9] provides a clean interface to load the pre-trained model and export it to ONNX. *Figure* 9.4 shows the example code to load the **"yolov12n.pt"** checkpoint for the YOLOv12n model. When the **YOLO** class from the ultralytics repository is instantiated, it automatically downloads the model if the specified checkpoint is not found in local storage. The **predict** method will run the model with the help of a sample image from the repository and return the resultant image with boxes plotted on the image. *Figure* 9.5 shows the output of YOLOv12n pre-trained model.

```
# Run YOLOv12 model in Pytorch first.
from ultralytics import YOLO

model = YOLO('yolov12n.pt')
res = model.predict()

for i, r in enumerate(res):
    r.save(f"res_{i}.jpg")
```

Figure 9.4: *YOLOv12n Pytorch Execution*

For the ONNX export, we will use the native export API provided within the ultralytics repository. As illustrated in *Figure* 9.6, the export process from PyTorch to ONNX is straightforward. We will utilize the **export** method native to the **YOLO** class, specifying **format='onnx'** to perform the conversion.

Figure 9.5: *YOLOv12n Pytorch outputs*

[8] https://github.com/ava-orange-education/Ultimate-ONNX-for-Optimizing-Deep-Learning-Models
[9] https://github.com/sunsmarterjie/yolov12

The **YOLO** class from the ultralytics module is designed to accept various YOLOv12 model variants as input parameters. Please note that during export we are specifying **simplify=True and nms=False** to the **export** method. The **simplify=True** parameter applies initial graph optimizations using the ONNX Slim package, though we recommend additional optimization with the more powerful ONNX Simplifier tool for production deployments. Keeping **nms=False** will not add NMS processing nodes in the graph and exported graph terminates at 2nd Concat layer as per *Figure* 9.3. This is done as the **nms** argument is not supported by the repository for ONNX export.

```
# Export to ONNX
from ultralytics import YOLO

model = YOLO('yolov12n.pt')
model.export(format="onnx", device="cpu", simplify=True, nms=False)
```

```
# Optimize the model using Onnx-Simplifier
!python -m onnxsim "./yolov12n.onnx" "./yolov12n.onnx"
```

Figure 9.6: *YOLOv12 ONNX export code*

Figure 9.7 illustrates the final portion of the exported ONNX graph. As we can see that there are three inputs to the Concat node. These three inputs correspond to three outputs from the three feature extractor part of the model. These feature extractors independently generate bounding box predictions and corresponding class probabilities. The Concat node merges these multi-scale predictions into a unified output stream.

Following the Concat node, the combined output undergoes processing through several key transformations. First, the tensor is split into separate components for box coordinates and classification scores. The scores pass through a sigmoid activation function to normalize probabilities within the **[0, 1]** range. Simultaneously, the box coordinates undergo conversion from the model's native xywh format (center coordinates with width/height) to the more conventional xyxy representation (top-left and bottom-right coordinates). These coordinates are then rescaled from their normalized **[0, 1]** range to the actual image dimensions of **[0, 640]**. The processed boxes and scores are subsequently combined through a second Concat node whose output serves as the graph's output.

Now that we have obtained the ONNX model, we will first execute it in FP32 precision to evaluate both its inference time and detection accuracy. It's important to note that the exported model is in FP32 precision by default. Running the model end-to-end involves three key steps: pre-processing the input image, performing model inference through ONNX Runtime, and post-processing the output boxes using a Non-Maximum

Suppression (NMS) algorithm. The accompanying Jupyter Notebook includes the complete implementation code for this pipeline.

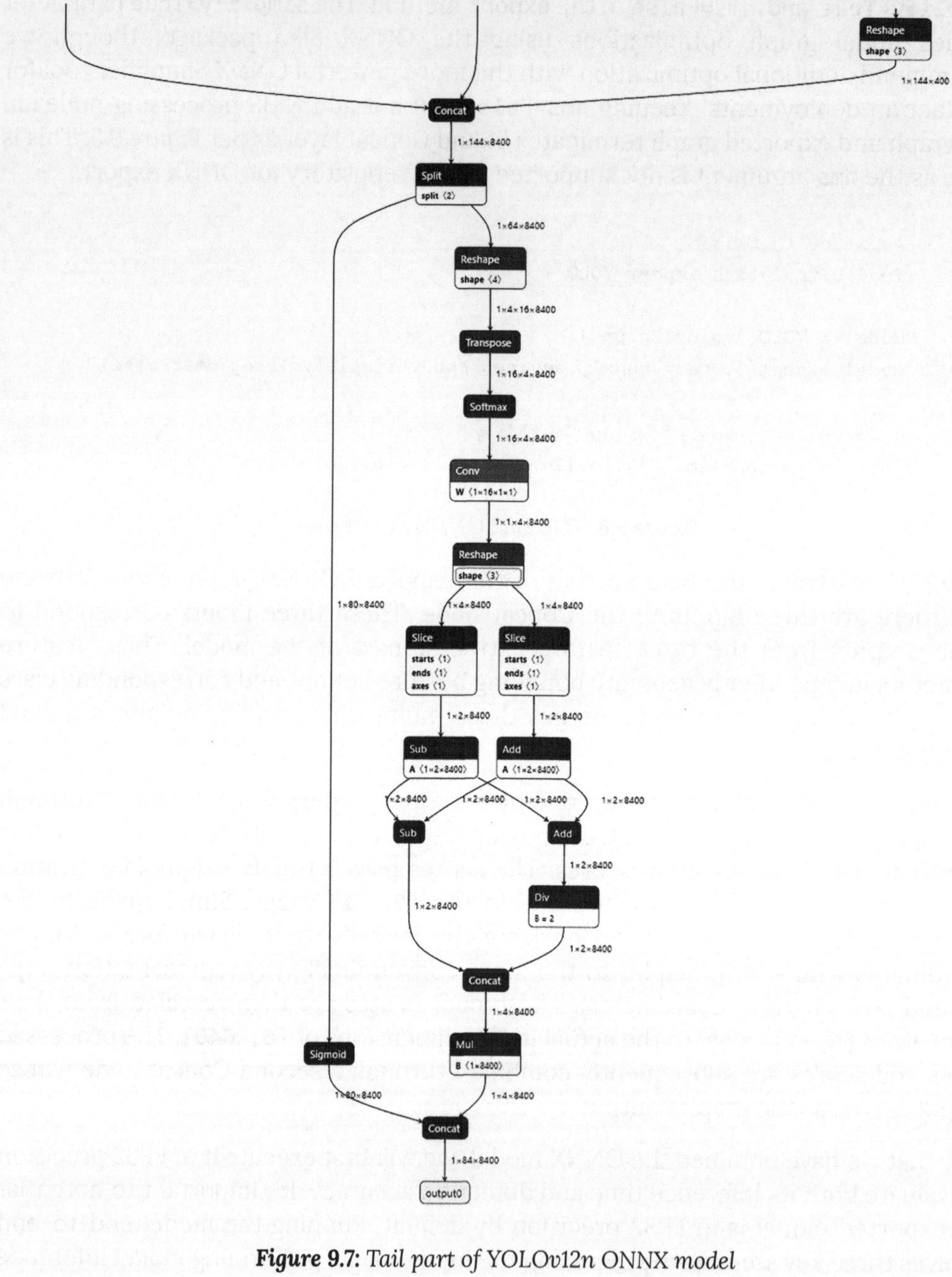

Figure 9.7: *Tail part of YOLOv12n ONNX model*

```
import cv2
from yolo_helper.inference import YOLOInference
from yolo_helper.visualization import draw_detections
from yolo_helper.postprocessing import get_class_names

# Configuration
MODEL_PATH = "yolov12/yolov12n.onnx"
IMAGE_PATH = "./yolov12/ultralytics/assets/zidane.jpg"
CLASS_NAMES = get_class_names()  # COCO class names
OUTPUT_PATH = "output_fp32.jpg"

# Initialize detector
detector = YOLOInference(MODEL_PATH)

# Run inference
result = detector(IMAGE_PATH, conf_thresh=0.25, iou_thresh=0.45)

if result is not None:
    image, detections = result

    # Draw and save results
    output_image = draw_detections(image, detections, CLASS_NAMES)
    cv2.imwrite(OUTPUT_PATH, output_image)
    print(f"Saved results to {OUTPUT_PATH}")
else:
    print("No detections found")
```

Figure 9.8: *Code example showing end to end execution of* YOLOv12n ONNX *model*

Figure 9.8 demonstrates the end-to-end execution code, which saves detection results to disk. It shows the usage of **`YOLOInference`** class which encapsulates the preprocessing, ONNX Runtime inference of the model and NMS filtering of the boxes and returns final results. When run, this implementation produces results as per *Figure* 9.9, which is similar to those shown in *Figure* 9.5. However, when deployed on a Raspberry Pi 3B+, the ONNX Runtime inference alone requires approximately **2.74 seconds** per execution. Given this substantial latency, we will run the model in lower precision (INT8) formats to achieve significant speed improvements while maintaining acceptable accuracy.

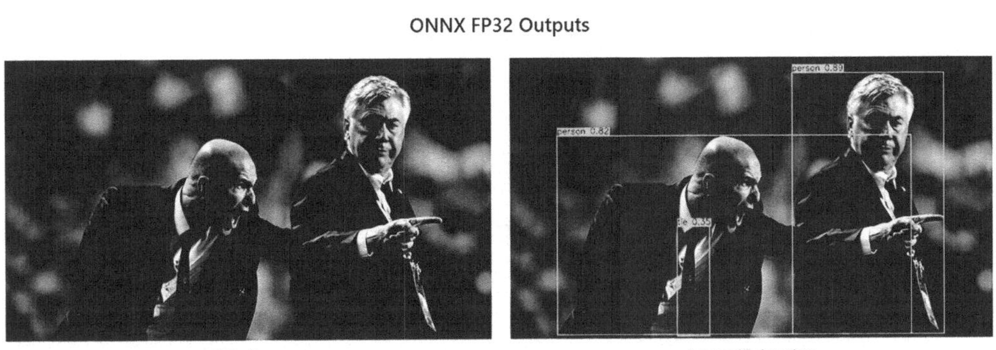

Figure 9.9: YOLOv12n ONNX FP32 *outputs*

Quantizing ONNX Model

To quantize the YOLOv12n model, we will apply the concepts covered in Chapter 5, utilizing static quantization methods. As established earlier, static quantization requires a calibration dataset to track activations and generate histograms for converting activations to lower precision. Since YOLOv12 is an object detection model trained on the COCO dataset[10], we will use the COCO validation set as our calibration dataset for quantizing the ONNX model.

Figure 9.10 presents the complete code for applying static quantization and dynamic quantization to the YOLOv12 model. The implementation closely resembles the BERT quantization example from Chapter 5. The accompanying Jupyter Notebook includes detailed implementations of the **`COCODataset`** and **`YoloDataReader`** classes used in static quantization.

```
import os
from yolo_helper.dataloader import COCODataset, YoloDataReader
from onnxruntime.quantization import quantize_static, quantize_dynamic, QuantType, CalibrationMethod
from onnxruntime.quantization.shape_inference import quant_pre_process

dataset = COCODataset("./datasets/val2017", sample=100)
data_reader = YoloDataReader(dataset)

fp32_path = "./yolov12/yolov12n.onnx"
fp32_path_preproc = "./yolov12/yolov12n_preproc.onnx"
int8_path_dynamic_quant = "./yolov12/yolov12n_int8_dynamic_quant.onnx"
int8_path_static_quant = "./yolov12/yolov12n_int8_static_quant.onnx"

# Firstly, apply shape inference and onnxruntime model optimization before quantizing the model.
quant_pre_process(fp32_path, fp32_path_preproc, skip_symbolic_shape=True)

# Apply dynamic quantization
quantized_model = quantize_dynamic(
    model_input=fp32_path_preproc,          # Input ONNX model
    model_output=int8_path_dynamic_quant,   # Output quantized model
    weight_type=QuantType.QUInt8            # Quantize only weights to uint8, activations will be quantize during runtime
)

print(f"Dynamic Quantized model saved at: {int8_path_dynamic_quant}")


# Apply static quantization
quantize_static(
    model_input=fp32_path_preproc,          # Input ONNX model
    model_output=int8_path_static_quant,    # Output quantized model
    calibration_data_reader=data_reader,
    weight_type=QuantType.QInt8,            # Quantize weights to int8
    activation_type=QuantType.QInt8,        # Quantize activations to int8
    calibrate_method=CalibrationMethod.MinMax,
    extra_options={"CalibStridedMinMax": 4}   # Process 4 images at a time for calibration
)

print(f"Static Quantized model saved at: {int8_path_static_quant}")
```

Figure 9.10: *Code example to showcase static and dynamic quantization of YOLOv12 model*

[10] https://cocodataset.org/

An important implementation note: we have specified the **extra_option** argument with **CalibStridedMinMax=4** during static quantization. This parameter is crucial because our calibration dataset contains 5,000 samples. Without this optimization, ONNX Runtime would consume excessive memory storing outputs for all samples to generate the final histogram. By using **CalibStridedMinMax**, the runtime processes the data in segments–in our case, generating histograms for 4 samples at a time and merging the results. This approach significantly reduces memory usage during the quantization process.

After obtaining the quantized ONNX model, we can execute it using the same inference code shown in *Figure* 9.8. However, initial runs with the static quantized model produce no detections, indicating that the quantization process has significantly affected the model's output behavior.

Here for the dynamic quantized model, we use **QuantType.QUInt8** for the weight type instead of **QuantType.QInt8**, as the latter causes runtime failures due to unsupported **ConvInteger** nodes in ONNX Runtime. While this configuration produces detection results consistent with our FP32 benchmarks (*Figure* 9.9), the Raspberry Pi 3B+ exhibits a **3.43 seconds** inference latency–slower than both static INT8 and native FP32 execution. This performance degradation occurs because dynamic quantization applies transformations during runtime, and in this case, the quantization overhead outweighs any potential speed benefits. Given these limitations, our best approach is to focus on debugging and fixing the static quantized model's accuracy issues.

Model Performance Debugging

It is time to systematically debug the static quantized model's accuracy problems. The most effective approach for analyzing quantization-related problems involves comparing both the final and intermediate outputs between the quantized and original FP32 models. Simply comparing final outputs would be insufficient; we need to examine intermediate node outputs to identify where the divergence begins.

```
=== Model Comparison Results ===
FP32 vs INT8 Model Output Analysis

=== Summary ===
Compared 548 outputs
548 outputs exceeded tolerance
Worst output: /model.6/m.1/m.1.1/attn/Sub_output_0
Average mismatch percentage: 91.11%

=== Detailed Output Comparison ===

Output: output0
  FP32 range: [0.000000, 637.011963]
  INT8 range: [0.000000, 641.186218]
  Max absolute difference: 331.866486
  Mean absolute difference: 0.402980
  Max relative difference: 6.748274 (674.83%)
  Mismatch percentage: 3.71%
  Absolute difference standard deviation: 3.75
  Within tolerance: No
  FP32 sample values: [ 2.9431 13.8634 21.8771 30.3228 35.2994]
  INT8 sample values: [ 5.321  10.6421 18.6237 26.6052 31.9263]

Output: /model.21/Mul_2_output_0
  FP32 range: [2.225511, 637.011963]
  INT8 range: [2.524338, 641.181824]
  Max absolute difference: 330.574463
  Mean absolute difference: 8.427004
  Max relative difference: 6.671295 (667.13%)
```

Figure 9.11: *Report generated by INT8 output inspection utility*

To facilitate this analysis, we have included an inspection utility called **`inspect_int8_outputs.py`** in the book's repository[11]. This tool performs comprehensive comparisons by:

- Converting all intermediate tensors into graph outputs for both FP32 and INT8 models
- Running inference with both models using the same input sample
- Comparing corresponding outputs for value ranges and numerical differences

Through this detailed comparison, we can get a rough idea about where quantization can introduce problematic deviations in the model architecture, thereby helping us identify the root cause of the detection failures.

---

11 https://github.com/ava-orange-education/Ultimate-ONNX-for-Optimizing-Deep-Learning-Models

As illustrated in *Figure* 9.11, the tool generates a comprehensive report covering all tensors, which includes the standard deviation of absolute differences between FP32 and INT8 tensor values. Ideally, these values should match with zero absolute difference. However, when the chosen quantization parameters fail to properly represent the FP32 output distribution within the INT8 range, substantial numerical discrepancies arise. By analyzing the standard deviation of these differences, we can quantify the magnitude of variation between FP32 and INT8 outputs and identify tensors showing substantial deviations.

To address accuracy issues, we can employ several strategies such as:

- **Selective Node Exclusion:**
    - Add problematic nodes to the **`nodes_to_exclude`** parameter in **`quantize_static`**, keeping them in FP32 precision while quantizing the rest of the model.
    - We can identify the problematic nodes by using the following sub-strategies:
        - **Sequential Method:** Progressively keep layers in FP32 starting from the output layer and moving backward, testing after each change until detections improve.
        - **Binary Search Method:** First, exclude either the first or second half of the model's nodes. If successful, reduce the excluded node set; if not, switch to the other half. Repeat the process with progressively smaller segments until identifying the minimal set of problematic nodes.
        - **Standard Deviation of Absolute Differences:** We can automatically flag problematic nodes by monitoring the standard deviation of absolute differences between FP32 and INT8 outputs. Any nodes exceeding our defined threshold (typically 0.5-1.0 for detection tasks) should remain in FP32 precision to restore model accuracy while maintaining optimal performance.
- **Quantization Parameter Tuning:**
    - The **`op_types_to_quantize`** parameter allows selective quantization of specific operator types. This is particularly useful because non-parametric operations (Gather, Concat) often struggle with INT8 range mapping due to their tensor transformations, while compute-intensive operations (Conv, MatMul) typically quantize well. By specifying only the latter, we maintain accuracy while still gaining quantization benefits.
    - Enable **`per_channel`** for channel-wise weight quantization, particularly beneficial for complex models like Transformers.

- The **calibrate_method** parameter offers multiple calibration techniques for optimal FP32-to-INT8 conversion. ONNX Runtime currently supports four approaches:
  - **MinMax:** Uses minimum/maximum activation ranges
  - **Entropy:** Optimizes for information preservation
  - **Percentile:** Reduces outlier sensitivity
  - **Distribution:** Matches statistical properties

While we acknowledge the importance of these methods, their detailed analysis falls beyond our current scope. For comprehensive implementation guidance, readers should consult *Footnote*[12].

In our case, the last output tensor "**output0**" produces a standard deviation of absolute differences around 3.75. The last Concat node in *Figure* 9.7 generates this tensor. We can add this node to the **nodes_to_exclude** list and verify whether it improves the results. *Figure* 9.12 shows the updated code for static quantization.

```
quantize_static(
    model_input=fp32_path_preproc,          # Input ONNX model
    model_output=int8_path_static_quant_w_concat_fp32,    # Output quantized model
    calibration_data_reader=data_reader,
    weight_type=QuantType.QInt8,            # Quantize weights to int8
    activation_type=QuantType.QInt8,        # Quantize activations to int8
    calibrate_method=CalibrationMethod.MinMax,
    nodes_to_exclude=["/model.21/Concat_5"],
    extra_options={"CalibStridedMinMax": 4}    # Process 4 images at a time for calibration
)
```

Figure 9.12: *Updated code for static quantization*

After excluding this single node, the model has started producing results matching *Figure* 9.5. These results are shown in *Figure* 9.13.

There is further explanation for this solution. As previously discussed, the Concat node takes processed boxes and processed scores as inputs. Post-processing scales the detected boxes' coordinates to pixel dimensions **[0, 640]**, while sigmoid nonlinearity transforms the classification scores into probability values bounded by **[0, 1]**. Combining these into a single tensor makes quantization difficult because we have 8400 boxes, each with 80 class predictions in the **[0, 1]** range and 4 coordinate predictions in the **[0, 640]** range. This creates many candidate values concentrated in **[0, 1]** while others are scattered across **[0, 640]**. The histogram of such a tensor shows a peak at **[0, 1]**. The FP32 range here is **[0, 640]**, which needs to be mapped to the INT8 range. During quantization, the resolution between values in the quantized range remains constant. With 256 discrete values in INT8 and 640 continuous values to represent, values in **[0, 2.5]** in FP32 range get mapped to **[-128, -127]** for

[12] https://quark.docs.amd.com/latest/onnx/config/calibration_methods.html#calibration-methods

INT8 and **`[0, 1]`** for UINT8. This creates unfair quantization for score predictions, making this Concat node particularly problematic. Readers are advised to verify this by plotting the histogram of the Concat node's output.

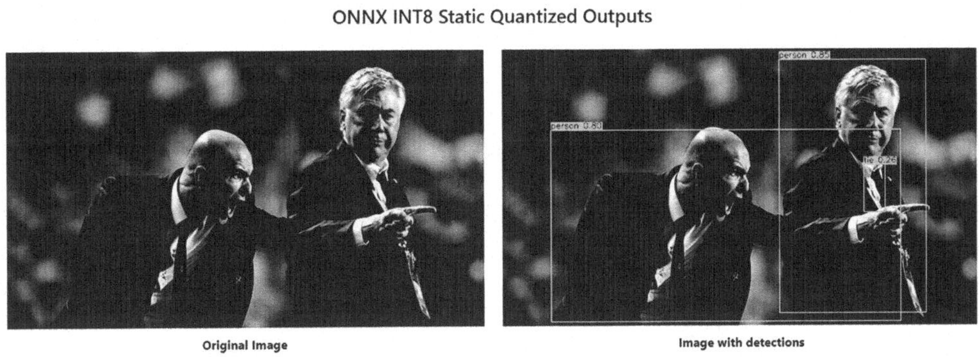

Figure 9.13: YOLOv12*n* ONNX INT8 *outputs*

Since we already have a complete end-to-end pipeline for this model, an alternative solution would be to modify the graph by removing the second Concat node entirely. Instead, we can configure the inputs to this Concat node (the processed boxes and scores) to serve as direct graph outputs. This modification will change the model's output structure from a single concatenated tensor to two separate outputs. Naturally, this architectural change will require corresponding adjustments to our post processing code, as we will now need to handle two distinct outputs from ONNX Runtime instead of one.

Since the model produces better results, we should not rely solely on a single image to assess quantization's impact on accuracy. It is always advisable to evaluate accuracy on a dedicated test or validation set for proper assessment of the quantized model's performance. Consider a model with 90% FP32 accuracy. For safety-critical applications like medical diagnosis or autonomous driving, the acceptable INT8 accuracy drop should be less than 1%. For general applications where speed is prioritized, a 3-5% accuracy drop may be acceptable. Some accuracy loss is inevitable, but quantization-aware training can improve INT8 accuracy.

Now that we have confirmed that the model generates correct outputs, testing it on a Raspberry Pi 3B+ shows execution time of **2.27 seconds**, which is better than the FP32 model.

It is worth noting that an execution time of **2.27 seconds** on an edge device like Raspberry Pi 3B+ is slow for real-time processing. To address this, we can explore pruning and knowledge distillation techniques to create smaller models with comparable accuracy. Another option is reducing input dimensions; instead of **`[640, 640]`** images, we could modify the ONNX model to accept **`[320, 320]`** inputs, thereby significantly improving speed at the cost of accuracy.

Furthermore, these inference speed measurements are based on Python implementation. Re-implementing the pre-processing, model inference, and post-processing pipelines in C++ could yield faster execution speeds compared to implementing it in Python.

Conclusion

This chapter explored object detection models, beginning with their historical evolution and architectural variants. We then focused specifically on YOLOv12, applying our prior knowledge to successfully export the PyTorch model to the ONNX model, and optimize it for deployment. Our quantization pipeline incorporated both static and dynamic quantization approaches, during which we identified and resolved challenges often observed in real-world deployment scenarios. Through systematic debugging strategies, we achieved functional INT8 precision while developing methodologies to address accuracy-loss and latency issues inherent in quantized models.

Building on these foundations, the next chapter will demonstrate an end-to-end application of these techniques to a speech recognition model, further solidifying our understanding of the subject.

CHAPTER 10

End to End Execution of Whisper Speech Recognition Model

Introduction

In the previous chapter, we explored the object detection task, using the YOLOv12 model as an example, and applied our knowledge in an end-to-end manner. To reinforce these concepts, this chapter will focus on the speech recognition task, which is a critical area for edge device deployment. First, we will delve into Automatic Speech Recognition (ASR) in detail. Then, we will examine the Whisper model as an example ASR system, analyzing its key components and building upon insights from earlier chapters.

Structure

This chapter covers the following topics:

- Overview of Speech Recognition Task
- Overview of Whisper ASR Model
- Exporting to ONNX Model
- End-to-End Model Inference
- Quantizing the ONNX Model

Overview of Speech Recognition Task

Processing audio data plays a crucial role in unlocking numerous real-world applications across industries. From voice assistants like Siri and Alexa to voice-controlled smart home systems, audio processing enables seamless human-machine interaction. It powers noise cancellation in headphones, fraud detection in call centers through voice biometrics, and even aids in emotion recognition for customer service enhancements. In security scenarios, audio analytics can detect gunshots or breaking glass, while in entertainment, they can enable the creation of music recommendation systems and contribute to automatic subtitling.

A compelling recent use case[1] comes from the call center industry, demonstrated by CARS24. The company analyzed customer care conversations to identify pain points, leading to a multifold improvement in service quality.

Another example[2] is Microsoft Teams' Copilot feature, that captures meeting audio, transcribes discussions, and generates summaries with actionable insights post-meeting.

Spotify[3] leverages audio processing to analyze user preferences, curating personalized playlists, and recommending music aligned with individual tastes.

Audio processing also plays a vital role in ecology. By automating biodiversity monitoring through sound, Machine Learning (ML) accelerates species identification, such as birdsong analysis, to track populations, assess forest health, and detect endangered or invasive species. Autonomous Recording Units (ARUs) capture large datasets, but manual analysis is slow and expertise-dependent. ML streamlines this process, aiding conservation efforts. Further details are articulated in below blogs[4].

Audio data processing involves several key sub-tasks, including Automatic Speech Recognition (ASR), audio denoising, speaker identification, keyword spotting, speech-to-speech translation, music generation, and sound classification. ASR converts spoken language into text, while audio denoising removes background noise to enhance audio quality. Speaker identification works alongside ASR to differentiate between speakers in conversations, and keyword spotting enables wake-word detection for voice assistants like Siri or Alexa. Speech-to-speech translation models allow direct conversion of spoken language from one language to another. In the music industry, AI models can generate background music based on user descriptions. Meanwhile, sound classification plays a crucial role in ecological research, such as identifying bird and animal vocalizations for biodiversity monitoring. While these tasks each have significant applications, in this chapter we will primarily focus on ASR.

---

[1] https://medium.com/cars24-data-science-blog/whos-been-listening-23e86f99e26c

[2] https://support.microsoft.com/en-us/office/use-copilot-in-microsoft-teams-meetings-0bf9dd3c-96f7-44e2-8bb8-790bedf066b1

[3] https://medium.com/beyond-the-build/the-inner-workings-of-spotifys-ai-powered-music-recommendations-how-spotify-shapes-your-playlist-a10a9148ee8d

[4] Bird species classification at Edge:
https://www.youtube.com/watch?v=reAm4HSyQl8
https://research.google/blog/separating-birdsong-in-the-wild-for-classification/

Overview of Whisper ASR Model

Whisper is an open-source, transformer-based model that can transcribe and translate speech across multiple languages with high accuracy. Trained on an extensive dataset of 680,000 hours of multilingual audio, it can process diverse accents, background noise, and even low-quality recordings remarkably well. This large-scale training allows Whisper to perform effectively in various real-world scenarios without separate acoustic or language models.

Before diving into Whisper's architecture, let us understand transformers, which is the foundation it is built upon. Transformers consist of two key parts: an encoder and a decoder. The encoder processes all input data at once, creating a comprehensive representation of the input. For Whisper, this input is audio, while for translation tasks it can be text in the source language. The decoder then uses this representation along with starter tokens (like beginning-of-sentence markers) to iteratively generate output tokens one at a time in the target format. *Figure* 10.1 shows an overview of the Transformer architecture.

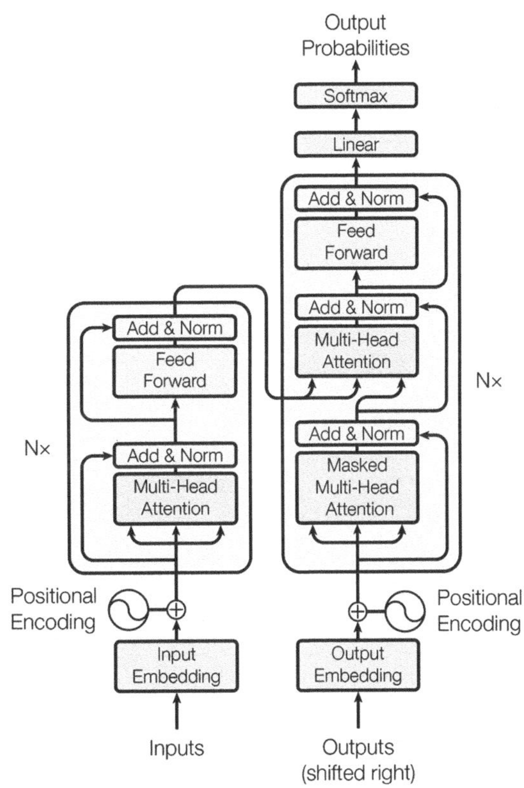

Figure 10.1: *Transformer Architecture (Source: Footnote*[5]*)*

[5] https://jalammar.github.io/illustrated-transformer/

Both the encoder and decoder contain stacked transformer blocks, each equipped with an attention mechanism and feed-forward network. The attention block is particularly clever in this regard, since it helps interpret each token's meaning in relation to others in the input. This context-awareness is crucial since words can have different meanings depending on their surroundings. The feed-forward network then further refines these representations. (For deeper technical details, see *Footnote*[5])

Now, let us see how Whisper implements this. The encoder processes audio sequences into meaningful representations that the decoder uses to generate text tokens iteratively. The process continues until the decoder produces an end-of-sentence token (**<|eos|>**), signaling completion. Check out *Figure* 10.2 for the architectural diagram, and original paper[6] of Whisper model.

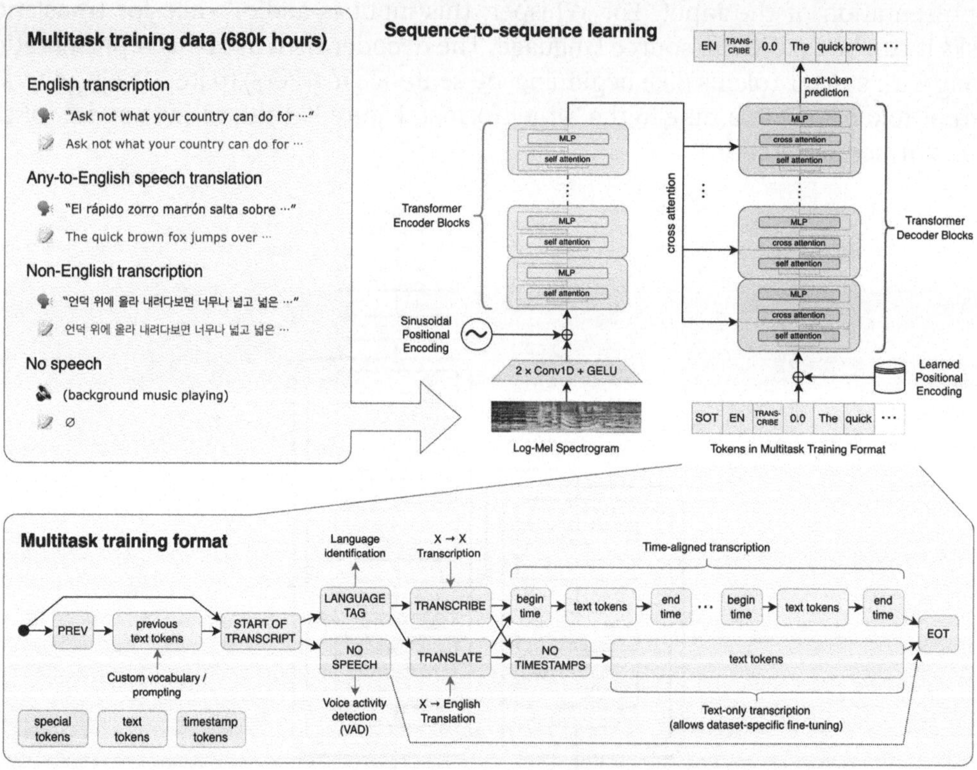

Figure 10.2: *Architecture of Whisper model (Source: Footnote*[6]*)*

Let us explore Whisper's input processing; it is fascinating how it transforms raw audio into understandable text! The journey begins with 16kHz audio waveforms that are normalized to consistent volume levels, ensuring stable performance across different recordings. This normalized audio then undergoes a series of transformations to convert the time-domain signal into a time-frequency representation. Whisper uses

[6] https://arxiv.org/abs/2212.04356

a Short-Time Fourier Transform (STFT) with a window size of 25 milliseconds and a hop length of 10 milliseconds, striking a balance between temporal and frequency resolution. The resulting spectrogram is converted to mel scale using 80 filter banks, which better approximates human auditory perception by emphasizing frequencies important for speech understanding. A logarithmic compression is then applied to the mel spectrogram to reduce the dynamic range and enhance quieter components of the signal.

Before being fed into the encoder, the log-mel spectrogram undergoes additional preprocessing. The model processes audio in 30-second chunks, padding shorter inputs with silence and truncating longer recordings. These spectrogram segments are then framed into overlapping windows that serve as input tokens to the Transformer encoder. The encoder's initial convolutional layers further process these features, using strided convolutions to reduce the sequence length while increasing the channel dimension, effectively creating a compressed yet information-rich representation of the audio input.

A crucial aspect of Whisper's input handling is its multilingual capability. The model doesn't require explicit language identification as input; instead, it can infer the language from the audio itself. However, users can optionally prepend task-specific tokens to guide the model's behavior, such as `<|transcribe|>` for direct transcription or `<|translate|>` to translate them into English. These special tokens condition the decoder's behavior, initiating an autoregressive generation process.

The decoder generates output tokens one at a time, conditioning each prediction on both the encoder's audio features and previously generated text tokens. At every step, the decoder uses cross-attention to focus on relevant parts of the encoded audio while maintaining context from prior tokens. This iterative process continues until the model predicts an end-of-sequence (`<|eos|>`) token, signaling completion. This approach allows Whisper to produce accurate, context-aware transcriptions while handling variable-length inputs and multiple languages seamlessly.

Exporting to ONNX Model

Now that we understand how the Whisper model works, let us explore how to use it in practice through code. We will load the model in PyTorch, run the inference, and export it as an ONNX model. Readers can run the code and reproduce the results by following the Jupyter Notebook of this chapter[7].

Figure 10.3 shows the sample code for loading the Whisper model and processor from Hugging Face's Transformers library. Whisper offers several model variants with

[7] https://github.com/ava-orange-education/Ultimate-ONNX-for-Optimizing-Deep-Learning-Models

different sizes and accuracy trade-offs - here we're using "**openai/whisper-tiny.en**", which can only transcribe English-spoken audio. Readers can further explore the other variants as shown in HuggingFace model card[8], which can provide multilingual capabilities.

In our example, we are using audio samples from the **LibriSpeech** dataset, but readers can easily substitute their own recordings. The **processor** handles the conversion of raw audio into log-mel spectrograms that the model expects. When we call **model.generate()**, it automatically handles the complete pipeline. First, the spectrogram input is fed to the encoder, which generates a rich, contextual representation of the audio. The decoder then takes this representation along with initial start tokens, iteratively predicting new tokens while incorporating its own previous predictions. This process continues until the decoder generates the **<|eos|>** (end-of-sentence) token, signaling completion of the transcription. The generated tokens are then decoded back into text using the **processor**. As we can see in *Figure* 10.3, the Whisper model is able to accurately generate the transcription in English text.

```
from transformers import WhisperProcessor, WhisperForConditionalGeneration
from datasets import load_dataset

# Load model and processor
processor = WhisperProcessor.from_pretrained("openai/whisper-tiny.en")
model = WhisperForConditionalGeneration.from_pretrained("openai/whisper-tiny.en")

# Load dummy dataset and read audio files
ds = load_dataset("hf-internal-testing/librispeech_asr_dummy", "clean", split="validation")
sample = ds[0]["audio"]
input_data = processor(sample["array"], sampling_rate=sample["sampling_rate"], return_tensors="pt")
input_features = input_data.input_features

# generate token ids
predicted_ids = model.generate(input_features)

# decode token ids to text
transcription = processor.batch_decode(predicted_ids, skip_special_tokens=True)
print(transcription)
```

```
[' Mr. Quilter is the apostle of the middle classes, and we are glad to welcome his gospel.']
```

Figure 10.3: *Sample code to load and run Whisper model*

Now, let us export this PyTorch model to the ONNX format. Unlike our approach in previous chapters, we will not export the entire Whisper model as a single unit. Instead, we will split it into three separate ONNX models: one for the encoder, and two distinct variants for the decoder. The encoder will be exported as a standalone model, while the decoder requires two specialized versions–an "init" model (also known as the "prefill" model) for the first inference step and a "step" model (also

[8] https://huggingface.co/openai/whisper-tiny.en

known as the "decode" model) for subsequent iterations. *Footnote*[9] describes these concepts in more detail.

This division is necessary as the model's complex execution flow prevents proper end-to-end export as a single unit. The decoder implementation particularly benefits from the KV Cache optimization technique[10], where attention keys and values from previous tokens are cached to avoid re-computation. This optimization necessitates the two decoder variants: the init model processes the initial input without any KV Cache but produces it as output, while the step model takes this cached state as input (either from the init model or its own previous iteration) and generates updated KV Cache along with the next token. Their fundamentally different operational requirements make separate ONNX exports essential for correct inference behavior. The decoder model's weights are identical in both init and step versions. *Figure* 10.4 shows the graphical overview of these three models, which we will export.

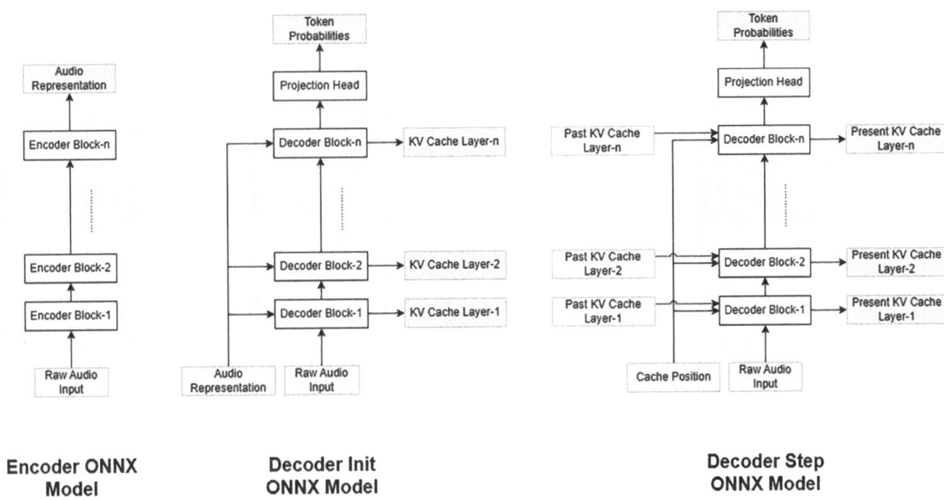

Figure 10.4: *Figure showing overview of Whisper encoder ONNX model, Whisper decoder init ONNX model and Whisper decoder step ONNX model*

As shown in *Figure* 10.5, we will export the Whisper encoder model following the same approach used for previous models, with the encoder specifically referenced through **`model.model.encoder`**. The encoder accepts input tensors of shape **`[1, 80, 3000]`**, a dimensionality derived from the model's 30-second audio processing capability at 16 kHz sampling. This 30-second window contains up to 480,000 raw samples (30 × 16,000), which are processed using 25 ms analysis windows with 10 ms hop lengths. Each hop advances the window by 160 samples (10 ms × 16,000 Hz), yielding 3000 total

[9] Prefill and decode models explained:
https://www.youtube.com/watch?v=3SBUCJzogj4
https://blog.premai.io/transformer-inference-techniques-for-faster-ai-models/
https://www.digitalocean.com/community/tutorials/llm-inference-optimization
[10] https://blog.dailydoseofds.com/p/kv-caching-in-llms-explained-visually

frames for a full 30-second input. Each frame is converted into an 80-dimensional mel-spectrogram using 80 filter banks, establishing the **[batch, 80, 3000]** input shape. To accommodate shorter sequences, we can make the third dimension dynamic. The encoder's output shape of **[batch, 1500, 384]** results from the initial convolutional layer's stride-2 downsampling, halving the temporal dimension, while producing a 384-dimensional latent representation of the input audio. The temporal dimension which was at the last axis in the input has moved to the middle axis in the output because of the internal transpose in the model.

```
# Export Whisper Encoder model to ONNX.
encoder_model_path = "whisper_encoder.onnx"
onnx_opset = 17

# Dummy input for encoder model: (batch_size=1, feature_dim=80, time_steps=3000)
dummy_input = torch.randn(1, 80, 3000)

# Export encoder
torch.onnx.export(
    model.model.encoder,
    (dummy_input,),
    encoder_model_path,
    input_names=["input_features"],
    output_names=["encoder_output"],
    dynamic_axes={
        "input_features": {0: "batch_size", 2: "time_steps"},
        "encoder_output": {0: "batch_size", 1: "time_steps"}
    },
    opset_version=onnx_opset,
)
print(f"Encoder exported as {encoder_model_path}")
```

Figure 10.5: *Whisper encoder model export code*

Now let us examine the decoder model implementation. *Figure 10.6* shows the custom class **WhisperDecoderInit** designed to simulate the decoder's init phase. This class's forward method accepts two critical inputs: **decoder_input_ids** (shaped as **[batch, 1]** with a fixed value of 50257 representing the start-of-transcription token) and **encoder_hidden_states** (the encoder's output with shape **[batch, 1500, 384]**). The class contains two core components: the main **decoder** module from the Whisper model and a projection layer (**proj_out**) that converts decoder outputs into token probabilities. The forward method produces two key outputs: **lm_logits** (representing token probabilities) and **past_key_values** (the generated KV cache).

```
class WhisperDecoderInit(torch.nn.Module):
    """Whisper decoder initialization model with projection head."""

    def __init__(self, decoder: torch.nn.Module, proj_out: torch.nn.Module):
        super().__init__()
        self.decoder = decoder
        self.proj_out = proj_out

    def forward(
        self,
        decoder_input_ids: torch.Tensor,
        encoder_hidden_states: torch.Tensor
    ) -> Tuple[torch.Tensor, ...]:
        """Forward pass for decoder initialization.

        Args:
            decoder_input_ids: Input token IDs for decoder
            encoder_hidden_states: Hidden states from encoder

        Returns:
            Tuple containing logits and past key values
        """
        output = self.decoder(
            input_ids=decoder_input_ids,
            encoder_hidden_states=encoder_hidden_states,
            use_cache=True,
        )
        lm_logits = self.proj_out(output[0])
        return (lm_logits,) + output.past_key_values
```

Figure 10.6: *Class representing Whisper decoder init model*

The model creates two distinct types of KV cache: self-attention cache and cross-attention cache. In self-attention, the Key (K) and Value (V) tensors originate from the same source as the Query (Q) tensor, whereas in cross-attention, K and V derive from the **`encoder_hidden_states`** while Q comes from the decoder inputs. Each layer consequently produces four cache components: two for self-attention (K and V) and two for cross-attention (K and V). The self-attention cache has dimensions **`[batch, num_heads, decoder_sequence, decoder_hidden_size]`** (specifically **`[1, 6, 1, 64]`** for our case), while the cross-attention cache uses **`[batch, num_heads, encoder_sequence, decoder_hidden_size]`** (**`[1, 6, 1500, 64]`**).

It is important to note that this init model operates without any pre-existing KV cache–its inputs consist solely of the forward method's parameters, which will directly translate to the ONNX model's inputs upon export. Similarly, the method's outputs will become the ONNX model's outputs. This class structure acts as the foundation for creating our init-phase ONNX model.

```
# Extract decoder and projection components
decoder = model.model.decoder
proj_out = model.proj_out

# Model configuration
config = model.config
batch = 1
decoder_seq_len = 1
encoder_seq_len = 1500      # depends on your audio length
hidden_size = config.d_model
num_layers = config.decoder_layers
num_heads = model.config.decoder_attention_heads
head_dim = hidden_size // num_heads

# Create dummy inputs
dummy_decoder_input_ids = torch.randint(
    0, config.vocab_size, (batch, decoder_seq_len)
)   # [batch, 1]
dummy_encoder_hidden_states = torch.rand(
    batch, encoder_seq_len, hidden_size
)   # [batch, 1500, 384]

# Define dynamic axes for inputs and outputs
dynamic_axes = {
    "decoder_input_ids": {0: "batch", 1: "seq_len"},
    "encoder_hidden_states": {0: "batch", 1: "encoder_seq_len"}
}
for i in range(num_layers):
    dynamic_axes[f"past_cross_key_{i}"] = {0: "batch", 2: "enc_seq_by_2"}
    dynamic_axes[f"past_cross_value_{i}"] = {0: "batch", 2: "enc_seq_by_2"}
    dynamic_axes[f"past_self_key_{i}"] = {0: "batch", 2: "past_seq"}
    dynamic_axes[f"past_self_value_{i}"] = {0: "batch", 2: "past_seq"}

# Initialize model
init_model = WhisperDecoderInit(decoder, proj_out)

# Prepare output names
init_model_output_names = []
for i in range(num_layers):
    init_model_output_names.extend([
        f"past_self_key_{i}",
        f"past_self_value_{i}",
        f"past_cross_key_{i}",
        f"past_cross_value_{i}"
    ])

# Export to ONNX
torch.onnx.export(
    init_model,
    (dummy_decoder_input_ids, dummy_encoder_hidden_states),
    decoder_model_init_path,
    input_names=["decoder_input_ids", "encoder_hidden_states"],
    output_names=["logits"] + init_model_output_names,
    dynamic_axes=dynamic_axes,
    opset_version=onnx_opset,
)

print(f"Decoder init model exported as {decoder_model_init_path}")
```

Figure 10.7: *Code showing export of Whisper decoder init model*

Figure 10.7 demonstrates the complete export process for the decoder initialization model, including the creation of dummy inputs, instantiation of the **`WhisperDecoderInit`** class, and the actual model export with properly configured output names and dynamic shape definitions.

```
class WhisperDecoderStep(torch.nn.Module):
    def __init__(self, decoder, proj_out):
        super().__init__()
        self.decoder = decoder
        self.proj_out = proj_out

    def forward(self, decoder_input_ids, cache_position, encoder_hidden_states, *past_key_values):
        # Reformat past_key_values
        num_layers = len(past_key_values) // 4
        past = []
        for i in range(num_layers):
            self_k = past_key_values[num_layers * i + 0]
            self_v = past_key_values[num_layers * i + 1]
            cross_k = past_key_values[num_layers * i + 2]
            cross_v = past_key_values[num_layers * i + 3]
            past.append((self_k, self_v, cross_k, cross_v))

        outputs = self.decoder(
            input_ids=decoder_input_ids,
            past_key_values=past,
            use_cache=True,
            cache_position=cache_position,
            encoder_hidden_states=encoder_hidden_states,
        )
        lm_logits = self.proj_out(outputs[0])
        return (lm_logits,) + outputs.past_key_values
```

Figure 10.8: *Class representing Whisper decoder step model*

We will follow a similar approach for the decoder step model. As illustrated in *Figure* 10.8, the **`WhisperDecoderStep`** class contains the same core components (**`decoder`** and **`proj_out`**) as in our previous implementation. However, this version introduces two critical additions to the forward method's inputs: **`cache_position`** and **`past_key_values`**.

```
def create_dummy_past_key_values(
    batch: int,
    num_layers: int,
    num_heads: int,
    decoder_seq_len: int,
    encoder_seq_len: int,
    head_dim: int
) -> List[torch.Tensor]:
    """Create dummy past key values for ONNX export.

    Args:
        batch: Batch size
        num_layers: Number of decoder layers
        num_heads: Number of attention heads
        decoder_seq_len: Length of decoder sequence
        encoder_seq_len: Length of encoder sequence
        head_dim: Dimension of each attention head

    Returns:
        List of dummy tensors for past key values
    """
    dummy_kvs = []

    self_attn_kv_shape = (batch, num_heads, decoder_seq_len, head_dim)
    cross_attn_kv_shape = (batch, num_heads, encoder_seq_len, head_dim)
    for _ in range(num_layers):
        # Self attention keys/values
        dummy_kvs.append(torch.rand(*self_attn_kv_shape))  # self_key
        dummy_kvs.append(torch.rand(*self_attn_kv_shape))  # self_value
        # Cross attention keys/values
        dummy_kvs.append(torch.rand(*cross_attn_kv_shape))  # cross_key
        dummy_kvs.append(torch.rand(*cross_attn_kv_shape))  # cross_value

    return dummy_kvs

# Create dummy inputs
dummy_decoder_input_ids = torch.randint(0, config.vocab_size, (batch, decoder_seq_len))
dummy_encoder_hidden_states = torch.rand(batch, encoder_seq_len, hidden_size)
dummy_cache_position = torch.tensor([0], dtype=torch.long)
dummy_past_key_values = create_dummy_past_key_values(
    batch, num_layers, num_heads, decoder_seq_len, encoder_seq_len, head_dim
)
```

Figure 10.9: *Code showing dummy input required for decoder step model export*

The **cache_position** parameter ensures that the proper positional encoding is applied to the **decoder_input_ids**, while **past_key_values** represents the cached attention states from either the init model's output or the previous step model iteration. Like the init model, this implementation produces two outputs: **lm_logits** (token probabilities) and updated **past_key_values**. Importantly, the output **past_key_values** expands dynamically with each iteration–the system takes the input cache and appends new key-value pairs generated from the current token's attention computation.

This growing cache mechanism enables efficient autoregressive generation while maintaining complete attention history.

```
# Prepare dynamic axes
dynamic_axes = {
    "decoder_input_ids": {0: "batch", 1: "seq_len"},
    "encoder_hidden_states": {0: "batch", 1: "encoder_seq_len"}
}

# Add dynamic axes for past key values
for name in init_model_output_names:
    if "cross" in name:
        dynamic_axes[name] = {0: "batch", 2: "enc_seq_by_2"}
    else:
        dynamic_axes[name] = {0: "batch", 2: "past_seq"}

# Prepare output names
step_output_names = []
for i in range(num_layers):
    step_output_names.extend([
        f"present_self_key_{i}",
        f"present_self_value_{i}",
        f"present_cross_key_{i}",
        f"present_cross_value_{i}"
    ])

# Initialize and export model
step_model = WhisperDecoderStep(model.model.decoder, model.proj_out)

torch.onnx.export(
    step_model,
    (dummy_decoder_input_ids, dummy_cache_position, dummy_encoder_hidden_states, *dummy_past_key_values),
    decoder_model_step_path,
    input_names=["decoder_input_ids", "cache_position", "encoder_hidden_states"] + init_model_output_names,
    output_names=["logits"] + step_output_names,
    dynamic_axes=dynamic_axes,
    opset_version=onnx_opset,
)
```

Figure 10.10: *Code showing export of Whisper decoder step model*

Figures 10.9 and 10.10 demonstrate the complete export process for the decoder step model, including the generation of dummy inputs and the actual ONNX model conversion. The **`decoder_input_ids`** maintain the same **`[batch, 1]`** shape configuration used in the init model. For positional tracking, we provide a 1D **`cache_position`** tensor that identifies the current token's sequence position. The **`past_key_values`** input follows the exact dimensional structure as previously discussed for the init model's KV cache outputs. Notably, the exported model prefixes all output cache tensors with "**`present_`**" to clearly distinguish them from input caches. To ensure flexibility with variable-length sequences, we have implemented dynamic axes configuration consistent with our earlier approach, allowing the model to adapt to different input sizes during inference. Besides this approach, readers can also explore the HuggingFace ONNX community[11] where the same Whisper model is available in ONNX form.

[11] https://huggingface.co/onnx-community/whisper-tiny.en

End-to-End Model Inference

We now have three ONNX models ready for use: one encoder and two decoder variants. Let us examine how these models work together in an end-to-end pipeline to convert audio input into text. Before execution, we will optimize these models using the ONNX Simplifier tool to improve inference performance.

```
# Load all three ONNX model
encoder_sess = ort.InferenceSession(encoder_path)
decoder_init_sess = ort.InferenceSession(decoder_init_path)
decoder_step_sess = ort.InferenceSession(decoder_step_path)

# Convert to log-mel spectrogram
inputs = processor(waveform, sampling_rate=16000, return_tensors="np")
input_features = inputs["input_features"]        # (1, 80, time)
print("Encoder input shape: ", input_features.shape)

# Run encoder model
encoder_hidden_states = encoder_sess.run(["encoder_output"],
                                         {"input_features": input_features})[0]
# (1, seq_len, hidden_size)
print("Encoder output shape: ", encoder_hidden_states.shape)

# Initial input for decoder
SOT_TOKEN = 50257             # Start of transcript token
EOS_TOKEN = 50256             # End of sentence token
decoder_input_ids = np.array([[SOT_TOKEN]], dtype=np.int64)

# Run decoder_init model
inputs = {
    "decoder_input_ids": decoder_input_ids,
    "encoder_hidden_states": encoder_hidden_states,
}
init_outputs = decoder_init_sess.run(None, inputs)

# Decode the decoder_init output
logits = init_outputs[0]
print("Logits shape: ", logits.shape)
generated_ids = [int(np.argmax(logits[0, -1]))]

# Fetch the KV caches which are generated
past_self_key = init_outputs[1::4]
past_self_value = init_outputs[2::4]
past_cross_key = init_outputs[3::4]
past_cross_value = init_outputs[4::4]
```

Figure 10.11: *Code showing inference of encoder model and decoder init model*

As illustrated in *Figure 10.11*, we will first load all three ONNX models into ONNX Runtime sessions. The audio waveform is processed through the Whisper processor, which converts it into a log-mel spectrogram with the expected **`[1, 80, 3000]`** dimensions. This tensor serves as input to the encoder model, which processes it to generate **encoder_hidden_states** – a **[1, 1500, 384]** dimensional representation of the audio features.

The decoder init model then takes two inputs: the **encoder_hidden_states** and **decoder_input_ids** containing the start token (**50257**). This special token signals the beginning of transcription and must always be the first input to the init model. The model produces 17 outputs: token probabilities followed by 16 KV cache tensors (4 layers × 2 attention types × 2 cache tensors each). We extract the predicted token by applying argmax to the probability scores, thereby effectively selecting the most likely token. The KV cache outputs are organized into separate lists for proper handling in the subsequent steps.

```
# Iteratively run decoder_step model
for step in range(num_iters):
    decoder_input_ids = np.array([[generated_ids[-1]]], dtype=np.int64)

    step_inputs = {
        "decoder_input_ids": decoder_input_ids,
        "cache_position": np.array([step + 1], dtype=np.int64),
    }

    # Flatten past_kv to feed as input
    for i in range(num_layers):
        step_inputs[f"past_self_key_{i}"] = past_self_key[i]
        step_inputs[f"past_self_value_{i}"] = past_self_value[i]
        step_inputs[f"past_cross_key_{i}"] = past_cross_key[i]
        step_inputs[f"past_cross_value_{i}"] = past_cross_value[i]

    # Run decoder step model
    step_outputs = decoder_step_sess.run(None, step_inputs)

    # Get the predicted token
    logits = step_outputs[0]
    next_token = int(np.argmax(logits[0, -1]))

    # Stop the loop if "End of Sentence" token is found.
    if next_token == EOS_TOKEN:
        break

    generated_ids.append(next_token)

    # Update KV cache for next step
    past_self_key = step_outputs[1::4]
    past_self_value = step_outputs[2::4]
    past_cross_key = step_outputs[3::4]
    past_cross_value = step_outputs[4::4]


# Display the combined prediction from decoder_init and decoder_step.
print("Generated token IDs:", generated_ids)
transcription = processor.batch_decode([generated_ids], skip_special_tokens=True)
print("Text transcription: ", transcription)
```

Figure 10.12: *Code showing iterative inference of decoder step model*

The iterative decoding phase (*Figure 10.12*) employs a for loop to repeatedly execute the decoder step model. Each iteration takes the previously predicted token as **decoder_input_ids**, along with its positional index and updated KV caches.

The **cache_position** starts from 1 (instead of 0) in the decoder step model because position 0 is already consumed during the init model's execution (which processes the starting token **<|startoftranscript|> (50257)** at position 0). After each step, we extract the new token prediction with highest probability and update both the **generated_ids** sequence and all cache tensors for the next iteration. This loop continues until either reaching the maximum token limit (100 in our case) or encountering the end-of-sequence token (**50256**). Finally, **processor.batch_decode** converts the accumulated token IDs into readable text, completing the transcription process.

This entire process implements a greedy decoding strategy, where the token with the highest probability is selected at every step. While effective, greedy search is just one of several decoding strategies[12] available; other common approaches include beam search, nucleus (top-p) sampling, and top-k sampling, which can often produce more fluent and creative outputs. A detailed discussion of these advanced techniques is beyond the scope of this book.

Quantizing ONNX Model

Now that we have successfully exported and integrated all ONNX models for end-to-end inference, let us explore quantizing these models to lower precision for improved efficiency. Given the transformer-based architecture of these models, we will use dynamic quantization instead of static quantization for our initial approach. While static quantization can be attempted using reference code from this chapter, preliminary experiments showed unsatisfactory results despite carefully excluding problematic nodes with high deviation. Readers are encouraged to investigate static quantization further, but we will proceed with dynamic quantization for its simplicity and reliability. *Figure* 10.13 illustrates a generic code that applies dynamic quantization uniformly across all three models.

```
# Firstly, apply shape inference and onnxruntime model optimization before quantizing the model.
quant_pre_process(fp32_path, fp32_path_preproc, skip_symbolic_shape=True)

# Apply dynamic quantization
quantize_dynamic(
    model_input=fp32_path_preproc,            # Input ONNX model
    model_output=int8_path_dynamic_quant,     # Output quantized model
    weight_type=QuantType.QUInt8              # Quantize only weights to uint8, activations will be quantize during runtime
)
```

Figure 10.13: *Generic code showing dynamic quantization of the exported models*

[12] https://huggingface.co/blog/mlabonne/decoding-strategies

The quantized models follow the same execution workflow demonstrated earlier in *Figures* 10.11 and 10.12. When this quantized model is executed using the earlier shown end-to-end pipeline, it generates the same results as the unquantized variant. We can deploy this optimized pipeline on edge devices like the Raspberry Pi 3B+ to evaluate both accuracy and performance gains. *Table* 10.1 shows the execution time of these models on Raspberry Pi 3B+. The benchmarking reveals that the encoder model consumes the majority of processing time, while both decoder init and step operations (single inference) complete in under a second. The sum of the encoder model's execution time, which generates the encoder representation, and the decoder init model's execution time, which establishes the initial KV caches, is often measured as Time to First Token (TTFT). Subsequent iterations through the decoder step model provide our Time per Output Token (TPOT) metric.

Dynamic quantization shows modest but consistent performance improvements over FP32 execution, suggesting potential for further optimization through static quantization by carefully analyzing and selecting nodes – a process similar to our YOLOv12 in earlier chapters. Beyond quantization, additional techniques like pruning and knowledge distillation could yield even more compact Whisper variants without significant accuracy loss, though these approaches remain for readers to explore independently.

Sr. No.	Model	FP32	INT8 (Dynamic)
1	Encoder	6.4352 sec	5.9880 sec
2	Decoder Init	0.8660 sec	0.6426 sec
3	Decoder Step (1 iteration)	0.1729 sec	0.1149 sec

Table 10.1: *Table showing execution time of all the models*

Conclusion

This chapter has provided readers with a comprehensive exploration of audio data processing. We examined various applications and use cases enabled through audio data analysis, focusing specifically on the Whisper model for Automatic Speech Recognition (ASR). Our study included an in-depth look at Whisper's architecture and components, followed by practical implementation, where we exported the model in segments and integrated them into a complete end-to-end inference pipeline for audio-to-text transcription. We further optimized the system by applying dynamic quantization and successfully deployed it on a Raspberry Pi edge device, thus demonstrating its real-world applicability.

Building on these concepts, the next chapter will apply similar methodologies to a Large Language Model (LLM). We will select a model with parameters suitable for the Raspberry Pi's computational capabilities and implement our accumulated knowledge from previous chapters. This will include the full pipeline from model preparation to end-to-end execution and strengthen our understanding of the learned concepts.

CHAPTER 11

End to End Execution of SmolLM Model

Introduction

In the last chapter, we learned about Whisper, which is an Automatic Speech Recognition (ASR) model, examined its different components, and applied our knowledge in an end-to-end implementation example. This chapter will follow a similar approach. Here, we will take a language model as an example, analyze its internal workings and components as we have done in previous chapters, and then apply our knowledge to optimize, quantize, and deploy it on edge devices.

Structure

This chapter covers the following topics:

- Overview of Language Models
- Overview of SmolLM Model
- Exporting to ONNX Model
- End-to-End Model Inference
- Quantizing the ONNX Model

Overview of Language Models

In the world of Natural Language Processing, language models are statistical machine learning models that can predict the probability distribution of words or sentences based on the given context. These models are trained on a large corpora of text data, which enables them to understand grammar, structure, and semantics. Such models have a wide range of applications like machine translation, speech recognition (as discussed in the previous chapter), chatbots like ChatGPT, and text generation.

From a mathematical perspective, if a sentence contains words $w_1, w_2, \ldots, w_{n-1}$, the language model's objective is to predict the probability of the next word w_n on the basis of the preceding words $w_1, w_2, \ldots, w_{n-1}$. The following equation illustrates this concept. The model aims to predict the most likely sequence of words, effectively determining the most probable sentence. The probability of the entire sentence can be computed by multiplying the conditional probabilities of each word given its preceding context.

$$
\begin{aligned}
P(w_1, w_2, \ldots, w_n) &= p(w_1)p(w_2|w_1)p(w_3|w_1, w_2)\cdots p(w_n|w_1, w_2, \ldots, w_{n-1}) \\
&= \prod_{i=1}^{n} p(w_i|w_1, \ldots, w_{i-1})
\end{aligned}
$$

Figure 11.1: *Equation to compute probability of a sentence*

The earliest language models relied primarily on statistical modeling. These models analyzed large text corpora to estimate word probabilities based on frequency counts. For example, in the sentence, "the cat sat on the mat", the probability of "cat" following "the" was determined by how often these words appeared together in the training data. Similarly, the likelihood of "sat" following "the cat" was calculated from their co-occurrence patterns. Later advancements in statistical modeling introduced an N-gram approach, where probabilities were estimated using sequences of N words rather than single preceding words. Bigram models, for instance, used two-word contexts - predicting "sat" from "the cat" and "on" from "cat sat." However, these methods had significant limitations as they could not handle spelling errors, lacked semantic understanding, performed poorly with rare word combinations, and were constrained by fixed context windows that struggled with long-range dependencies in text.

The advancement of neural networks led to the development of neural language models utilizing RNN and LSTM architectures, followed by transformer-based models. These models successfully addressed the shortcomings of traditional statistical approaches by capturing longer contextual dependencies and better understanding semantic meaning through learned parameters (weights) trained on extensive text corpora. Modern neural language models have achieved such remarkable scale that they now surpass human performance on numerous benchmarks. Applications such as ChatGPT, Claude, DeepSeek, and Gemini are examples of these advanced systems trained on Terabytes of text data containing trillions of tokens. To effectively process and learn from such massive datasets, these models require architectures scaled to billions of parameters, which is why they are called Large Language Models (LLMs).

Overview of SmolLM Model

Now that we have explored Large Language Models, we will use the **SmolLM2** language model[1] as our working example. This model offers three variants–1.7B (billion parameters), 360M (million parameters), and 135M (million parameters). To align with our edge deployment requirements, we will focus on the smallest variant. Strictly speaking, this 135M model does not qualify as a Large Language Model due to its modest parameter count of 135 million, placing it in the Small Language Model category. Nevertheless, it delivers a strong performance across various tasks compared to other models with similar parameter sizes.

The **SmolLM2** model builds upon the Llamav2 architecture, which implements only the decoder component of the original Transformer model. This decoder-only design processes input text and generates output autoregressively, producing one token at a time in an iterative manner. Earlier, we studied the Whisper model's encoder-decoder structure, but here we focus solely on the decoder part. It is worth noting that Llamav2 introduces several architectural modifications compared to the original transformer design; more detailed comparisons can be found in Llama related blogs[2].

In this chapter, we will specifically use the **SmolLM2-135M-Instruct** model[3]. This model differs from the standard **SmolLM2** language model in its approach to training. While the base **SmolLM2** model was trained on a large corpus of general text, including books, web data, and code, the Instruct variant undergoes further instruction fine-tuning. This technique adapts the model to follow instructions in a manner similar to ChatGPT or Gemini, enabling it to respond to user queries based on its understanding of the subject.

Instruction fine-tuning typically employs Q&A and instructional datasets to enhance the model's task-following capabilities, align responses with human intent, and mitigate harmful or undesirable behavior. For example, if presented with the prompt "The capital of France is", a vanilla language model might autocomplete with "a beautiful city with many museums." In contrast, when asked "What is the capital of France?", the instruction-tuned model directly answers "Paris." Such models are particularly suited for applications like chatbots, virtual assistants, and task-solving systems.

---

[1] https://arxiv.org/abs/2502.02737
[2] Llama2 architecture:
https://cameronrwolfe.substack.com/p/llama-2-from-the-ground-up
https://ai.plainenglish.io/understanding-llama2-kv-cache-grouped-query-attention-rotary-embedding-and-more-c17e5f49a6d7
https://www.youtube.com/watch?v=oM4VmoabDAI
https://www.youtube.com/watch?v=5T99hAg3oVg
[3] https://huggingface.co/HuggingFaceTB/SmolLM2-135M-Instruct

Exporting to ONNX Model

Before exporting the **SmolLM2** model to ONNX, let us first load the model from Hugging Face and run it to understand its behavior. This section and the following sections are further elaborated in the Jupyter Notebook provided for this chapter[4].

```
from transformers import AutoModelForCausalLM, AutoTokenizer

# Load the model from Huggingface and run it in Pytorch
model_name = "HuggingFaceTB/SmolLM2-135M-Instruct"

tokenizer = AutoTokenizer.from_pretrained(model_name)
model = AutoModelForCausalLM.from_pretrained(model_name,
                                             attn_implementation="eager",
                                             use_cache=True)

messages = [{"role": "user", "content": "What is gravity?"}]
input_text = tokenizer.apply_chat_template(messages, tokenize=False)
inputs = tokenizer(input_text, return_tensors="pt")
outputs = model.generate(**inputs, max_new_tokens=1000)

# Decode only the new tokens
input_length = inputs.input_ids.shape[1]
output_text = tokenizer.decode(outputs[0][input_length:])

print("===== Input to the model =====")
print(input_text)
print("===== Model's prediction =====")
print(output_text)
```

Figure 11.2: *Sample code to run the SmolLM2 model*

Figure 11.2 shows the code to load and run the **SmolLM2-135M-Instruct** model from Hugging Face using PyTorch. When initializing the model with **`AutoModelForCausalLM.from_pretrained`**, two key arguments are specified: **`attn_implementation="eager"`** and **`use_cache=True`**. Setting **`attn_implementation`** to **`"eager"`** ensures that the model uses a standard attention mechanism rather than an optimized version tailored for NVIDIA GPUs. This is necessary for successful ONNX export, as some optimized attention implementations are not compatible with ONNX conversion. Enabling **`use_cache=True`** allows the model to utilize KV caching during inference. KV caching[5] is an optimization technique that stores previously computed key-value states to avoid redundant computations for past tokens, thereby improving efficiency.

[4] https://github.com/ava-orange-education/Ultimate-ONNX-for-Optimizing-Deep-Learning-Models

[5] https://blog.dailydoseofds.com/p/kv-caching-in-llms-explained-visually

The input to an instruction-tuned model like **SmolLM2-135M-Instruct** must follow a specific structured format. As shown in *Figure* 11.2, the input is provided as a dictionary with **role** and content **keys**, which are then processed using the tokenizer's **apply_chat_template** method. This method formats the input into a structured conversation with special tokens. The processed input, illustrated in *Figure* 11.3, includes a system message, that serves as an initial instruction to guide the model's behavior. The system message is followed by the user's query, with each segment enclosed in **<|im_start|>** and **<|im_end|>** tags to delineate different parts of the conversation.

```
===== Input to the model =====
<|im_start|>system
You are a helpful AI assistant named SmolLM, trained by Hugging Face<|im_end|>
<|im_start|>user
What is gravity?<|im_end|>

===== Model's prediction =====
<|im_start|>assistant
Gravity is a fundamental force of nature that attracts objects with mass towards each othe
r. It is a result of the interaction between mass, energy, and space itself. In the context
of our universe, gravity is a result of the curvature of spacetime caused by the presence o
f mass and energy.

Imagine spacetime as a trampoline. When you place a heavy object, like a bowling ball, on t
he trampoline, it creates a depression in the surface. This depression is caused by the obj
ect's mass and the energy it contains. The more massive the object, the larger the depressi
on.

Now, when you move an object, such as a bowling ball, it creates a gravitational pull on th
e surrounding space. This gravitational pull is what causes the bowling ball to move toward
s the center of the trampoline. The more massive the object, the stronger the gravitational
pull.

Gravity is a universal force that acts between all objects in the universe, regardless of t
heir mass or energy. It is a fundamental aspect of the universe and plays a crucial role in
shaping the behavior of celestial bodies, including planets, stars, and galaxies.<|im_end|>
```

Figure 11.3: *Input provided to the SmolLM2 Instruct model and output generated by the model*

When the model generates a response, it continues from the formatted input, producing an assistant reply that adheres to the same structured format. The **generate** method iteratively runs the model, producing one token at a time. The generation process stops either when the **<|eos|>** (end-of-sequence) token is encountered or when the maximum token limit (set to 1000 via **max_new_tokens**) is reached. The output is then decoded, skipping the input tokens to extract only the newly generated text. The final response explains gravity as a fundamental force resulting from the curvature of space time, using an analogy of a trampoline to illustrate how mass influences gravitational attraction. This structured interaction ensures the model generates coherent and contextually appropriate responses, as it was fine-tuned to follow such conversational patterns.

Now that we understand the working of the model in PyTorch, let us try to export the model to ONNX. As SmolLM2 model is a decoder only model, we will follow the same approach we used to export the Whisper model. We will export the model in two variants– the "init" model (also known as the "prefill" model), which is used for the first inference that generates token predictions and the KV caches; and the "step" model (also known as the "decode" model), which is used for the subsequent inferences on the basis of the past KV cache and generating token probabilities and new KV caches. Just like our earlier Whisper decoder model export, the decoder model's weights are identical between the init and step versions, with the differences being limited to their input and output interfaces. *Figure* 11.4 explains the idea using a high-level diagram.

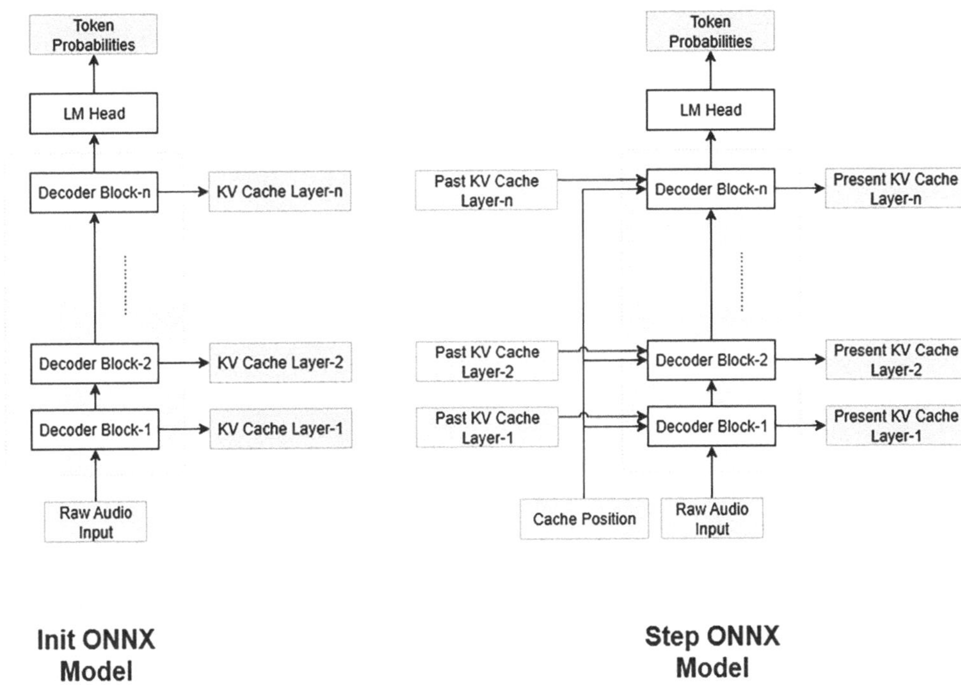

Figure 11.4: *Overview of SmolLM2 Init ONNX model and SmolLM2 Step ONNX model*

The **SmolLMInit** class, as depicted in *Figure* 11.5, initializes the SmolLM model. This init model takes **input_ids** of shape **[batch, seq_len]** and outputs both **logits** (token probabilities) and **past_key_values** (KV cache). The **logits** tensor, with a shape of **[batch, seq_len, vocab_size]** (where **vocab_size** is 49152 for SmolLM), provides probability distributions for each token in the input sequence across the entire vocabulary. However, only the probability of the final token in the sequence is utilized by the step model for subsequent iterative generation. The KV cache comprises key (K) and value (V) tensors, each having a shape of **[batch, num_heads, seq_len, head_dim]**. For the SmolLM model, with 3 attention heads and a head dimension of 64, the shape of each K and V tensor within a single KV cache is **[batch, 3, seq_len, 64]**. Since SmolLM is a 30-layer decoder-only model, it maintains 30 such KV cache pairs. Unlike encoder-decoder architectures like Whisper, SmolLM does not have Cross Attention KV caches.

```
class SmolLMInit(torch.nn.Module):
    """Smol LM init model with lm head."""

    def __init__(self, model: torch.nn.Module, lm_head: torch.nn.Module):
        super().__init__()
        self.model = model
        self.lm_head = lm_head

    def forward(
        self,
        input_ids: torch.Tensor,
    ) -> Tuple[torch.Tensor, ...]:
        """Forward pass for decoder initialization.

        Args:
            input_ids: Input token IDs for decoder

        Returns:
            Tuple containing logits and past key values
        """
        output = self.model(
            input_ids=input_ids,
            use_cache=True,
        )
        lm_logits = self.lm_head(output[0])
        return (lm_logits,) + output.past_key_values.to_legacy_cache()
```

Figure 11.5: *Class representing SmolLM init model*

```
batch = 1
seq_len = 16

# Create dummy inputs
input_ids = torch.randint(0, model.config.vocab_size, (batch, seq_len))    # [batch, seq]

# Initialize model
init_model = SmolLMInit(model.model, model.lm_head)

# Add inputs and outputs in dynamic axes
dynamic_axes = {
    'input_ids': {0: 'batch', 1: 'sequence_length'},
    'logits': {0: 'batch', 1: 'sequence_length'},
}

# Prepare output names
init_input_names = ["input_ids"]
init_output_names = ["logits"]
for i in range(model.config.num_hidden_layers):
    init_output_names.append(f'past_key_values.{i}.key')
    init_output_names.append(f'past_key_values.{i}.value')
    dynamic_axes[f'past_key_values.{i}.key'] = {0: 'batch', 2: 'sequence_length'}
    dynamic_axes[f'past_key_values.{i}.value'] = {0: 'batch', 2: 'sequence_length'}

# Export to ONNX
torch.onnx.export(
    init_model, (input_ids), init_model_path,
    input_names=init_input_names, output_names=init_output_names,
    dynamic_axes=dynamic_axes, opset_version=onnx_opset,
)
```

Figure 11.6: *Code showcasing the export of SmolLM init model*

Figure 11.6 illustrates the code for exporting the SmolLM init model to the ONNX format.

Notably, it demonstrates using the **`dynamic_axes`** argument, which allows the model to handle inputs and generate outputs of varying lengths.

```python
class SmolLMStep(torch.nn.Module):
    """Smol LM step model with lm head."""

    def __init__(self, model: torch.nn.Module, lm_head: torch.nn.Module):
        super().__init__()
        self.model = model
        self.lm_head = lm_head

    def forward(
        self,
        input_ids: torch.Tensor,
        cache_position: torch.Tensor,
        *past_key_values: Tuple[torch.Tensor, ...]
    ) -> Tuple[torch.Tensor, ...]:
        """Forward pass for decoder initialization.

        Args:
            input_ids: Input token IDs for decoder
            cache_position: Position index for caching
            *past_key_values: Past key-value pairs for attention

        Returns:
            Tuple containing logits and updated key values
        """
        # Reformat past_key_values into expected structure
        num_layers = len(past_key_values) // 2
        reformatted_past = []

        for i in range(num_layers):
            layer_past = (
                past_key_values[2 * i],     # self_key
                past_key_values[2 * i + 1], # self_value
            )
            reformatted_past.append(layer_past)

        dynamic_cache = DynamicCache.from_legacy_cache(reformatted_past, num_layers)
        outputs = self.model(
            input_ids=input_ids,
            past_key_values=dynamic_cache,
            use_cache=True,
            cache_position=cache_position,
        )

        lm_logits = self.lm_head(outputs[0])
        return (lm_logits,) + outputs.past_key_values.to_legacy_cache()
```

Figure 11.7: *Class representing SmolLM step model*

Figure 11.7 illustrates the **SmolLMStep** class, which manages the step-by-step generation of tokens. It receives **input_ids**, **cache_position** and **past_key_values**, outputting **logits** (token probabilities) and updated KV caches. Similar to the Whisper model, this step model predicts probabilities for a single token during every iteration. This predicted token then serves as input for the subsequent iteration. The initial iteration of this step model utilizes the **past_kv_cache** from the init model's output KV caches. The step model generates an updated **present_kv_cache**, which is used as input in the next iteration of the step model.

The **input_ids** for this SmolLM step model have a shape of **[batch, 1]**, while the input KV cache maintains the same shape as the init model's output KV cache: **[batch, 3, seq_len, 64]**. In each iteration, the key-value (KV) cache size increases linearly. For instance, the **present_kv_cache** from the first iteration of the step model has a shape of **[batch, 3, seq_len + 1, 64]**. Subsequently, in the next iteration, its shape becomes **[batch, 3, seq_len + 2, 64]**, and this pattern of linear growth continues with every subsequent iteration. A scalar **cache_position** tensor, indicating the current token's position in the generated sentence, is also provided as the input.

```
def create_dummy_past_key_values(
    batch: int,
    num_layers: int,
    num_heads: int,
    past_seq_len: int,
    head_dim: int
) -> List[torch.Tensor]:
    """Create dummy past key values for ONNX export.

    Args:
        batch: Batch size
        num_layers: Number of decoder layers
        num_heads: Number of attention heads
        past_seq_len: Length of past sequence
        head_dim: Dimension of each attention head

    Returns:
        List of dummy tensors for past key values
    """
    dummy_kvs = []

    self_attn_kv_shape = (batch, num_heads, past_seq_len, head_dim)
    for _ in range(num_layers):
        # Self attention keys/values
        dummy_kvs.append(torch.rand(*self_attn_kv_shape))  # self_key
        dummy_kvs.append(torch.rand(*self_attn_kv_shape))  # self_value

    return dummy_kvs


# Create dummy inputs
dummy_input_ids = torch.randint(0, model.config.vocab_size, (batch, step_seq_len))
dummy_cache_position = torch.tensor([0], dtype=torch.long)
dummy_past_key_values = create_dummy_past_key_values(
    batch, model.config.num_hidden_layers, model.config.num_key_value_heads, past_seq_len, model.config.head_dim
)
```

Figure 11.8: *Code showing dummy input required for step model export*

Figures 11.8 and 11.9 illustrate the code for creating dummy inputs that are required for exporting a step model and the subsequent code for converting it to an ONNX model. These dummy **input_ids**, dummy **cache_position**, and dummy **past_key_values** tensors are shaped as previously discussed. The model export utilizes **dynamic_axes**, enabling it to process inputs with varying sequence lengths. The output's updated KV cache is named **present_key_value** to distinguish it from the input KV cache.

```
past_seq_len = 16
step_seq_len = 1
batch = 1

# Prepare dynamic axes
dynamic_axes = {
    "input_ids": {0: 'batch', 1: "curr_seq_len"},
    "logits": {0: 'batch', 1: "curr_seq_len"},
}
# Prepare output names
step_output_names = ["logits"]
step_input_names = ["input_ids", "cache_position"]
past_kv_dynamic_axes = {0: 'batch', 2: "past_seq"}
present_kv_dynamic_axes = {0: 'batch', 2: "past_seq_plus_curr_seq_len"}
for i in range(model.config.num_hidden_layers):
    dynamic_axes[f'past_key_values.{i}.key'] = past_kv_dynamic_axes
    dynamic_axes[f'past_key_values.{i}.value'] = past_kv_dynamic_axes
    dynamic_axes[f'present_key_values.{i}.key'] = present_kv_dynamic_axes
    dynamic_axes[f'present_key_values.{i}.value'] = present_kv_dynamic_axes
    step_input_names.append(f'past_key_values.{i}.key')
    step_input_names.append(f'past_key_values.{i}.value')
    step_output_names.append(f'present_key_values.{i}.key')
    step_output_names.append(f'present_key_values.{i}.value')

# Initialize and export model
step_model = SmolLMStep(model.model, model.lm_head)

torch.onnx.export(
    step_model,
    (dummy_input_ids, dummy_cache_position, *dummy_past_key_values),
    step_model_path,
    input_names=step_input_names, output_names=step_output_names,
    dynamic_axes=dynamic_axes, opset_version=onnx_opset,
)
```

Figure 11.9: *Code showing export of SmolLM step model*

The exported models occupy about 622 MB of storage space, since they use FP32 precision for their weights. Interestingly, while we have exported two separate models, they share the same set of weights. The difference lies in how each model utilizes them during operation. Additionally, readers can also explore the HuggingFace[6], where the same SmolLM2-135M Instruct model is available in ONNX form.

[6] https://huggingface.co/HuggingFaceTB/SmolLM2-135M-Instruct/tree/main/onnx

End-to-End Model Inference

Once we export both ONNX models, let us try to run both these using an end-to-end pipeline, which is similar to what we did with the Whisper model. It involves loading both models. The init model is run first and its output is then used as input for the step model. Specifically, the predicted token (which is based on the last token's probability), the KV caches from the init model, and **`cache_position`** are fed into the step model.

```
def run_models(init_model, step_model, inputs, tokenizer, max_iters=100):
    past_seq_len = inputs["input_ids"].shape[1]
    print("Inputs shape: ", inputs['input_ids'].shape)

    # Run init model
    outputs = init_model.run(None, inputs)
    logits = outputs[0]
    print("Logits shape: ", logits.shape)
    generated_ids = [int(np.argmax(logits[0, -1]))]

    step_inputs = {}
    step_inputs["input_ids"] = np.array(generated_ids[-1]).reshape(1, -1)

    num_layers = (len(outputs) - 1) // 2
    for i in range(num_layers):
        step_inputs[f'past_key_values.{i}.key'] = outputs[i * 2 + 1]
        step_inputs[f'past_key_values.{i}.value'] = outputs[i * 2 + 2]

    for i in range(max_iters):
        step_inputs["cache_position"] = np.array([past_seq_len + i], dtype=np.int64)

        # Run step model iteratively
        step_outputs = step_model.run(None, step_inputs)
        logits = step_outputs[0]
        pred_token = int(np.argmax(logits[0, -1]))

        if pred_token == tokenizer.eos_token_id:
            print("Stopping generateion as EOS token reached.")
            break

        generated_ids.append(pred_token)

        step_inputs["input_ids"] = np.array(pred_token).reshape(1, -1)
        for i in range(num_layers):
            step_inputs[f'past_key_values.{i}.key'] = step_outputs[i * 2 + 1]
            step_inputs[f'past_key_values.{i}.value'] = step_outputs[i * 2 + 2]

    predicted_text = tokenizer.decode(generated_ids)
    print("Predicted text:", predicted_text)
    return predicted_text
```

Figure 11.10: *Inference pipeline for SmolLM model*

The step model then iteratively produces probabilities for new tokens and generates new KV caches. These new tokens with highest probability and KV caches along with next **cache_position** are subsequently fed back into the step model for the next iteration. This approach, which selects the most probable token at each timestep, is known as greedy decoding. While straightforward and efficient, it is worth noting that alternative decoding strategies, such as beam search, top-k sampling, and nucleus sampling, exist and can often yield better results. A full exploration of these methods is outside the scope of this book; hence, readers are advised to visit this blog[7] for a comprehensive understanding of the subject.

This process repeats until either 1,000 tokens are generated or the model outputs the end-of-sentence token (**<|eos|>**). For optimal execution speed in the pipeline, we will also apply graph optimizations using ONNX Simplifier to these models beforehand.

```
# Helper function for inference
def preprocess(user_text, tokenizer):
    messages = [{"role": "user", "content": user_text}]
    input_text = tokenizer.apply_chat_template(messages, tokenize=False)
    input_ids = tokenizer(input_text, return_tensors="np").input_ids
    return {"input_ids": input_ids}

# Run exported models
init_model_path = "smol_lm_init.onnx"
step_model_path = "smol_lm_step.onnx"
init_model = ort.InferenceSession(init_model_path)
step_model = ort.InferenceSession(step_model_path)

inputs = preprocess("What is gravity?", tokenizer)
predicted_text = run_models(init_model, step_model, inputs, tokenizer, max_iters=1000)
```

Figure 11.11: *End-to-end execution of SmolLM model using pipeline*

Figures 11.10 and 11.11 illustrate the end-to-end inference pipeline, including the preprocessing function and the process of running the model end-to-end to obtain predictions.

Figure 11.10 presents the **run_models** function. This function accepts the ONNX Runtime Inference session object for init and step models, preprocessed inputs for the init model, a tokenizer for decoding the predicted tokens, and **max_iters** to set the generation limit. The **run_models** function begins by executing the init model with an inputs dictionary, which is created using the preprocess function as shown in *Figure* 11.11. The primary output of the init model is the token probabilities. As mentioned earlier, only the probability of the last token, representing the newly predicted token, is considered. Additionally, the init model generates 30 KV caches pairs, which will be used by the step model.

[7] https://huggingface.co/blog/mlabonne/decoding-strategies

Following the execution of the init model, the step model is iteratively executed. It takes the token generated either by the init model, or the previous step model iteration as input (a single token with shape **`[batch, 1]`**). The step model's execution also depends on the **`cache_position`** tensor. Its value is determined by the initial sequence length plus the current step model iteration count, ensuring the input token is assigned the correct position within the generated sequence. The final input to the step model is the KV cache from either the init model or the prior step model execution. Based on these three inputs, the step model produces token probabilities and new KV caches. The generated token is appended to the **`generated_ids`** list, which serves as the input for the next step model iteration. Similarly, the new KV caches are used as input in the subsequent iteration. This loop continues until either **`max_iter`** iterations are completed or the model generates the end-of-sentence token (**<|eos|>**). Once the loop terminates, all generated tokens are stored in **`generated_ids`**. The **`tokenizer.decode`** function converts these tokens into readable words. Finally, the **`run_models`** function returns this decoded text.

Figure 11.11 demonstrates the loading process for the init and step models. It also illustrates the preprocessing of a sample input text: "What is gravity?". *Figure 11.12* shows the expected output when this tokenized input is processed by the **`run_models`** function.

```
Predicted text: <|im_start|>assistant
Gravity is a fundamental force of nature that attracts objects with mass towards each other.
It is a result of the interaction between mass, energy, and space itself. In the context of o
ur universe, gravity is a result of the curvature of spacetime caused by the presence of mass
and energy.

Imagine spacetime as a trampoline. When you place a heavy object, like a bowling ball, on the
trampoline, it creates a depression in the surface. This depression is caused by the object's
mass and the energy it contains. The more massive the object, the larger the depression.

Now, when you move an object, such as a bowling ball, it creates a gravitational pull on the
surrounding space. This gravitational pull is what causes the bowling ball to move towards th
e center of the trampoline. The more massive the object, the stronger the gravitational pull.

Gravity is a universal force that acts between all objects in the universe, regardless of the
ir mass or energy. It is a fundamental aspect of the universe and plays a crucial role in sha
ping the behavior of celestial bodies, including planets, stars, and galaxies.
```

Figure 11.12: *Generated output from the ONNX Runtime execution of SmolLM models*

Quantizing ONNX Model

Now that we have exported our ONNX model, we will quantize it to make it suitable for edge deployment. We have found through practical testing that running unquantized models directly on devices like Raspberry Pi 3B+ causes significant issues such as overheating and system unresponsiveness due to increased computational demands. This makes quantization not just beneficial, but essential for successful deployment on resource-constrained hardware.

Since we are working with a transformer-based architecture in SmolLM, we will implement dynamic quantization like we did on Whisper. Readers are encouraged to explore the static quantization path as well. For consistency, we are reusing the dynamic quantization code from our Whisper implementation. In *Figure* 11.13, we clearly demonstrate how to apply the **apply_dynamic_quantization** function to both our init and step models.

```
def apply_dynamic_quantization(fp32_path):
    root, ext = os.path.splitext(fp32_path)
    fp32_path_preproc = f"{root}_preproc{ext}"
    int8_path_dynamic_quant = f"{root}_int8_dynamic_quant{ext}"

    # Firstly, apply shape inference and onnxruntime model optimization before quantizing the model.
    quant_pre_process(fp32_path, fp32_path_preproc, skip_symbolic_shape=True)

    # Apply dynamic quantization
    quantize_dynamic(
        model_input=fp32_path_preproc,           # Input ONNX model
        model_output=int8_path_dynamic_quant,    # Output quantized model
        weight_type=QuantType.QUInt8             # Quantize only weights to uint8,
                                                 # activations will be quantize during runtime
    )

    print(f"Dynamic Quantized model saved at: {int8_path_dynamic_quant}")

    # Compare model sizes
    fp32_size = os.path.getsize(fp32_path) / 1024 / 1024
    dynamic_quant_size = os.path.getsize(int8_path_dynamic_quant) / 1024 / 1024

    print(f"FP32 Model Size: {fp32_size:.2f} MB")
    print(f"Dynamic Quantized Model Size: {dynamic_quant_size:.2f} MB")

    return int8_path_dynamic_quant
# Quantize SmolLM init model
init_model_path_int8 = apply_dynamic_quantization(init_model_path)

# Quantize SmolLM step model
step_model_path_int8 = apply_dynamic_quantization(step_model_path)
```

Figure 11.13: *Code showing the dynamic quantization of SmolLM init and step model*

When we execute these quantized models through our established pipeline (*Figure* 11.10), we obtain the results shown in *Figure* 11.14. Comparing these with the original unquantized outputs in *Figure* 11.12, we observe them to be remarkably close, though not identical. This variance comes from inherent quantization errors when we convert the weights using dynamic quantization. To assess the impact properly, we should evaluate performance metrics across test datasets. This analysis helps us understand the accuracy trade-offs and potentially develop compensation strategies. Readers are advised to conduct this evaluation before actually using these models in the production.

When we run these quantized models on a Raspberry Pi 3B+ using our test question "What is gravity?", we observe some interesting performance metrics. The init model takes approximately **1.239 seconds** for its first inference (what we call Time to First Token or TTFT), while the step model completes each subsequent inference in about **0.2198 seconds** (known as Time per Output Token or TPOT). This translates to a generation speed of roughly 5 tokens per second - quite respectable for an edge device like the Pi 3B+.

It is worth noting that we are currently working with the 135 million parameter version of SmolLM. If this does not meet our specific use case requirements, we could explore the larger parameter variants, though we should expect slower performance with those models. For those looking to push performance further, we might consider experimenting with static quantization techniques or upgrading to more powerful edge devices like the Raspberry Pi 5 or Jetson Nano. These alternatives can potentially offer better speed and efficiency for our inference tasks.

```
Predicted text: <|im_start|>assistant
Gravity is a fundamental force of nature that attracts objects with mass towards each othe
r. It is a result of the interaction between mass, energy, and space. The force of gravity
is a result of the curvature of spacetime caused by the presence of mass and energy.

The force of gravity is not a force that acts between two objects, but rather a force that
acts between objects that are moving towards each other. This is because the presence of ma
ss causes the gravitational field to become stronger, pulling objects towards each other.

The strength of the gravitational field depends on the mass of the objects and the distance
between them. The stronger the gravitational field, the stronger the force of gravity. The
strength of the gravitational field is also affected by the strength of the gravitational f
ield of the other objects, as well as the distance between them.

Gravity is a universal force that acts across the entire universe, and it is the reason why
objects fall towards the ground, and why planets orbit around stars. It is a fundamental fo
rce of nature that is responsible for many natural phenomena, such as the tides, the orbits
of planets, and the rotation of the Earth.

In summary, gravity is a fundamental force of nature that attracts objects with mass toward
s each other, and it is a result of the curvature of spacetime caused by the presence of ma
ss and energy.
```

Figure 11.14: *Generated output from dynamically quantized SmolLM ONNX models*

Conclusion

Throughout this chapter, we have explored the fascinating world of Language Models in Natural Language Processing (NLP). We started by understanding the fundamentals of how these models operate and the outputs they generate. After reviewing the latest LLM advancements, we chose SmolLM for our tests due to its lightweight architecture and efficient performance on resource-constrained hardware. We explored its architecture in more detail and implemented a complete end-to-end workflow–from exporting the model to ONNX format to applying dynamic quantization techniques. We also successfully deployed our optimized model on a Raspberry Pi 3B+, proving how these concepts work in practical scenarios.

Looking ahead, our next chapter will tackle more advanced aspects of the ONNX ecosystem. We will build an ONNX model completely from scratch, bypassing the usual PyTorch or TensorFlow export path. Then, we will push further into advanced territory by learning how to create custom ONNX operators to essentially expand ONNX's capabilities to suit our specific needs. Mastering these complex topics will provide us an insight into using powerful tools for real-world deployment challenges that often require customized solutions.

CHAPTER 12

ONNX Model from Scratch and Custom Operators

Introduction

Till now, we have explored the ONNX model's structure, quantized and optimized the ONNX model and deployed it using the ONNX Runtime. Later, we learned about various real-world models and applied our knowledge in an end-to-end manner. Now, we will dive into some advanced topics, which would not be required in general usage of ONNX, but are good to know about. In this chapter, we will learn about how to construct an ONNX model using pure ONNX APIs and ONNX Script tool. Then we will learn about custom operators and how to enable them in ONNX using ONNX APIs, ONNX Script and Pytorch export.

Structure

This chapter covers the following topics:

- Constructing ONNX Model Using ONNX APIs
- Constructing ONNX Model Using ONNX Script
- Extending ONNX via Custom Operators
- Custom Ops Using ONNX APIs
- Custom Ops Using ONNX Script
- Custom Ops Using Pytorch Export

Constructing ONNX Model Using ONNX APIs

In Chapter 2, we learned about the building blocks of an ONNX model. We saw that the ONNX model is constructed in the form of a ModelProto. The ModelProto contains GraphProto and FunctionProto. The GraphProto is composed of TensorProto, ValueInfoProto, NodeProto, and AttributeProto, while the FunctionProto contains ValueInfoProto, NodeProto, and AttributeProto. *Figure* 12.1 illustrates the overall hierarchy of these objects for better understanding.

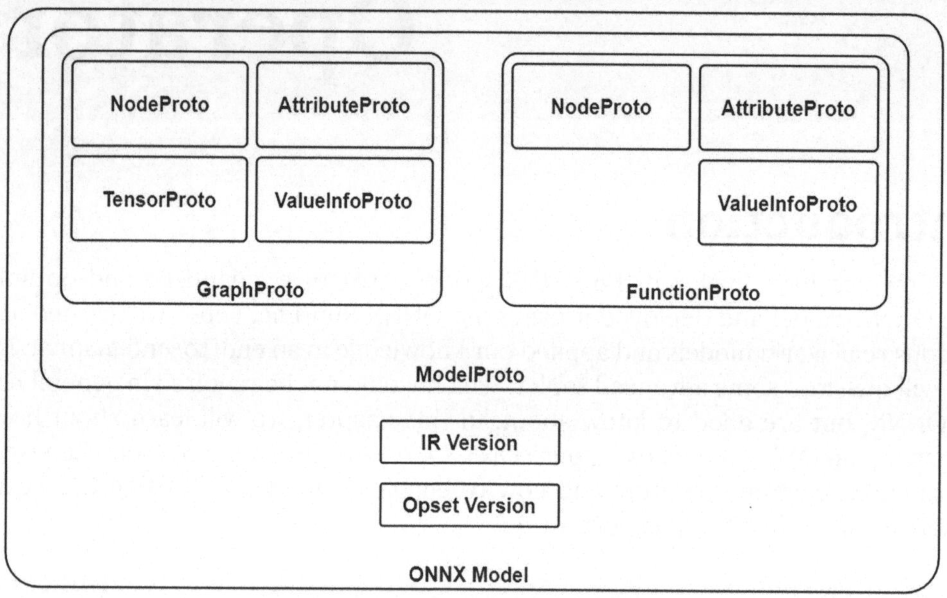

Figure 12.1: ONNX *model structure*

When we export a PyTorch or TensorFlow model to an ONNX model, the constant tensors are converted into TensorProto. Each layer of the PyTorch or TensorFlow model is converted into a corresponding ONNX NodeProto. The shapes of the input and output tensors for each NodeProto, as well as the graph inputs and outputs, are stored in ValueInfoProto. If the NodeProto has any attributes, they are stored in AttributeProto. This conversion is handled automatically by PyTorch in the case of PyTorch-to-ONNX conversion, whereas for TensorFlow, it is done by the **`tf2onnx`** utility. Under the hood, both frameworks convert the source model into the corresponding building blocks of the ONNX model.

Here, we will construct an ONNX model by building its different components in a hierarchical pattern. For this, we will use an example of a 2-layer model consisting of MatMul nodes followed by an Add node and a ReLU activation between the layers. *Figure* 12.2 provides a visual representation of the model we will construct.

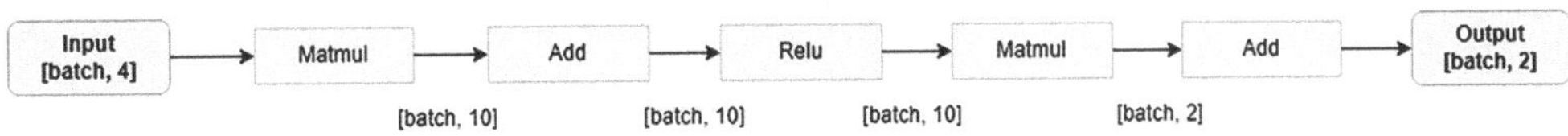

Figure 12.2: *Visual representation of sample model*

First, we will define the model's input and output. For this example, we will consider an input shape of **["batch", 4]** and an output shape of **["batch", 2]**. The inputs and outputs are defined using ValueInfoProto, and ONNX provides the **make_tensor_value_info** function under the **onnx.helper** module. As shown in *Figure* 12.3, the **make_tensor_value_info** function takes the tensor's name, datatype, and shape as arguments. Here, we define one input named **"input"** with a **float32** datatype and a shape of **["batch", 4]**, and one output named **"output"** with a **float32** datatype and a shape of **["batch", 2]**.

```
# Model specification
input_size = 4
hidden_size = 10
output_size = 2

# Define input tensor (with dynamic batch size)
X = helper.make_tensor_value_info(
    name="input",
    elem_type=TensorProto.FLOAT,
    shape=["batch", input_size]  # [batch_size, input_size]
)

# Define output tensor
Y = helper.make_tensor_value_info(
    name="output",
    elem_type=TensorProto.FLOAT,
    shape=["batch", output_size]  # [batch_size, output_size]
)
```

Figure 12.3: *Input-Output value info creation in ONNX model*

Next, we will define the model's constants as initializers. The model will have two weights for the MatMul nodes and two biases for the Add nodes following each MatMul. The initializers are defined using TensorProto and can be created using the **make_tensor** function under the **onnx.helper** module. *Figure* 12.4 demonstrates the creation of weights and biases as initializers. The **make_tensor** function takes the constant's name, datatype, shape, and values as arguments. For our example, we define random weights and biases. The first layer's weights have a shape of **[4, 10]**, since we use 10 as the intermediate layer dimension, and the bias has a 1D shape of **[10]**. Similarly, the second layer's weights have a shape of **[10, 2]**, and the biases have a shape of **[2]**.

```
# Weights and biases for the first layer (input -> hidden)
W1 = helper.make_tensor(
    name="W1",
    data_type=TensorProto.FLOAT,
    dims=[input_size, hidden_size],
    vals=np.random.randn(input_size, hidden_size).astype(np.float32).flatten().tolist()
)

B1 = helper.make_tensor(
    name="B1",
    data_type=TensorProto.FLOAT,
    dims=[hidden_size],
    vals=np.random.randn(hidden_size).astype(np.float32).flatten().tolist()
)

# Weights and biases for the second layer (hidden -> output)
W2 = helper.make_tensor(
    name="W2",
    data_type=TensorProto.FLOAT,
    dims=[hidden_size, output_size],
    vals=np.random.randn(hidden_size, output_size).astype(np.float32).flatten().tolist()
)

B2 = helper.make_tensor(
    name="B2",
    data_type=TensorProto.FLOAT,
    dims=[output_size],
    vals=np.random.randn(output_size).astype(np.float32).flatten().tolist()
)
```

Figure 12.4: *Initializer creation in ONNX model*

Afterward, we will create nodes corresponding to each layer. We will create a total of five nodes: two MatMul nodes, two Add nodes, and one ReLU node. The nodes in ONNX are generated using the NodeProto object. The **make_node** function under the **onnx.helper** module constructs NodeProto. As shown in *Figure* 12.5, the **make_node** function requires the **op_type** to define the node's type, the names of the input and output tensors, and the node's name. For nodes like Conv, attributes such as **kernel_shape**, **pads**, and **strides** can also be provided as keyword arguments.

When defining an ONNX node, we must carefully specify the inputs and outputs, as they form the edges of the graph. In our case, the input of the first MatMul node is the graph input named "**input**" and the weight "**W1**". The output of this MatMul node is named "**matmul1_out**". This same tensor is then fed into the next node, an Add node, which takes "**matmul1_out**" as one input and the constant bias tensor "**B1**" as the other.

Similarly, each node's inputs and outputs are connected to ensure the graph edges are correctly formed.

```
# Node 1: X * W1 + B1
node_matmul1 = helper.make_node(
    op_type="MatMul", inputs=["input", "W1"], outputs=["matmul1_out"], name="matmul1"
)

node_add1 = helper.make_node(
    op_type="Add", inputs=["matmul1_out", "B1"], outputs=["add1_out"], name="add1"
)

# Node 2: ReLU activation
node_relu = helper.make_node(
    op_type="Relu", inputs=["add1_out"], outputs=["relu_out"], name="relu"
)

# Node 3: relu_out * W2 + B2
node_matmul2 = helper.make_node(
    op_type="MatMul", inputs=["relu_out", "W2"], outputs=["matmul2_out"], name="matmul2"
)

node_add2 = helper.make_node(
    op_type="Add", inputs=["matmul2_out", "B2"], outputs=["output"], name="add2"
)
```

Figure 12.5: *Node creation in ONNX model*

The **op_type** accepts supported operators from the list provided in ONNX documentation[1]. Note that the list of supported operators expands with different opset versions as new operators are incrementally added. Additionally, the operator's signature, such as keyword arguments and required inputs, may change with opset updates. Therefore, it is advisable to review the operator's documentation for the specific opset being used.

Now that all components are ready, we can construct the graph. We have the nodes, initializers, and input-output tensors. As shown in *Figure* 12.6, we use the **make_graph** function from **onnx.helper** to create the ONNX GraphProto. This function takes the nodes, graph name, inputs, outputs, initializers, and value info as arguments. Here, we do not explicitly specify value info since we have not defined the shapes of intermediate tensors (for example, "**matmul1_out**", "**add1_out**", etc.), as this step is optional. Instead, this information can be populated later by applying shape inference to the model using the **onnx.shape_inference.infer_shapes** API.

[1] https://onnx.ai/onnx/operators/index.html

```
graph = helper.make_graph(
    nodes=[node_matmul1, node_add1, node_relu, node_matmul2, node_add2],
    name="2_layer_mlp",
    inputs=[X],
    outputs=[Y],
    initializer=[W1, B1, W2, B2]
)
```

Figure 12.6: *Graph creation in ONNX model*

Once the ONNX GraphProto object is constructed, we will use the **make_model** function from **onnx.helper** to convert it into a ModelProto and save it to disk. *Figure* 12.7 shows the code snippet for constructing the model from the graph. The function takes the **graph**, **producer_name** (to identify the model generation process), **opset_import** (to enforce a specific opset for all nodes), and **ir_version** (to specify the graph's IR version). The **""** and "**ai.onnx**" in **opset_import** represent the default domain for all operators, indicating that operators without a domain or with the "**ai.onnx**" domain should follow the given opset. This serves as a namespace in the ONNX graph. For example, a ReLU node from the default domain with opset 17 and another ReLU node from the "**abc**" domain with opset 1 can coexist in the model and may have different functionalities if defined differently.

```
model = helper.make_model(
    graph,
    producer_name="onnx-mlp-example",
    opset_imports=[helper.make_opsetid("", onnx_opset)],
    ir_version=ir_version, # ONNX opset version
)

# Save the model
onnx.save(model, onnx_model_path)
```

Figure 12.7: *Model creation in ONNX model*

The generated model is saved to the disk. We can use the Netron utility to visualize the model and ONNX Runtime to verify that it executes without errors. *Figure* 12.8 shows the Netron view of the generated model. As seen in the model properties, the **producer** and **graph** properties are set to the values we provided. The imports field shows "**ai.onnx**" followed by "**v18**", indicating that the model uses opset 18 for the "**ai.onnx**" domain. We can also verify the input and output tensors, along with their shapes and datatypes.

Note that we have not used AttributeProto or FunctionProto here. AttributeProto is required for nodes like Conv that have attributes in their signatures. FunctionProto will be needed when we discuss custom operators in the next sections. The detailed documentation for all APIs under **`onnx.helper`** can be found in ONNX documentation[2].

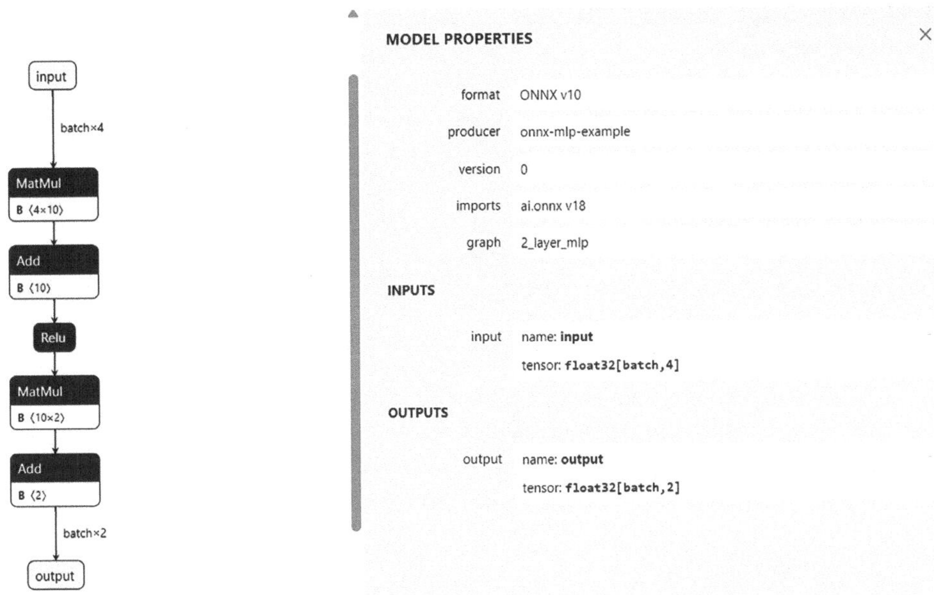

Figure 12.8: *Netron visualization of model generated through* ONNX APIs

Constructing ONNX Model Using ONNX Script

So far, we have manually constructed ONNX models using its low-level building blocks defining constants, initializers, inputs, outputs, nodes, and the graph itself. While this approach offers fine-grained control, it is often error-prone and requires deep expertise.

To address these challenges, we can use ONNX Script, which is a Python-based tool that simplifies ONNX model creation. Instead of dealing with complex manual graph construction or error-prone export steps, ONNX Script defines models using intuitive Python code.

The model we constructed in the previous section can be recreated in just a few lines using the ONNX Script, as shown in *Figure 12.8*. We will now explore how this is achieved and examine the key components of the ONNX Script tool:

[2] https://onnx.ai/onnx/api/helper.html

```
import onnxscript
from onnxscript import opset18 as op
from onnxscript import FLOAT, ir
import numpy as np

onnx_model_path_onnxscript = "mlp_model_onnxscript.onnx"

# Define model
@onnxscript.script()
def two_layer_nn(input: FLOAT["batch", 4]) -> FLOAT["batch", 2]:
    # Layer 1: Linear (X * W1 + B1)

    # Define weights and biases as constants
    W1 = op.Constant(value=np.random.randn(4, 10).astype(np.float32))
    B1 = op.Constant(value=np.random.randn(10).astype(np.float32))
    # Define Matmul Layer followed by Add
    hidden = op.Add(op.MatMul(input, W1), B1)

    # ReLU activation
    hidden = op.Relu(hidden)

    # Layer 2: Linear (hidden * W2 + B2)
    # Define weights and biases as constants
    W2 = op.Constant(value=np.random.randn(10, 2).astype(np.float32))
    B2 = op.Constant(value=np.random.randn(2).astype(np.float32))
    # Define Matmul Layer followed by Add
    output = op.Add(op.MatMul(hidden, W2), B2)

    return output

# Convert to ONNX model
model = two_layer_nn.to_model_proto()

# Save to ONNX model
onnx.save(model, onnx_model_path_onnxscript)
```

Figure 12.9: *ONNX model generation using ONNX Script tool*

As seen in *Figure 12.9*, we define a function named **`two_layer_nn`**, which contains most of the model logic. The function takes an argument named "**`input`**" with a **`FLOAT`** datetype and a shape of **`["batch", 4]`**. When executed, the function name (**`two_layer_nn`**) becomes the graph name in the generated ONNX model (visible in Netron). The graph input retains the name "**`input`**" with a float datatype and shape **`["batch",`**

4]. The function returns a variable named "**output**" with a **FLOAT** datatype and shape **["batch", 2]**, which becomes the graph output in the ONNX model.

In *Figure* 12.9, we import **opset18** from **onnxscript** as **op**. If a different opset is required, we simply import the corresponding version. The **op** object is used to define constant initializers and nodes like MatMul. When we call **op.Constant** with a NumPy array, it automatically converts the array into an ONNX initializer. The initializer's name is derived from the variable assigned to **op.Constant**, which in this case is **W1**, **B1**, **W2**, and **B2**.

Similarly, nodes like MatMul, Add, and Relu are defined using **op.MatMul**, **op.Add**, and **op.Relu**, respectively. The graph edges are formed based on the inputs passed to these operations. For example, **op.MatMul** takes "**input**" and "**W1**" as inputs and its output is passed to **op.Add** along with "**B1**", establishing the necessary connections between nodes.

This seamless conversion is enabled by the **@onnxscript.script()** decorator applied to the **two_layer_nn** function. This decorator instructs ONNX Script to parse the function and generate an internal representation of the ONNX model. Calling **two_layer_nn.to_model_proto()** converts the Python code into an ONNX ModelProto, which can then be saved to disk.

As seen previously, we can validate the model using ONNX Runtime and visualize it with Netron. *Figure* 12.10 shows how Netron visualizes the ONNX Script-generated model. We can see that the ONNX Script-generated model looks the same as *Figure* 12.8:

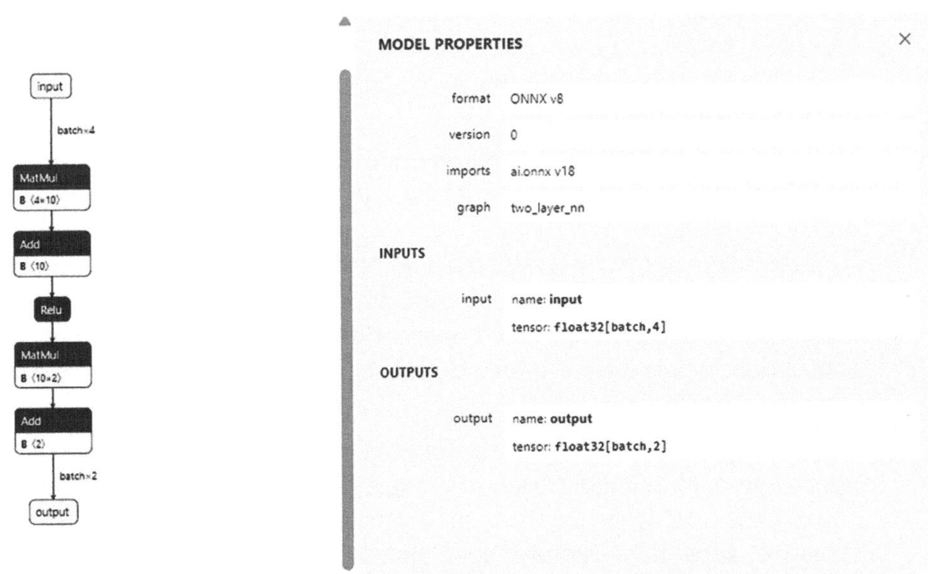

Figure 12.10: *Netron visualization of model generated through* ONNX *Script*

Extending ONNX via Custom Operators

ONNX was designed as a universal translator for deep learning, enabling AI models to work seamlessly across frameworks like PyTorch and TensorFlow. However, since the field evolves quickly, and real-world needs become diverse, no standard operation set can possibly include every innovation or specialized requirements for businesses. This is why ONNX allows custom operators, or specialized extensions that fill the gaps when built-in operations fall short.

Architecturally, systems that support user extensions tend to be modular, promote separation of concerns, and improve maintainability through well-defined plug-in mechanisms. Custom operators in ONNX serve this purpose, offering flexibility for unique scenarios.

The need for custom operators arises in several key situations such as:

- **Cutting-Edge Research:** Machine learning evolves rapidly, with new architectures and layers emerging constantly. While ONNX maintains a stable core of operators, researchers often experiment with novel activation functions, attention mechanisms, or specialized layers that are not yet standardized. Custom operators let these innovations exist in ONNX without waiting for official adoption.
- **Framework-Specific Operations:** Deep learning frameworks often introduce unique operations. For instance, PyTorch has dedicated operators for **`LayerNormalization`** and **`RMSNormalization`**, which only became part of ONNX in opset 17 and 23, respectively. Before that, PyTorch's **`nn.LayerNorm`** had to be translated into primitive ONNX operations like **`Sub`**, **`Add`**, and **`Div`**. Custom operators bridge such gaps, ensuring that even highly specialized models remain portable.
- **Hardware Optimization:** Not all compute architectures are created equal. AI accelerators, whether they are NPUs, GPUs, or custom ASICs, often rely on highly optimized kernels that go beyond standard ONNX operations. Hardware vendors like Intel (with oneDNN) and NVIDIA (with TensorRT plugins) use custom operators to expose chip-specific optimizations. For example, some accelerators fuse **`Conv+BN+ReLU`** operations into a single kernel during model translation, while others offer specialized implementations for transformer attention blocks.
- **Domain-Specific Needs:** Certain fields require calculations that standard AI operations cannot handle. Medical imaging might need custom preprocessing, autonomous vehicles depend on proprietary sensor fusion, and privacy-sensitive apps may require specialized security layers. Without custom operators, developers will face clunky workarounds or abandon ONNX entirely for these critical use cases.

- **Unforeseen and Unique Requirements:** Despite its extensive library of built-in operators, ONNX cannot anticipate every possible computational need. Some operations are either too specialized to break down into existing primitives or are still being considered for future versions. For example, applications working with complex numbers may need dedicated operators that support complex arithmetic. Custom operators serve as flexible solutions, whether interim or long-term, while maintaining model portability even when standard operators do not yet cover specific requirements.

In the following sections, we will demonstrate how to extend ONNX models with custom operators with a practical example. We will take the SwiGLU activation function as our candidate custom operator and use it to replace the ReLU activation in our previously exported model. This hands-on approach will illustrate the complete process of implementing and integrating custom operators in ONNX.

Custom Ops Using ONNX APIs

First, let us explore how to implement custom operators using ONNX's APIs. In the ONNX framework, custom operators behave just like standard operators (nodes). To add a custom node to an ONNX graph, we use the **`make_node`** function from **`onnx.helper`**. However, unlike standard operators that belong to either the default domain (**`""`**) or "**`ai.onnx`**", custom operators must use a different domain name. The default domains are reserved exclusively for official ONNX operators defined in the specification.

Simply defining a custom operator in the graph is not enough, we also need to provide its implementation for the model to work with ONNX Runtime. The only exception is when the model is meant for specialized hardware that directly translates the ONNX model to its native format and has its own implementation of the custom operator.

To implement our custom operator, we need to create a FunctionProto object. Similar to GraphProto, FunctionProto contains its own subgraph. When ONNX Runtime encounters a custom operator whose **`op_type`** matches a FunctionProto's **`fname`**, it uses the subgraph defined in the FunctionProto as the operator's implementation. For detailed documentation on **`make_function`**, see ONNX documentation[3].

[3] https://onnx.ai/onnx/api/helper.html#onnx.helper.make_function

```
# Build the Model Graph
def construct_graph(custom_op_domain):
    # Define Model Weights (Initializers)
    # Layer 1: 4x10 weight + 10 bias
    W1 = numpy_helper.from_array(np.random.randn(4, 10).astype(np.float32), name="W1")
    B1 = numpy_helper.from_array(np.random.randn(10).astype(np.float32), name="B1")

    # SwiGLU: Two 10x10 weights (W and V)
    W_swiglu = numpy_helper.from_array(np.random.randn(10, 10).astype(np.float32), name="W_swiglu")
    V_swiglu = numpy_helper.from_array(np.random.randn(10, 10).astype(np.float32), name="V_swiglu")

    # Layer 2: 10x2 weight + 2 bias
    W2 = numpy_helper.from_array(np.random.randn(10, 2).astype(np.float32), name="W2")
    B2 = numpy_helper.from_array(np.random.randn(2).astype(np.float32), name="B2")

    graph = helper.make_graph(
        name="SwiGLU_Linear_Model",
        inputs=[
            helper.make_tensor_value_info("input", TensorProto.FLOAT, ["batch", 4]),
        ],
        outputs=[
            helper.make_tensor_value_info("output", TensorProto.FLOAT, ["batch", 2]),
        ],
        nodes=[
            # Layer 1: MatMul -> Add
            helper.make_node("MatMul", ["input", "W1"], ["matmul1_out"], name="matmul1"),
            helper.make_node("Add", ["matmul1_out", "B1"], ["add1_out"], name="add1"),

            # SwiGLU
            helper.make_node(
                "SwiGLU",
                inputs=["add1_out", "W_swiglu", "V_swiglu"],
                outputs=["swiglu_out"],
                domain=custom_op_domain,
                name="swiglu",
            ),

            # Layer 2: MatMul -> Add
            helper.make_node("MatMul", ["swiglu_out", "W2"], ["matmul2_out"], name="matmul2"),
            helper.make_node("Add", ["matmul2_out", "B2"], ["output"], name="add2"),
        ],
        initializer=[W1, B1, W_swiglu, V_swiglu, W2, B2],
    )
    return graph
```

Figure 12.11: *ONNX model graph construction with Custom Operator for SwiGLU node*

Let us put this into practice by modifying our earlier model to use SwiGLU activation instead of ReLU. The key difference lies in their mathematical formulation (*Equations* 1 and 2). It takes three parameters: the input tensor **X** and two weight matrices **W** and **V**. The operation first computes **XW** (matrix multiplication of input with **W**), then applies a sigmoid gate to this result. The **XW** and sigmoid of **XW** are multiplied element-wise. This gated output is then multiplied element-wise with **XV** (the matrix product of input and **V**). The complete operation can be represented as **SwiGLU(X) = ((XW) ⊙ σ(XW)) ⊙ XV**, where **σ** is the sigmoid function and ⊙ denotes element-wise multiplication. Since

ONNX version 1.18 (opset 23) lacks a native SwiGLU operator, it serves as an excellent example of custom operator implementation.

$$\text{ReLU}(x) = \max(0, x) \tag{1}$$

$$\text{SwiGLU}(x, W, V) = (xW \cdot \sigma(xW)) \odot (xV) \tag{2}$$

Figure 12.12: *Equations for ReLU and SwiGLU activation function*

The graph construction follows similar steps to *Figures* 12.3-12.6, consolidated in *Figure* 12.11's **construct_graph()** function. The notable difference is the addition of our SwiGLU node with three inputs and one output, assigned to a custom domain ("**my.custom_op**") instead of the default domain.

```
# Build SwiGLU ONNX Function Proto
def get_swiglu_function_proto(op_name, input_names, output_names, domain, opset):
    # Define SwiGLU as a FunctionProto
    x_inp, W_inp, V_inp = input_names
    output = output_names[0]

    swiglu_fn = helper.make_function(
        domain=domain,  # Custom domain to avoid conflicts
        fname=op_name,
        inputs=input_names,
        outputs=output_names,
        nodes=[
            # xW = MatMul(x, W)
            helper.make_node("MatMul", [x_inp, W_inp], ["xW"], name="matmul_xW"),
            # sigmoid_xW = Sigmoid(xW)
            helper.make_node("Sigmoid", ["xW"], ["sigmoid_xW"], name="sigmoid"),
            # swish_xW = Mul(xW, sigmoid_xW)
            helper.make_node("Mul", ["xW", "sigmoid_xW"], ["swish_xW"], name="swish"),
            # xV = MatMul(x, V)
            helper.make_node("MatMul", [x_inp, V_inp], ["xV"], name="matmul_xV"),
            # output = Mul(swish_xW, xV)
            helper.make_node("Mul", ["swish_xW", "xV"], [output], name="mul_swish"),
        ],
        opset_imports=[helper.make_opsetid("", opset)],  # ONNX opset version
    )
    return swiglu_fn
```

Figure 12.13: ONNX *FunctionProto for SwiGLU*

Figure 12.13 demonstrates how we implement the SwiGLU operator using FunctionProto. The **make_function** call requires several key components: the same domain name used in our SwiGLU node definition, an **fname** that matches the SwiGLU node's **op_type**, and the input/output tensor names for the subgraph. Additionally, we need to define the subgraph's nodes (constructed similarly to our main graph) and specify the opset for nodes within this subgraph.

```
# Create and Save the Model
def construct_model_proto(custom_op_domain, custom_op_opset, model_opset, ir_version):
    swiglu_fn = get_swiglu_function_proto(
        "SwiGLU", ["x", "W", "V"], ["output"], custom_op_domain, model_opset
    )

    graph = construct_graph(custom_op_domain)

    model = helper.make_model(
        graph,
        functions=[swiglu_fn],
        opset_imports=[
            helper.make_opsetid("", model_opset), # ONNX opset
            helper.make_opsetid(custom_op_domain, custom_op_opset), # Custom domain
        ],
        ir_version=ir_version,
    )
    return model


custom_op_domain = "my.custom_op"
custom_op_opset = 1
model_opset = 18
ir_version = 10
model = construct_model_proto(custom_op_domain, custom_op_opset, model_opset, ir_version)

swiglu_model_onnx_apis = "swiglu_model_onnx_apis.onnx"
onnx.save(model, swiglu_model_onnx_apis)
```

Figure 12.14: *ONNX ModelProto construction with SwiGLU custom operator*

With both GraphProto and FunctionProto prepared, we can now construct the complete ModelProto as shown in *Figure 12.14*. The **`make_model`** function integrates several key components: our main graph from **`construct_graph()`**, the SwiGLU ONNX function implementation from **`get_swiglu_function_proto()`**, the opset imports (including the default "**`ai.onnx`**" domain at opset 18 and our custom "**`my.custom_op`**" domain at opset 1), along with the IR version. Importantly, we maintain consistency by using "**`my.custom_op`**" for both the SwiGLU node definition and its ONNX function implementation. Once assembled, we can save the final model for execution in ONNX Runtime and visualization in Netron.

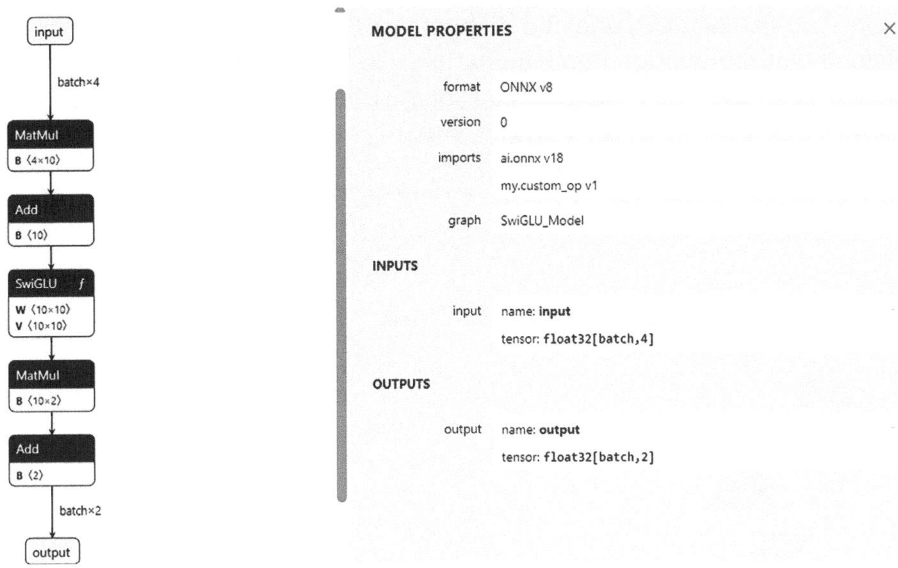

Figure 12.15: *Visualization of generated ONNX model with SwiGLU custom operator*

Figure 12.15 shows the visualization of our generated ONNX model with the SwiGLU custom operator. The model properties clearly display both domains, which are the default "**`ai.onnx`**" at opset 18 and our custom "**`my.custom_op`**" domain at opset 1 for the SwiGLU implementation.

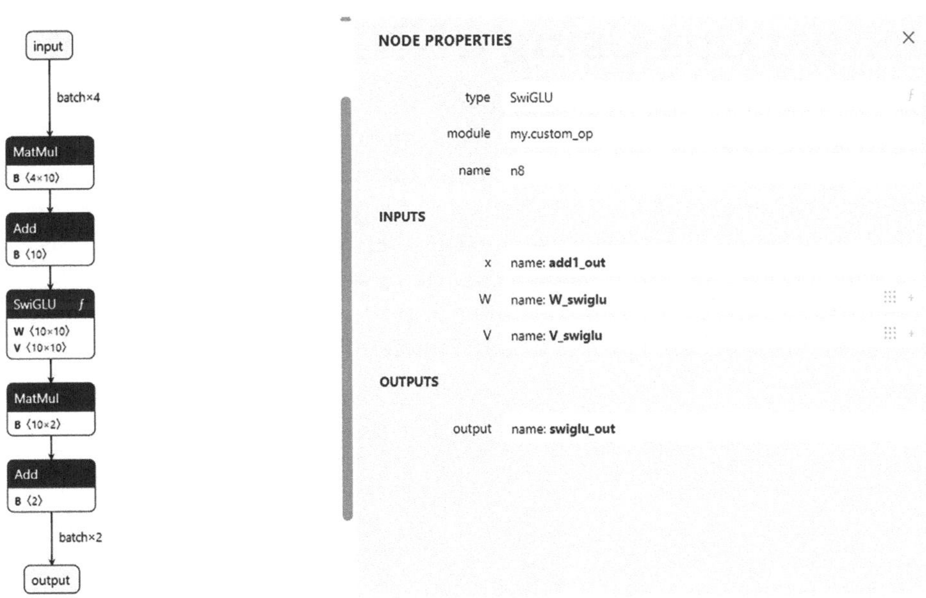

Figure 12.16: *Node properties of SwiGLU*

When examining the SwiGLU node properties in *Figure* 12.16, we observe several key details: the custom domain "**`my.custom_op`**" appears as the module, the node type is specified as "**SwiGLU**", and the distinctive "**f**" indicator reveals the presence of a subgraph within function implementation. The complete implementation appears in *Figure* 12.17 when selecting the "**f**" icon and reveals the subgraph that precisely matches the node structure we defined in **get_swiglu_function_proto()**.

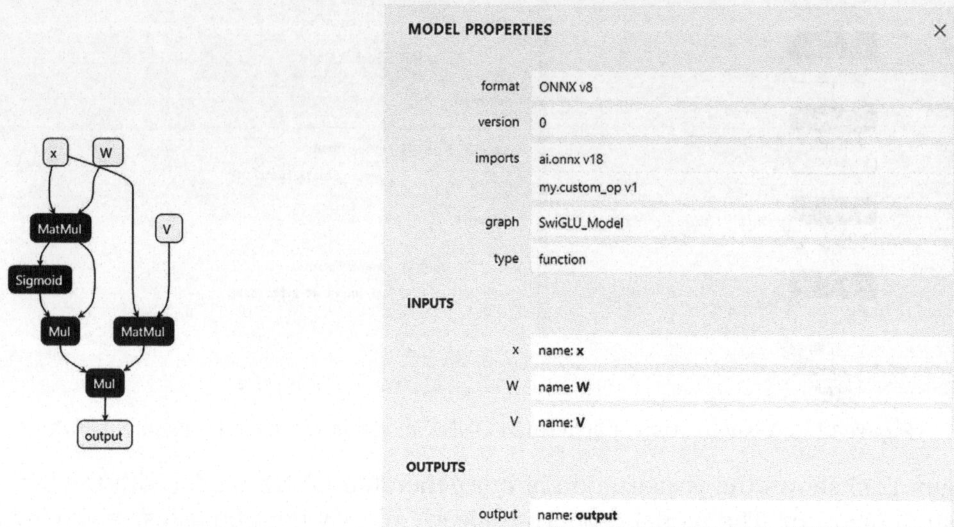

Figure 12.17: *Subgraph associated with SwiGLU custom operator*

Custom Ops Using ONNX Script Tool

Let us now rebuild the same ONNX model with our SwiGLU custom operator, this time using the ONNX Script tool. The implementation is shown in *Figures* 12.18 and 12.19. In *Figure* 12.18, we define a **SwiGLU** function that takes three float-type inputs (the [...] notation after FLOAT indicates tensors of any shape with floating-point values). Similarly as in *Figure* 12.9, we will use the **@onnxscript.script** decorator, but with one key difference–we are now passing a **custom_opset** parameter that specifies custom op domain ("**my.custom_op**") and custom op opset version (1). This decorator converts our Python function into a proper ONNX FunctionProto implementation.

```
import numpy as np
import onnxscript
from onnxscript import opset18 as op
from onnxscript import FLOAT, script

custom_op_domain = "my.custom_op"
custom_op_opset = 1
model_opset = 18
ir_version = 10
custom_opset = onnxscript.values.Opset(custom_op_domain, custom_op_opset)

# Define the custom SwiGLU function using ONNX Script
@onnxscript.script(opset=custom_opset)
def SwiGLU(x: FLOAT[...], W: FLOAT[...], V: FLOAT[...]) -> FLOAT[...]:
    xW = op.MatMul(x, W)
    sigmoid_xW = op.Sigmoid(xW)
    swish_xW = op.Mul(xW, sigmoid_xW)
    xV = op.MatMul(x, V)
    output = op.Mul(swish_xW, xV)
    return output
```

Figure 12.18: *SwiGLU custom operator definition in ONNX Script*

Figure 12.19 demonstrates how we incorporate this **SwiGLU** function within our main model definition through the **SwiGLU_model** function. This follows the same pattern as our earlier **two_layer_nn** function from *Figure 12.9*, with the addition of the **SwiGLU** node and its associated weight matrices (**W_swiglu** and **V_swiglu**). When we call **SwiGLU_model.to_model_proto()**, it automatically generates the complete ONNX ModelProto object ready for saving. The resulting model, when viewed in Netron, will match the structure shown in *Figure 12.15*.

This example clearly shows how much simpler model construction becomes compared to the manual approach we used in the previous section.

```
# Define the main model
@onnxscript.script()
def SwiGLU_Model(input: FLOAT["batch", 4]) -> FLOAT["batch", 2]:
    # Layer 1 weights
    W1 = op.Constant(value=np.random.randn(4, 10).astype(np.float32))
    B1 = op.Constant(value=np.random.randn(10).astype(np.float32))

    # SwiGLU weights
    W_swiglu = op.Constant(value=np.random.randn(10, 10).astype(np.float32))
    V_swiglu = op.Constant(value=np.random.randn(10, 10).astype(np.float32))

    # Layer 2 weights
    W2 = op.Constant(value=np.random.randn(10, 2).astype(np.float32))
    B2 = op.Constant(value=np.random.randn(2).astype(np.float32))

    # Layer 1: MatMul -> Add
    matmul1_out = op.MatMul(input, W1)
    add1_out = op.Add(matmul1_out, B1)

    # SwiGLU
    swiglu_out = SwiGLU(add1_out, W_swiglu, V_swiglu)

    # Layer 2: MatMul -> Add
    matmul2_out = op.MatMul(swiglu_out, W2)
    output = op.Add(matmul2_out, B2)

    return output

# Convert to ONNX model
model = SwiGLU_Model.to_model_proto()

# Save the model
swiglu_model_onnx_script = "swiglu_model_onnx_script.onnx"
onnx.save(model, swiglu_model_onnx_script)
```

Figure 12.19: *ONNX model with SwiGLU custom operator constructed via ONNX Script tool*

Custom Ops Using Pytorch Export

Beyond using ONNX APIs and the ONNX Script tool, we can also leverage PyTorch to export our ONNX model with the SwiGLU custom operator. Building a simple ONNX model through PyTorch is usually straightforward. We just need to create an **nn.Module** subclass. Typically, we need to define the layers in **__init__** and specify the implementation of layers in **forward** function. However, our case is different because we are working with a custom SwiGLU operator. This requires special handling.

Figure 12.20 shows the **SwiGLUModel** class inherited from **nn.Module**, which includes two **nn.Linear** layers and a custom **SwiGLU** layer implemented via **SwiGLUFunction.apply**. Unlike standard activation functions like ReLU that exist in **torch.nn**, **SwiGLU** requires custom implementation. Normally, for pure PyTorch usage (without ONNX export), we could implement this as another **nn.Module**. However, for ONNX export, we need to create a **torch.autograd.Function** subclass with both **forward** and **symbolic** methods, as shown in *Figure* 12.21:

```
# 2. Create PyTorch model
class SwiGLUModel(nn.Module):
    def __init__(self, in_dim, out_dim, hidden_dim):
        super().__init__()
        self.linear1 = nn.Linear(in_dim, hidden_dim, bias=True)
        self.W_swiglu = nn.Parameter(torch.randn(hidden_dim, hidden_dim))
        self.V_swiglu = nn.Parameter(torch.randn(hidden_dim, hidden_dim))
        self.linear2 = nn.Linear(hidden_dim, out_dim, bias=True)

    def forward(self, x):
        x = self.linear1(x)
        x = SwiGLUFunction.apply(x, self.W_swiglu, self.V_swiglu)
        return self.linear2(x)
```

Figure 12.20: *SwiGLU Pytorch nn.Module class*

The **forward** method in the **SwiGLUFunction** implements the actual computation for the **SwiGLU** layer during inference. It takes several parameters: the context object (**ctx**), along with our layer inputs **x**, **W**, and **V**. The **ctx** parameter plays a critical role during training as it stores tensors and other information needed for gradient calculation in the backward pass. While we are not implementing the **backward** method for this example (since we are focused on inference), it is important to understand that in a complete implementation, **backward** would use these stored values to compute gradients during training.

The **symbolic** method serves a different but equally important purpose because it defines how the operation of the class **SwiGLUFunction** translates to ONNX. As shown in *Figure* 12.21, this method receives a graph context object (**g**) that lets us build the ONNX representation. The **g.onnxscript_op** call connects our Python implementation (from *Figure* 12.20) to the ONNX graph defined using ONNX Script (from *Figure* 12.22). To be precise, the **g.onnxscript_op** call takes the **SwiGLU** function defined in *Figure* 12.22. We also use **setType** to precisely define the output characteristics and ensure that the exported model has clear type and shape information for all operations.

```
# 1. Define the SwiGLU custom PyTorch operation
class SwiGLUFunction(torch.autograd.Function):
    @staticmethod
    def forward(ctx, x, W, V):
        ctx.save_for_backward(x, W, V)
        xW = torch.matmul(x, W)
        sigmoid = torch.sigmoid(xW)
        swish = xW * sigmoid
        xV = torch.matmul(x, V)
        return swish * xV

    @staticmethod
    def symbolic(g, x, W, V):
        return g.onnxscript_op(SwiGLU, x, W, V).setType(
            x.type().with_sizes([None, V.type().sizes()[1]])
        )
```

Figure 12.21: *SwiGLU torch.autograd.Function class for ONNX export via Pytorch*

The ONNX Script implementation of the **SwiGLU** layer in *Figure* 12.22 mirrors what we saw earlier. It defines the **SwiGLU** operation's computational graph using ONNX Script APIs.

```
import torch
import torch.nn as nn
import onnxscript
from onnxscript import opset18 as op

custom_op_domain = "my_custom_op"
custom_op_opset = 1
model_opset = 18
swiglu_model_pytorch_export = "swiglu_pytorch_exported.onnx"
custom_opset = onnxscript.values.Opset(custom_op_domain, custom_op_opset)

# Define the custom SwiGLU function using ONNX Script
@script(opset=custom_opset)
def SwiGLU(x: FLOAT[...], W: FLOAT[...], V: FLOAT[...]) -> FLOAT[...]:
    xW = op.MatMul(x, W)
    sigmoid_xW = op.Sigmoid(xW)
    swish_xW = op.Mul(xW, sigmoid_xW)
    xV = op.MatMul(x, V)
    output = op.Mul(swish_xW, xV)
    return output
```

Figure 12.22: *SwiGLU ONNX Script implementation to be used in Pytorch class*

To ensure PyTorch uses the **SwiGLUFunction**'s **symbolic** method during ONNX export, we must register it in PyTorch's custom operator registry. As shown in *Figure* 12.23, we accomplish this by calling **torch.onnx.register_custom_op_symbolic()**. This registration function requires three key pieces of information: first, the custom operator's domain name and ONNX operator name (combined as a single string argument); second, our symbolic implementation function for custom operator; and third, the target opset version for our custom operator, which we specify through the **opset_version** keyword argument. This process ensures that the same Pytorch model can be executed in Pytorch eager execution and exported as an ONNX model for deployment. Readers can find more details about this registration process in Pytorch documentation[4].

```
# 3. Register the custom symbolic function
torch.onnx.register_custom_op_symbolic(
    f"{custom_op_domain}::SwiGLU",
    SwiGLUFunction.symbolic,
    opset_version=model_opset,
)

# 4. Create and export the model
model = SwiGLUModel(4, 2, 10)
dummy_input = torch.randn(1, 4)  # Single example

# Export to ONNX
torch.onnx.export(
    model,
    dummy_input,  # Pass the tensor directly
    swiglu_model_pytorch_export,
    input_names=["input"],
    output_names=["output"],
    dynamic_axes={"input": {0: "batch"}, "output": {0: "batch"}},
    opset_version=model_opset,
    custom_opsets={custom_op_domain: custom_op_opset},  # Must match registration domain
)

print("Successfully exported PyTorch model with custom SwiGLU op!")
```

Figure 12.23: *SwiGLU symbolic custom op registration and ONNX export*

With all pieces in place, we can now instantiate our **SwiGLUModel** and export it using **torch.onnx.export** as shown in *Figure* 12.23. This export process requires special attention as we must pass the **custom_opset** parameter, which is a dictionary specifying our custom operator's domain name and corresponding opset version.

[4] https://github.com/vladalonso/onnx-tutorials/blob/main/PyTorchCustomOperator/README.md#export-the-operator-to-onnx

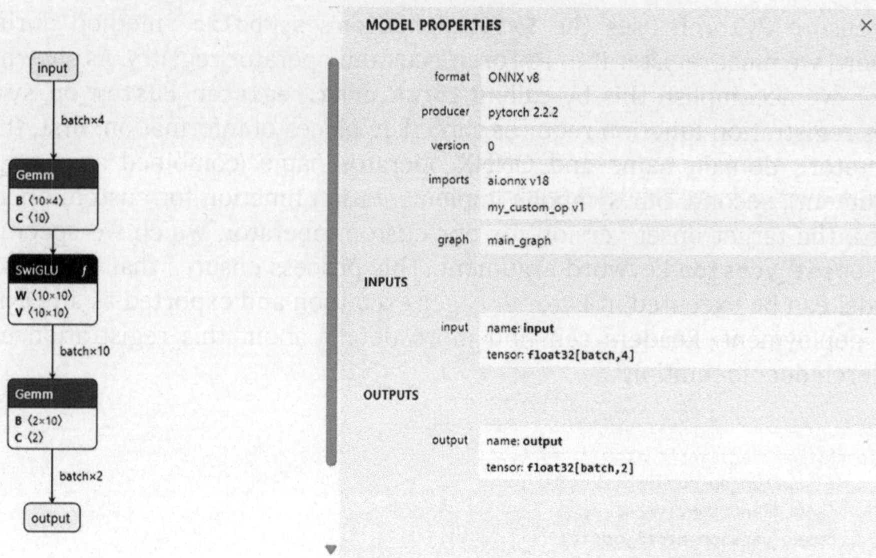

Figure 12.24: *SwiGLU custom operator model exported via Pytorch*

After a successful export, we can visualize the model using Netron. As shown in *Figure 12.24*, the exported model maintains the same structure we built earlier, with some notable differences. The separate MatMul and Add operations have been consolidated into Gemm layers, because we have used PyTorch's **`nn.Linear`** implementation. Most importantly, the visualization clearly shows our **`SwiGLU`** custom operator node in the graph, along with its complete subgraph implementation matching our original design.

Conclusion

In this chapter, we explored how to construct an ONNX model from scratch using ONNX's core building blocks. We then examined the ONNX Script tool and rebuilt the same model using its APIs, demonstrating how it simplifies the model creation process. Later in the chapter, we discussed custom operators, what they are and when they are required. Using SwiGLU as our example, we implemented a custom operator in an ONNX model through both the native ONNX APIs and the ONNX Script tool. Finally, we covered the modifications required for PyTorch-to-ONNX export to support custom operators.

In the next chapter, we will examine real-world case studies of model deployment at the edge. We will explore critical deployment considerations including safety measures and industry best practices. The discussion will then shift to emerging trends in both ONNX and edge AI technologies.

CHAPTER 13
Real-World Applications, Best Practices, Security, and Future Trends in ONNX for Edge AI

Introduction

Throughout this book, we have explored nearly every aspect of the ONNX ecosystem through hands-on exercises to enrich our understanding. Now, we will take a step back to see how these concepts come together in the real world. This chapter focuses on practical implementations of ONNX in edge computing, industry best practices for deployment, and critical security considerations for model deployment. We will also look at emerging trends in edge computing, AI, and ONNX. Together, these discussions will provide you a comprehensive bird's-eye view of the entire ecosystem.

Structure

In this chapter, we will cover the following topics:

- Real-World Applications of ONNX in Edge AI
- Best Practices for ONNX Model Deployment on Edge Devices
- Security Challenges and Mitigations
- Future Trends in ONNX for Edge AI

Real-World Applications of ONNX in Edge AI

Throughout this book, we have explored various AI models—object detection, image classification, speech-to-text, and language models—along with their practical applications. In this chapter, we will expand our perspective by examining real-world use cases that demonstrate the growing relevance of ONNX in edge computing today.

Drones: Eyes in the Sky

Modern drones, like those from DJI, now incorporate onboard AI capabilities for object identification and tracking. These autonomous systems serve diverse purposes like crowd surveillance, wildlife monitoring, and precision agriculture for targeted pesticide spraying. Inspection companies leverage drones to assess tall structures and wind turbines, identifying defects in locations that might be costly or dangerous for human access.

These intelligent drones operate in dynamic environments, using onboard computation to detect obstacles and adjust flight paths in real time. Specialized AI processors handle tasks such as object detection (often using YOLO models) and object tracking (employing either statistical methods, or deep learning models, depending on available compute resources). Many integrate LiDAR or radar sensors, fusing multiple data streams to enhance perception and navigation.

Self-Driving Cars: AI on the Road

Autonomous vehicles are one of the most critical applications of edge AI and have to uphold the paramountcy of safety. These systems combine powerful onboard AI with real-time sensor data processing to construct 3D environmental models, determine vehicle positioning, and navigate safely. Continuous object tracking enables dynamic trajectory adjustments to make split-second decisions that can protect human lives.

Manufacturing: The Smart Factory

Edge devices such as Jetson Nano, Raspberry Pi, and FPGAs (Field-Programmable Gate Array) deploy ONNX-based object detection models to identify defective products on assembly lines. Semiconductor manufacturers particularly rely on such automated defect detection in wafer production. Other specialized edge systems monitor machinery health in real-time through vibration and noise pattern analysis, using either time-series or classical machine learning models deployed via ONNX.

Space: AI in Orbit

China's recent AI-equipped satellite constellation is a breakthrough in space technology. Unlike traditional satellites that struggle with bandwidth-limited data transmission, these systems process climate and sensor data onboard. They form an interconnected network using laser communication, powered by solar energy and naturally cooled by space's vacuum, pushing the boundaries of edge deployment[1].

Agriculture: Smart Farming

Specialized edge devices now analyze soil composition, measuring mineral content and moisture levels to recommend optimal crops and fertilizers—all processed locally without depending on the cloud.

Healthcare: AI for All

AI-powered edge devices are transforming healthcare in rural India by providing critical diagnostic services such as diabetic retinopathy screening and cardiovascular risk assessment directly to underprivileged communities[2].

Fitness: Personalized Coaching

The fitness revolution now includes mobile apps that analyze workout form through pose estimation, providing real-time feedback on yoga postures or exercise techniques by tracking key body joints.

Urban Surveillance: Smart Cities

AI-enabled CCTV cameras process video feeds locally, identifying vehicles, people, and animals before transmitting only relevant insights to central servers, enabling efficient monitoring of traffic, crowds, and security threats.

Retail: Checkout-Free Shopping

Autonomous grocery stores[3] allow customers to scan in, pick items, and leave, with AI systems tracking purchases and processing payments automatically through camera networks.

Automotive: Voice-Enabled Vehicles

Budget cars now feature onboard voice assistants capable of handling everything from climate control to diagnostics, processing audio locally for instant response[4].

These examples merely scratch the surface of edge AI's potential. Across countless fields, ONNX-enabled solutions are solving real-world challenges by bringing intelligence directly to devices. Our goal is to showcase these possibilities, helping readers understand the different models for specific scenarios and how ONNX facilitates these innovative deployments.

---

1 https://www.livescience.com/technology/computing/china-is-building-a-constellation-of-ai-supercomputers-in-space-and-just-launched-the-first-pieces
2 https://www.youtube.com/watch?v=WdSGE7MHVg0
3 https://www.youtube.com/watch?v=rhj7iYY0vuY
4 https://www.youtube.com/watch?v=fsZJ_CK1uc0

Best Practices for ONNX Model Deployment on Edge Devices

Throughout this book, we have explored various optimization techniques, including pruning, knowledge distillation, graph optimizations, and quantization. In real-world deployments, these methods are typically applied in combination to achieve optimal performance.

Modern pruning techniques intelligently identify and remove redundant weights while minimizing accuracy loss. While we have covered basic approaches earlier, different model architectures often benefit from specialized pruning methods. Advanced pruning methods analyze layer activation distributions to determine which weights to remove[5], while others transform weight matrices to identify minimal essential sets[6]. The ultimate goal remains consistent: create compact models that meet edge device resource constraints while maintaining acceptable performance. For video processing applications, this typically means achieving real-time 30-60 FPS throughput. In text generation scenarios like ChatGPT-like systems, the target becomes generating tokens at a human-readable pace. For safety-critical applications involving human lives, such as autonomous vehicles or medical diagnostics, the performance requirements become even more stringent, often demanding additional validation steps.

After pruning, we often need to recover some of the lost accuracy. This is where knowledge distillation proves invaluable. The smaller "**`student`**" model, which is either trained from scratch or fine-tuned, learns to mimic the behavior of the larger "**`teacher`**" counterpart. By aligning the output distributions or values (typically from the final layer), we can significantly improve the pruned model's accuracy without increasing its parameter count, which is a crucial advantage for deployment.

Framework-trained models (PyTorch/TensorFlow) often contain training-specific operations that become redundant for inference. While ONNX Simplifier and ONNX Runtime provide excellent baseline optimizations, real-world deployments sometimes require custom graph optimizations. These involve:

- Pattern matching to identify subgraphs for fusion
- Replacing matched patterns with more efficient equivalents
- Implementing hardware-specific fused operations as custom operators

The timing of these optimizations matters significantly. While typically applied pre-quantization (to avoid interference from QDQ nodes), some scenarios demand post-quantization optimizations to clean up quantization artifacts. Special cases may

[5] Wanda pruning paper: https://arxiv.org/abs/2306.11695
[6] SliceGPT pruning paper: https://arxiv.org/abs/2401.15024

require hardware-aware optimizations, like splitting large matrix multiplications in LLMs (Large Language Models) to fit within limited device memory, either through graph transformations or custom operators that handle the operation in chunks.

Quantization represents our final optimization frontier, trading some accuracy for significantly improved execution speed through lower precision arithmetic. While we have explored various ONNX Runtime quantization techniques, the field continues to evolve. Emerging methods such as GPTQ[7] and AWQ[8] are particularly promising for LLMs on edge devices, as they use innovative 4-bit weight storage with runtime dequantization. To fully leverage these in ONNX, we need to implement custom operators that maintain the 4-bit storage while handling dequantization during execution. The quantization landscape remains rich with opportunities for further exploration and implementation.

Security Challenges and Mitigations

While ONNX's interoperability accelerates AI deployment, it also exposes models to unique risks like adversarial manipulation, data leakage, and compromised model integrity during updates or on-device execution. These threats can be tackled by security strategies tailored to ML systems when conventional safeguards often fall short. This section explores critical vulnerabilities and mitigations that preserve both model performance and trust across deployment environments.

On Device Security

When deploying ONNX models on edge devices like Raspberry Pi for customer use, we face significant intellectual property risks. Since the model exists as a standard file in the device's file system, customers with access could potentially extract and redeploy it on unauthorized hardware. In commercial applications, these models typically combine proprietary architectures with valuable training data, which is either custom-built from open-source foundations or is developed entirely in-house. The model's architecture, trained weights, and underlying dataset collectively form trade secrets that could enable competitors to replicate the entire solution if compromised.

We can employ multiple protection strategies to prevent model theft. The most fundamental one is AES-256 encryption of the ONNX file, prior to deployment. The model only decrypts in-memory during execution using hardware-anchored keys from Trusted Platform Modules (TPMs) or Hardware Security Modules (HSMs), ensuring it remains bound to authorized devices. For less sensitive scenarios where exposing the model structure is acceptable, we can selectively encrypt the weights. This allows the user to visualize the model graph through tools like Netron while rendering outputs

[7] https://arxiv.org/abs/2210.17323
[8] https://arxiv.org/abs/2306.00978

meaningless without proper decryption. To implement such encryption, tools such as OpenSSL[9] and TensorFlow Model Encryption[10] are commonly used. These encryption techniques are typically deployed via C++ rather than Python, as compiled C++ code offers stronger protection against reverse engineering compared to Python libraries.

Running ONNX Runtime within a Trusted Execution Environment (TEE) provides robust protection for AI models, safeguarding both the weights and computations from unauthorized access or modification. This hardware-enforced isolation ensures confidentiality and integrity throughout the inference process. Leading implementations include Intel's Software Guard Extensions (SGX) for x86 processors, ARM TrustZone for mobile and embedded systems, AMD's Secure Encrypted Virtualization (SEV) for cloud deployments, Nvidia's Confidential Computing for GPU acceleration, and Samsung Knox for mobile device security, with each offering hardware-rooted protection tailored for different computing platforms.

Securing OTA Updates

The problem does not end after the model is deployed on the edge device. In the real world, the model might need to be updated based on recent data. Hence, it is usually updated in such cases via an Over-the-Air (OTA) update. When we send a machine learning model to a device OTA, we need to make sure that nobody tampers with it along the way. To do this, the model is encrypted so that only the device can read it. Then it is signed with a digital signature (like a unique fingerprint) to prove that it came from a trusted source. The device checks this signature with a pre-installed certificate to confirm that the update is legitimate before accepting it.

While a hacker might intercept and copy the encrypted model, signature, and certificate in an attempt to spoof the device, multiple safeguards prevent such attacks from succeeding. First, updates incorporate timestamps and version numbers, enabling devices to detect and reject outdated or replayed updates. Secondly, the system uses short-lived signing keys that expire quickly, rendering any stolen credentials useless shortly after compromise. Thirdly, built-in firmware security checks verify certificate validity and ensure updates represent genuine version progressions.

On top of that, the most secure systems use hardware protections such as a Trusted Platform Module (TPM) or Hardware Security Module (HSM), to store the keys and verify updates. This means that even if someone gets inside the device's software, they cannot easily fake an update because the keys are locked away in a secure chip.

Real-world systems such as smartphones, cars, and cloud services use these techniques to make sure that the updates stay safe. Apple, Tesla, and AWS, for example, all rely

[9] https://www.openssl.org/

[10] https://github.com/tf-encrypted/tf-encrypted

on similar methods to prevent hackers from pushing malicious updates. So, while an attacker might grab the encrypted model, signature, and certificate, they still cannot do much with them because of all these layered protections.

Data Privacy and Result Leakage

When deploying ONNX models on edge devices such as security cameras, voice assistants, and facial recognition systems, we can face serious privacy and security risks that go beyond protecting the AI model. Imagine a high-security office building that uses facial recognition for door access. In such a setting, an attacker could manipulate the camera feed by digitally replacing an unauthorized person's face with an authorized employee's face in real-time, essentially creating a sophisticated "digital mask" to trick the system. This is not just hypothetical; such attacks have been demonstrated by researchers in the real world. The raw video feeds that these systems process contain extremely sensitive biometric data, and if hackers gain access to the device's memory during processing, they could not only steal facial images, but potentially reverse-engineer the system to identify weaknesses.

Even more concerning, the model's outputs, such as granting access or logging someone's identity, could be intercepted and manipulated. Unlike traditional security systems, these AI-powered devices make decisions autonomously at the edge, meaning a compromised device might grant access without any red flags appearing at a central monitoring station. The physical exposure of edge devices makes them vulnerable; a hacker does not need sophisticated digital skills if they can simply plug into an exposed USB port on the camera. This is why protecting these systems requires multiple layers of security, such as encrypted video feeds, tamper-proof hardware, and continuous monitoring for anomalies in the recognition patterns, so that the systems do not grant access to someone whose facial features don't perfectly match the movement patterns of a real human face.

Adversarial Attacks

Deep learning models, despite their impressive capabilities, face inherent vulnerabilities due to their training on finite datasets. These models, with their high parameter counts, tend to learn dataset-specific patterns, making them susceptible to manipulation. This has led to the emergence of adversarial attacks as a critical research area, focusing on identifying subtle input perturbations that can dramatically alter a model's outputs while remaining undetectable to humans. *Figures* 13.1 and *Figure* 13.2 illustrate this phenomenon through concrete examples.

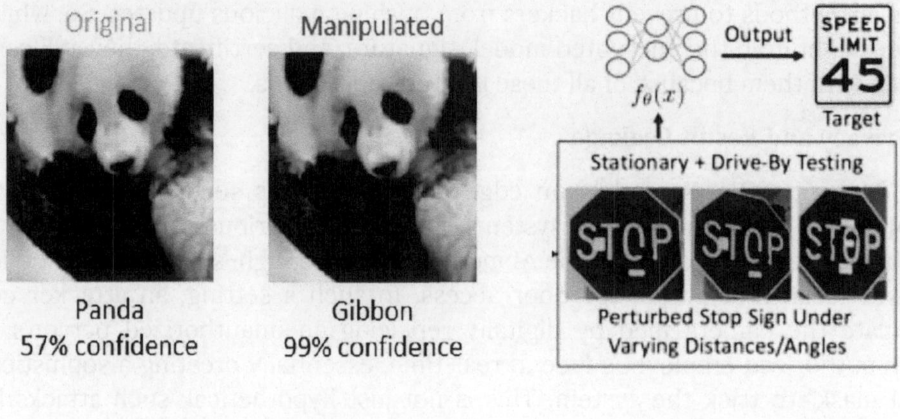

(a) Image classification (b) Image classification

Figure 13.1: *Overview of adversarial attacks*[11] *on image classification models*

Figure 13.1 demonstrates how imperceptible modifications can deceive image classifiers. A panda image, which is visually unchanged to human observers, gets misclassified as a gibbon. Similarly, a stop sign can be interpreted as a 45 mph speed limit sign.

Figure 13.2: *Overview of adversarial attacks*[11] *on object detection models*

[11] Adversarial attack:
https://medium.com/subex-ai-labs/adversarial-attacks-a-detailed-review-part-1-20fac7ccfc1a
https://analyticsindiamag.com/ai-features/how-to-fool-ai-with-adversarial-attacks/
https://www.youtube.com/watch?v=MIbFvK2S9g8

Figure 13.2 shows comparable vulnerabilities in object detection systems, where a person wearing a specially patterned shirt becomes invisible to the model while others can be detected. Additional examples and analysis can be found in *Footnote*[11].

These attacks pose serious real-world risks. Consider autonomous vehicles; if an attack like *Figure* 13.2's "invisible person" scenario occurred, it could lead to catastrophic consequences. Adversarial techniques work under both white-box conditions (with full model access) and more concerning black-box scenarios (without weight knowledge). Black-box attacks pose a greater threat because they represent generic attacks that can successfully fool models with different architectures, even when those models were trained on entirely different datasets for the same task. This transferability makes them particularly dangerous and underscores the critical importance of developing robust defenses against such attacks.

Adversarial training offers an effective defense against adversarial attacks. In this approach, we maintain fixed model weights while processing inputs to compute the standard task loss. However, instead of minimizing this loss through gradient descent, we deliberately maximize it by strategically manipulating the input image. This involves calculating the input gradient and performing gradient ascent to create carefully perturbed images that would degrade model performance. By exposing the model to these adversarial examples during training, we can strengthen its resilience against such attacks.

Additionally, since adversarial images often contain characteristic noise artifacts, computer vision systems can employ spatial smoothing techniques to suppress these distortions and mitigate attack effectiveness.

While most research focuses on unquantized models, the nature of quantization, which compresses model precision, likely introduces additional vulnerabilities to adversarial attacks. The reduced numerical precision and altered weight distributions in quantized models make them particularly susceptible to manipulation, requiring specific defensive strategies.

Future Trends in ONNX for Edge AI

The landscape of model deployment is rapidly evolving. Advancements in chip design are making edge devices more powerful, while cloud computing grows increasingly affordable and accessible. For many applications, the distinction between edge and cloud computing is blurring, with hybrid approaches gaining traction, processing some computations locally while offloading others to the cloud.

The rise of LLMs has driven ONNX to expand its operator set, with recent additions such as Rotary Embedding, RMSNorm, and advanced attention nodes in opset 23 and ONNX Runtime's contrib ops[12]. Staying updated about these developments is crucial.

The ONNX ecosystem continues to evolve with new technologies that enhance model manipulation and runtime efficiency. This includes various open-source tools adopted by different repositories, each serving specific purposes in the model development pipeline.

ONNX Runtime GenAI[13]

This specialized library supports generative AI workflows within ONNX, handling everything from tokenization and preprocessing to inference, logits processing, search/sampling, and KV cache management. It offers state-of-the-art open-source decoder models and facilitates their iterative execution.

ONNX Graphsurgeon[14]

Developed by Nvidia as part of TensorRT's toolset, this utility converts ONNX graphs into an internal representation for easy graph modification. Like the ONNX Simplifier, it includes basic graph optimization capabilities.

ONNX MLIR[15]

This compiler transforms ONNX models into optimized Multi-Level Intermediate Representation (MLIR) code. It performs graph optimizations (such as fusion, constant folding, and so on) and compiles models for diverse hardware backends (like CPUs, GPUs, accelerators). It also supports ONNX Runtime-like inference through its modular design.

Community Tools

The open-source nature of ONNX has spurred various community-developed tools:

- **ONNX Slim[16]**: A tool similar to ONNX Simplifier that enables graph optimization through its own pattern-matching infrastructure and optimization passes.
- **ONNX Tool[17]**: Provides infrastructure for implementing custom optimization passes via ONNX graph pattern matching.
- **Simple ONNX Processing Tools[18]**: A collection of lightweight utilities for model manipulation and inspection.

---

[12] https://github.com/microsoft/onnxruntime/blob/main/docs/ContribOperators.md
[13] https://onnxruntime.ai/docs/genai/
[14] https://github.com/NVIDIA/TensorRT/tree/release/10.12/tools/onnx-graphsurgeon
[15] https://onnx.ai/onnx-mlir/
[16] https://github.com/inisis/OnnxSlim
[17] https://github.com/ThanatosShinji/onnx-tool
[18] https://github.com/PINTO0309/simple-onnx-processing-tools

While these tools address many common use cases, complex scenarios often demand custom optimization passes. Developers can leverage existing infrastructure or build specialized solutions. This capability demonstrates ONNX's flexibility when it is fully mastered.

Throughout this book, we have primarily focused on deploying ONNX models through ONNX Runtime. However, ONNX model deployment extends beyond this single pathway. For Nvidia hardware, TensorRT provides optimized deployment capabilities. Intel devices benefit from OpenVINO's specialized toolchain. Apache TVM[19] offers a versatile solution, supporting deployment across diverse edge devices including CPUs, GPUs, NPUs, and even microcontrollers, with particular optimization for Arm-based processors like those in Raspberry Pi. For Arm-specific architectures, the ArmNN[20] library enables efficient deployment across Arm CPUs, GPUs, and NPUs. All these libraries can directly consume ONNX models and enable optimized deployment on their respective target devices.

As the landscape of edge computing and AI continues to evolve at a rapid pace, staying informed about the latest technologies and model advancements becomes increasingly critical.

Conclusion

This chapter provides a comprehensive look at how ONNX enables AI deployment across diverse edge computing applications. We examined real-world implementations, where ONNX-based solutions are making significant impacts, followed by a detailed walkthrough of the end-to-end deployment workflow, including practical considerations and challenges. The discussion then turned to critical safety aspects of edge deployment and strategies to mitigate potential risks. Finally, we explored emerging trends in edge AI and ONNX's evolving role, along with specialized open-source tools for advanced use cases.

[19] https://tvm.apache.org/

[20] https://github.com/ARM-software/armnn

Index

P

Q

R